Routledge Philosophy GuideBook to

Mill

on Utilitarianism

■ Roger Crisp

First published 1997
by Routledge
11 New Fetter Lane,
London EC4P 4EE

Simultaneously published in the
USA and Canada
by Routledge
29 West 35th Street,
New York NY 10001

Reprinted 2001

*Routledge is an imprint of the
Taylor & Francis Group*

© 1997 Roger Crisp

Typeset in Times and Frutiger by
Ponting–Green Publishing
Services, Chesham,
Buckinghamshire

Printed and bound in Great Britain
by Clays Ltd, St Ives plc

*British Library Cataloguing in
Publication Data*
A catalogue record for this book is
available from the British Library

*Library of Congress Cataloging in
Publication Data*
Crisp, Roger
  Routledge philosophy guidebook
to Mill on utilitarianism /
Roger Crisp.
    p.   cm. – (Routledge philosophy
guidebooks)
  Includes bibliographical
references and index.
  1. Mill, John Stuart, 1806–1873.
  Utilitarianism.
2. Utilitarianism.   I. Title.   II. Series.
B1603.U873C75   1997
171′.5–dc21

                                      97–1476
                                           CIP

ISBN 0–415–10977–9 (hbk)
ISBN 0–415–10978–7 (pbk)

Routledge Philosophy GuideBook to

Mill

on Utilitarianism

'This is the only comprehensive study of Mill's *Utilitarianism* which I would recommend to students as a reliable guide.'

(John Skorupski, *University of St Andrews*)

'It is written throughout in a style which readers, including those who are new to philosophy, should find accessible. Wherever possible it avoids jargon and needless technicality.'

(Wayne Sumner, *University of Toronto*)

'The interpretations of Mill are sensible and clear-headed, and the criticisms of Mill judicious.'

(Thomas Hurka, *University of Calgary*)

John Stuart Mill's *Utilitarianism* is one of the most important philosophical works of the nineteenth century. Its advocacy of utilitarianism – the view that individual and political action should be directed at the 'greatest happiness' – not only influenced British political life but attracted, and still attracts, a great deal of criticism. This is the first book dedicated to the interpretation and critical discussion of this seminal text.

Ideal for those new to *Utilitarianism* and to moral philosophy, this book will also be essential reading for scholars. Written from the point of view of contemporary ethics, this GuideBook reveals how much this text still has to offer today.

Roger Crisp is Fellow and Tutor in Philosophy at St Anne's College, Oxford. He has edited the Oxford Philosophical Text of Mill's *Utilitarianism*, and *How Should One Live? Essays on the Virtues*. He is also the editor of *Utilitas*.

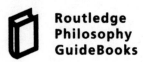

**Routledge
Philosophy
GuideBooks**

Edited by Tim Crane and Jonathan Wolff
University College London

Heidegger and *Being and Time*
Stephen Mulhall

Locke on Government
D.A. Lloyd Thomas

Locke on Human Understanding
E.J. Lowe

Plato and the *Republic*
Nickolas Pappas

Spinoza and the *Ethics*
Genevieve Lloyd

Wittgenstein and the *Philosophical Investigations*
Marie McGinn

LONDON AND NEW YORK

To my parents

Contents

7 Justice   155

8 Utilitarianism and freedom: *On Liberty*   173

9 Utilitarianism and equality: *The Subjection of Women*   201

Acknowledgements

I am grateful to the following for extremely helpful comments on all, or almost all, of a penultimate draft: James Griffin, Edward Harcourt, Brad Hooker, Thomas Hurka, Derek Parfit, John Skorupski, Wayne Sumner, Eric Tsui-James, Jonathan Wolff; and for equally useful comments on substantial parts of the text: John Broome, Tim Endicott, Cécile Fabre, Alan Haworth, Andrew Mason, Andrew Moore, Mark Nelson, Ingmar Persson, Peter Sandøe and Tony Shooman. I am pleased to be able to thank the staff and students of the Department of Philosophy, University of Bucharest, for their insightful remarks on lectures on Mill's *Utilitarianism* I delivered in Cîmpulung Moldovenesc, August 1995. I thank especially Valentin Muresan for inviting me to give these lectures. I learned much from a seminar on a draft of the book, organized in April 1996 by the Bioethical Research Group at the University of Copenhagen. I would like to thank Klemens Kappel, Nils Holtug, Karsten Jensen and Kasper Lippert-Rasmussen. I was helped by Michael Rosen's response to a paper on the liberalisms of Mill and Tocqueville I delivered at a conference on Mill and the French thought of his time, at the Maison Française, Oxford, December 1995. I am indebted also to those students who participated in graduate seminars on Mill I held in Oxford, Michaelmas Term, 1995, and to many of the undergraduates with whom I have studied Mill over the last ten years. I am grateful to Philip Schofield for advice on Bentham, and to Bernard Williams for help in interpreting his views on integrity. I owe thanks to the Principal and Fellows of St Anne's College, Oxford, to the British Academy, and to Oxford University for grants of sabbatical leave which greatly expedited the writing of this book. The dedication of the book to my mother and father, Daphne and Tony Crisp, is a meagre return for their constant support.

Roger Crisp
September 1996

A note on texts and references

Utilitarianism was first published in 1861 as a series of three essays in volume 64 of *Fraser's Magazine* (October: chs 1 and 2, November: chs 3 and 4, December: ch. 5). It was first published as a book in 1863. The second edition was published in 1864, and the third in 1867. The text I have used is the fourth, of 1871, the last published in Mill's lifetime (London: Longmans, Green, Reader and Dyer). This text is also that used in the *Collected Works* (Mill 1961–91) and in my Oxford Philosophical Text of *Utilitarianism* (Mill 1997).

All self-standing references (e.g. 2.2) are to chapters and paragraphs of *Utilitarianism*. This is the case even when the self-standing reference is preceded by a reference with a prefix (e.g. *L* 1.9; cf. 2.2).

References to *On Liberty* and *The Subjection of Women* are also by chapter and paragraph, and prefixed by *L* and *SW* respectively (e.g. *L* 1.9). Quotations from these books are from the *Collected Works* (vols 18 and 21 respectively).

All other references to Mill's writings are to the *Collected Works*, by volume and page number. Prefixes refer to the following works:

A	*Autobiography*, 1873.
AC	*Auguste Comte and Positivism*, 1865.
AP	*James Mill's Analysis of the Phenomena of the Human Mind*, 1869.
B	'Bentham', 1838.
BHM	'Blakey's *History of Moral Science*', 1833.
E	*An Examination of Sir William Hamilton's Philosophy*, 1865.
O	'On Marriage', 1832–3
R	'Remarks on Bentham's philosophy', 1833.
S	*A System of Logic Ratiocinative and Inductive*, 1843.
SD	'Sedgwick's discourse', 1833.
TD	'Tocqueville on democracy in America', 1835; 1840.
TL	'Thornton on labour and its claims', 1869.
W	'Whewell's moral philosophy', 1852.

Chapter 1

A teacher in an age of transition

Mill's life

Utilitarianism is one of the most significant works in moral philosophy, ranking in importance alongside Aristotle's *Nicomachean Ethics* and Immanuel Kant's *Groundwork of the Metaphysic of Morals*. Its author was the greatest British philosopher of the nineteenth century, John Stuart Mill.

John Stuart Mill's father, James Mill (1773–1836), was also a philosopher. James came from a poor background in Scotland, but his mother was ambitious. Not only did she scorn the local porridge, but she changed the family name from the less distinguished 'Milne' and took care to cultivate the acquaintance of local dignitaries. James worked hard at school, and at 17, having been chosen as tutor to the daughter of Sir John Stuart, was sent to the University of Edinburgh. By 1798, James was qualified as a preacher, but his sermons were above the heads of most congregations and he failed to gain a living. In 1802, Sir John Stuart offered him a seat in his carriage to London, and James began to make his living there as an editor and writer. Three years later, he married Harriet Burrow, the daughter of a Yorkshire widow whose wealth came from keeping a mental hospital. The son they named after James's patron was conceived soon afterwards, and born on 20 May 1806.

James Mill's view of the mind was influenced by the work of the English philosopher John Locke (1632–1704) (see Locke 1690). James believed that the mind was like a blank sheet of paper, and that ideas were based purely on sense-experience (*empiricism*) and then related to one another by general laws of association (*associationism*). James began writing on his son's blank sheet early, starting him on Greek and arithmetic at the age of 3. By the time John was 7, he was acquainted with the first six Platonic dialogues, reading the others over the following five years. At 11, he was helping his father correct the proofs of his *History of India*, and shortly afterwards he began logic and political economy. The bibliography of Mill's first few years in his 1873 *Autobiography*, which, incidentally, does not mention his mother, is quite staggering.

Mill did not go to school, but learned under the guidance of his father, explaining on daily walks in the countryside what he had read the day before. James Mill was closely acquainted with another important philosopher of the time, Jeremy Bentham (1748–1832). Bentham too followed Locke in thinking that all knowledge is ultimately based on sense-experience; but he was also a *utilitarian*, who believed that human actions and institutions should be directed at promoting the greatest overall 'utility', by which he meant happiness or pleasure (this he called *the greatest happiness principle*). Bentham himself had started young; at 3, on a visit to a country house, he was bored by the conversation of his elders and retreated to the library to carry out some historical research. It was probably Bentham who first suggested to James that young John be educated as the torchbearer for empiricism, associationism and utilitarianism.

The sheet of paper analogy should not be exaggerated, since James's main aims were to enable John to think for himself and to teach his young siblings. But his father's influence, along with that of the kindly economist David Ricardo (1772–1823), and of Bentham, with whom the family spent several summers, was enormous, and John was later stung by criticism that he was a 'manufactured man'. The emphasis in his thought on the importance of individuality, autonomy and self-culture began to emerge as soon as he moved out of the 'mental crisis' he suffered at 20, partly as a result of the hothouse upbringing which culminated in a hard year editing Bentham's vast *Rationale of Judicial Evidence*.

Mill's depression lifted when, on being moved to tears by Marmontel's recollections of his father's death, he realized that he was not a mere calculating machine. This period also marked Mill's first intellectual steps in directions away from his father and Bentham. He immersed himself in poetry, especially that of Wordsworth, and began to seek insights from thinkers such as the radical and influential Scottish essayist Thomas Carlyle (1795–1881) and the English poet and philosopher Samuel Taylor Coleridge (1772–1834), as well as the founder of French socialism, Claude Henrie de Rouvroy Saint-Simon (1760–1825), the originator of sociology, Auguste Comte (1798–1857) and the historian and political theorist, Alexis de Tocqueville (1805–59). France, the home of the last three, had been dear to Mill since a teenage visit, but he sought inspiration from elsewhere on the Continent, primarily from German Romantics such as Wilhelm von Humboldt (1767–1835). But this was not some kind of conversion. Mill was an Aristotelian, not a Platonist, at heart, believing that intellectual advance would come not from revisionist theory but from insight gathered systematically from different perspectives and various sources. Henceforth Mill sought to combine respect for rigour and philosophical analysis with genuine attention to culture and emotion, and it is in this attempt to expand on his Enlightenment heritage that much of his historical importance as a philosopher consists.

James Mill kept his son from university as well as from school. Sir John Stuart had left five hundred pounds in his will for John to go, but his father believed that it was wrong for one to be required to swear allegiance to a church before admittance, that

John already knew more than he could be taught at Cambridge, and that he should anyway have a secure income to provide for his siblings if necessary. Instead, John began to study law under the great utilitarian jurist John Austin (1790–1859). Around this time, John read a French edition of Bentham's *Traités de Législation*, and henceforth he never deserted the greatest happiness principle:

> It gave unity to my conceptions of things. I now had opinions; a creed, a doctrine, a philosophy; in one among the best senses of the word, a religion; the inculcation and diffusion of which could be made the principal outward purpose of a life.
>
> (*A* 1.69)[1]

Mill saw himself as an advocate, an evangelist even, for utilitarianism, telling us later that he never gave up the greatest happiness principle (*A* 1.185). One of his first moves was to establish a group of fellow sympathizers, which met in a disused room at Bentham's house. Unsurprisingly, he called the group the Utilitarian Society, and it met fortnightly for three years.[2]

James Mill's career in the East India Company, a private institution which largely ran India on behalf of the British Government, flourished, and when he was promoted in 1823 a vacancy remained to be filled by his son. John's career in the Company lasted until its dissolution in 1858, by which time he held a position on a level with a Secretary of State. At first he was paid little, but the rewards became large as he progressed. In addition, he found that his job, the official working hours of which by modern standards were anyway far from excessive, could be done in three to four

---

1 In an earlier draft, Mill uses the word 'aim' instead of 'purpose' (*A* 1.68). The change is perhaps to be put down to his awareness that often the best way to achieve a goal is not consciously to aim at it. I shall discuss this in the context of his utilitarianism in ch. 5.

2 In a footnote to 2.1, Mill suggests that he was the first to bring the term 'utilitarian' into use. His biographer, Packe, criticizes him for this (1954: 53, n.), noting that Bentham had employed the term in a letter of 1802. But there is of course a difference between using a term and bringing it into use. In *Utilitarianism*, Mill himself notes that the term had been used before him by Henry Galt, in a novel of 1821.

hours a day, leaving him plenty of time for discussion with friends and other activities. Several of his manuscripts, indeed, are written on East India Company notepaper.

The Utilitarian Society was not the only intellectual circle in which Mill moved. There was also, for example, a group of young men who met before work to discuss texts such as James Mill's own *Elements of Political Economy*, and the London Debating Society, where Mill came across novel political views. Mill also began to write serious critical articles for *The Westminster Review*, set up by Bentham in 1824 to represent the views of the political and intellectual group known as the 'Philosophical Radicals'.

In 1830, Mill attended a dinner party and met Harriet Taylor, a beautiful young woman of 22, and they were soon in love. Matters were complicated by the fact that Harriet herself was hosting the party with her husband John, while their children slept upstairs. Nevertheless, Harriet and Mill continued their relationship, although any sexual desire either may have felt for the other was not fulfilled until after their marriage in 1851, John Taylor, a man of remarkable forbearance, having died in 1849. Mill's marriage lasted until only 1858, when Harriet died at Avignon.

Mill believed his wife to be a genius, and began to see himself as a conduit for their joint intellectual efforts. His love was not blind, but somewhat myopic. Taylor was no genius, but she had a lively, forthright and imaginative intelligence, and there is no doubting the great influence she had on the direction of Mill's thinking. It was at her suggestion, for example, that he began to take socialism more seriously, and her interest in feminism served greatly to increase his own. A few years before she died, she and Mill planned a list of essays, and this list became the basis for his publications after her death. Three of the subjects were 'Foundation of Morals', 'Liberty' and 'Family', which led respectively to *Utilitarianism* (1861), *On Liberty* (1859) and *The Subjection of Women* (1869).

James Mill's death in 1836 brought on another mental crisis for Mill. Freed from his father's direct influence, Mill drew up a programme for advancing the utilitarian cause. Mill was, as the legal author A.V. Dicey puts it, 'a teacher created for, and assured of a welcome in, an age of transition'.[3] His was to be a 'utilitarianism which takes into account the whole of human nature', and in it 'Feeling' was to be 'at least as valuable as Thought, & Poetry not only on a par with, but the necessary condition of, any true and comprehensive Philosophy' ('Letter to Bulwer' (1836) 12.312). A few years afterwards, Caroline Fox wrote in her journal of how much she had enjoyed time spent in Cornwall with Mill, discussing poetry, beauty and truth (Fox 1882: 69–88). Fox notes that not only had Mill set himself the task of being a beneficiary of his age, but that the daunting task ahead of him was 'sufficiently attested by his careworn and anxious . . . countenance'. But Mill was not quite as dour as this might suggest. When he and his companions were leaving Pendennis Cavern, Mill proposed leaving their candles as an offering to the gnomes, and at a lunch in the open air he remarked on 'the extreme elation of spirits he always experienced in the country, and illustrated it, with an apology, by jumping'.

At around this time, Mill completed a draft of his first major work, the *System of Logic*, eventually published in 1843, in which the empiricist seeds sown by his father and Bentham came to fruition. Mill argued that *all* knowledge – including mathematics and logic – is based ultimately on the evidence of the senses. But, we might ask, our knowledge that $2 + 3 = 5$ surely cannot be based on our seeing that putting two objects besides three objects consistently gives us five objects? Rather, we know that it just could not be otherwise. Mill would respond that we cannot *imagine* how it could be otherwise, but that does not show that it could not. This response is important for anyone studying Mill's *Utilitarianism*, as we shall see shortly.

In 1848, the year of revolutions in Continental Europe, Mill published his *The Principles of Political Economy*, which soon became a standard textbook. In it, Mill showed more concern for the position of the working class than any political economist before him, and in 1865 he was asked by a group of citizens in Westminster to stand in the General Election as the candidate for the working

---

3 Harvie 1976: 40; cited in Thomas 1985: 126.

class. At a meeting before the election, Mill was asked whether he had accused the lower classes of being 'habitual liars', and his honest admission was met with tumultuous applause. His election allowed the intellectual left to combine for the first time with the working class, and played an important part in the foundation of modern socialism in Britain. At first, he worked closely with Gladstone, and when the Tories took power in 1866 he managed to prevent a meeting of Reformers in Hyde Park from becoming a riot. When Disraeli proposed a Bill to extend the vote to all house-holders, Mill suggested that the word 'person' be substituted for 'man', and a substantial minority voted with him. Mill was defeated by the Tory candidate in 1868, largely because of his contribution to the election expenses of a widely disliked working-class candidate.

Mill spent the last years of his life with his step-daughter Helen at Avignon, where he was able to pursue further his life-long interest in botany. He continued to write essays and letters until his death from a fever in 1873. He had failed to convert the world to utilitarianism, and, it may well have appeared to him, in his attempts to bring about radical reform in the British political system. But Mill realized that no single person could have accomplished these goals, and his last words to his step-daughter suggest that he was satisfied with his achievements: 'You know that I have done my work'.

The development of Mill's ethics

The idea at the heart of utilitarianism is that actions and institutions should increase the overall amount of happiness in the world. Mill, as we saw above, was converted to the doctrine early, and decided to dedicate his life to developing and propagating it. In so far as Mill was an evangelist, *Utilitarianism*, first published as a series of three essays in 1861, can be seen as his bible.[4] Though it was not written in the high and polished style of *On Liberty* or *The*

---

4   *Fraser's Magazine*, in which *Utilitarianism* first appeared, was a general intellectual journal.

Subjection of Women, it was clearly intended to be the summation, and defence, of his thoughts on the doctrine which provided the foundation for his views in other areas. If we look briefly at some of the other important ethical works he published before *Utilitarianism*, we can see that some of the main lines of thought expressed in *Utilitarianism* had been developing for some time.

Ethics and metaethics

Mill's philosophical opponents in ethics and elsewhere were the so-called *intuitionists*. In an early and spirited critique published in 1835 of a particular intuitionist, Adam Sedgwick, Mill characterizes intuitionism in ethics as the view that the distinction between right and wrong is an ultimate and inexplicable fact, perceived by a special faculty known as a 'moral sense' (*SD* 10.51). Against intuitionism he sets the view that the recognition of right and wrong can be explained without postulating any faculty other than our intellects and senses. Mill connects this latter view directly with utilitarianism, the idea, which I shall discuss further in chapter 4, being that our senses (or rather our desires) suggest that happiness is the only good, and then our intellects recognize that this is what makes them morally good or right. Ethics is *inductive*, that is, based upon experience and observation (*SD* 10.37; cf. 1.3).

On the face of it, the difference between intuitionists and inductivists in ethics concerns how we *find out* what is morally required of us, not what it is that we are required to do by morality. Mill to a certain extent realized that the connection between views about morality and moral views themselves, such as utilitarianism, was not quite as tight as his arguments against Sedgwick might imply. In a yet earlier essay, 'Remarks on Bentham's philosophy', published in 1833, Mill had pointed out that intuitionists could claim that they were not merely restating moral views resting only on sentiment and inculcated into them as children, but referring to certain laws or principles which were at odds with utilitarianism (*R* 10.5). The question then arises of why one should not be an intuitionist who refers only to the greatest happiness principle. In the first chapter of *Utilitarianism*, Mill again sets up the debate as between intuitionists and inductivists, but in a later chapter we find him saying:

> If there be anything innate in the matter, I see no reason why the feeling which is innate should not be that of regard to the pleasures and pains of others. If there is any principle of morals which is intuitively obligatory, I should say it must be that. If so, the intuitive ethics would coincide with the utilitarian, and there would be no further quarrel between them.

(3.7)

So the intermingling of ethics and metaethics, of moral questions themselves and questions concerning the nature of ethics and our knowledge of it, runs throughout Mill's ethical writings. In *Utilitarianism* he sees that intuitionism and utilitarianism might sit perfectly well together, but it was for the next great writer in the utilitarian tradition, Henry Sidgwick (1838–1900), fully to develop the idea.[5] This failure sharply to distinguish metaethics and ethics perhaps led Mill to take the ethical views of his opponents less seriously than he might have done. He tended to see those who denied utilitarianism as committed to what he viewed as bizarre metaphysics and metaethics, and this left his faith in utilitarianism largely unquestioned and the potential attractions of non-utilitarian views uninvestigated.

First principle, secondary principles and proof

The first chapter of *Utilitarianism* stresses the importance of having a first principle in ethics, but the second goes on to emphasize what Mill calls 'secondary principles'. According to utilitarianism, the first principle of ethics is that one's actions should produce the greatest happiness overall. But Mill points out that this need not mean that one should always be attempting to guide one's actions by referring to this first principle. The first principle itself may

---

5   Primarily in his magisterial *Methods of Ethics*, first published in the year after Mill's death.

support certain more everyday principles, such as 'Do not lie', on the ground that following these everyday principles will prove the most effective way of acting in accordance with the first principle.

In another attack on intuitionism, 'Blakey's *History of Moral Science*', published in 1833, we find Mill claiming:

> The real character of any man's ethical system depends not on his first and fundamental principle, which is of necessity so general as to be rarely susceptible of an immediate application to practice, but upon the nature of those secondary and intermediate maxims, *vera illa et media axiomata*, in which, as Bacon observes, real wisdom resides.
>
> (*BHM* 10.29)

Mill makes the same point in another, fuller, essay on Bentham of 1838 (*B* 10.100–11; cf. *SD* 10.64; *W* 10.173–4[6]), and goes on to note in both the Blakey and the later Bentham essays, as indeed he does in *Utilitarianism*, that the first principle will be required in the case of conflict between secondary principles. But by the time of the essay on Sedgwick, he places yet more stress on the idea of a first principle and begins to show an impatience with the intuitionists, noting that their view, since it tended in the main to be a rehash of common sense or 'customary' morality, had conservative implications which Mill felt were quite at odds with the progressive and reforming tendencies of utilitarianism (*SD* 10.73–4; cf. *W* 10.168–9, 178–9). He thought that Bentham was correct that intuitionists were dressing up their unreflective sentiments in vague philosophical language in the hope of converting others to their point of view (*B* 10.84–8); and, he believed, they ignored those aspects of customary morality with which they themselves disagreed (*W* 10.178–9).

It is here that we can see the relationship between Mill's ethics and the rest of his philosophy. Mill believed that if you were an intuitionist in ethics, you should be an intuitionist about science

---

6 'Whewell's moral philosophy', published in 1852, was a discussion of a book by Mill's arch-opponent, the Cambridge professor William Whewell (1794–1866).

and accept that there are laws which can be intuited independently of experience (*W* 10.171). But he also thought that what many people saw as plausible in intuitionism in science – the apparent *obviousness* of certain fundamental principles in mathematics or physics – could be taken to support intuitionism in ethics (see *A* 1.233, 235). Mill believed, however, that just as you should not assume that what appears self-evident in science is correct, nor should you assume this in ethics either. The attack on intuitionism in the *System of Logic* is all of a piece with his attack on intuitionism in ethics. In both spheres, Mill believes, you should base your views on 'observation and experience', and it is the task of the inductivist utilitarian philosopher to provide an empirical justification for his views. 'Those who maintain that human happiness is the end and test of all morality are bound to prove that the principle is true', he said in 1835 (*SD* 10.52; cf. *R* 10.6). That proof is exactly what he attempts in the fourth chapter of *Utilitarianism*.[7]

Character, happiness and moral motivation

We have already seen how after his mental crisis of 1826 Mill began to look for inspiration from writers other than those in the utilitarian tradition in which he had been trained. One of the effects of this was on his conception of utility or happiness itself. As early as the 1833 essay on Bentham, we can see Mill pointing out what he saw to be Bentham's failure to understand the importance of *character* (*R* 10.9). Utilitarianism says not only that one should perform those actions that produce the most happiness, but that one's very character should also be directed to the same end. In the later essay on Bentham, Mill expands on this notion. Mill sees morality as concerned not only with the regulation of actions, but with the self-education of the sentiments (*B* 10.98, 112; cf. *SD* 10.55–6). This is so not merely because the character one has affects the actions one does, which in turn affect the level of happiness overall, though of course this matters. Rather, self-education is important in coming

---

7   A central component of the proof – the claim that human beings desire only pleasure – is present in the essay on Whewell (*W* 10.184, n.).

to understand the nature of happiness itself, and is itself a constituent of happiness. Bentham's empiricism is 'the empiricism of one who has had little experience' (*B* 10.92). Mill saw Bentham as a child with a child's limited imagination, and believed that the most important sources of happiness lay in the adult world of noble morality and the arts. The sense of dignity, which was one of the many omissions Mill saw in Bentham's 'Table of the springs of action' (*B* 10.95–6), reappears in the second chapter of *Utilitarianism* as what enables those human beings who possess it to understand the important difference between 'higher' and 'lower' pleasures.

An account of human motivation – the 'springs of action' – should have something plausible to say about moral motivation. Here again Mill believed Bentham to be deficient. In particular, he omits from his list the notions of conscience and duty (*R* 10.13; *B* 10.95). Mill was particularly annoyed at Whewell's suggestion that utilitarians had to choose between speaking of human happiness and of duty (*W* 10.172). Two years after the publication of the essay on Whewell in 1852, Mill wrote the first draft of the essays which were to become *Utilitarianism*. In the third chapter of *Utilitarianism*, he recognizes that customary morality alone presents itself to us as obligatory, but he goes on to point out that education of the natural sympathy human beings have for one another may allow that feeling of obligatoriness to ground a practical utilitarian morality.[8] He suggests that such a form of moral motivation may itself come to be a vital constituent of human happiness itself, thus distancing himself from Bentham's view that self-interest will almost always predominate over social concern (*R* 10.15).

So we can see that many of the issues discussed in *Utilitarianism* were foreshadowed in earlier essays by Mill: the foundation of ethics and ethical understanding, the importance of first and secondary principles, the proof of utilitarianism, the sources of human happiness, moral motivation and the 'sanctions' of morality. The one central topic of *Utilitarianism* not covered in much detail in these earlier essays is justice, the subject of the longest and final

---

8 Mill speaks of sympathy as natural in the essay on Sedgwick (*SD* 10.60).

chapter of *Utilitarianism*.[9] This chapter was originally written as a separate essay, and Mill did not seek to tie it closely to what came to make up the earlier chapters of *Utilitarianism*. But in his incorporating it into the text, we can perhaps see the emergence, as he came to the end of his life, of an awareness of the particular power of the notion of justice, resting as it does on the fact that we are each independent individuals with our own lives to lead. Again, Mill was seeing beyond the utilitarianism of his father and Bentham, but it was not until the latter half of the twentieth century, in the writings of John Rawls and others, that the problems of justice for utilitarianism were posed in all their starkness.

Interpreting Mill

Mill's self-avowed purpose in life was to be an advocate for the greatest happiness principle. Very early in his literary career, we can see that he is quite conscious of the effects of writing itself upon its readers. Sedgwick had complained of utilitarianism that it was degrading. In his essay on Sedgwick (*SD* 10.62–72), Mill takes pains to point out the difference between the truth of a claim and its effect on its readers. But only two years before this, in the first essay on Bentham, Mill criticizes Bentham's doctrine that self-interest takes priority over social concern for the harmful effects it has on its readers. Those who might be tempted to virtue will be put off, and those who probably would not be tempted will be corrupted (*R* 10.15). Mill says that if only a threshold number of people could be persuaded to be benevolent, the happiness of all would be greatly increased.

---

9   The discussion in 'Bentham' (*B* 10.112–13) of the three aspects of human action – moral, aesthetic and sympathetic – does prefigure the distinction between conduct required by duty and conduct not required by duty but which we should like someone for doing in 5.14. Further, in the Whewell essay (*W* 10.184–5), Mill suggests that the origin of the moral feelings is an important metaphysical question, and this is one of the questions he seeks to answer in his discussion of justice. This essay also includes the argument of 5.26–31 that only the principle of utility provides an escape from the conflict which arises from the plurality of principles in intuitionism.

There is, however, a problem for the potentially benevolent individual acting alone, in that individual actions may have little or no effect. In that respect, ethical writing is itself ethical – an attempt to solve a problem of co-ordination, by inspiring sufficient people in a single period to work for good. Its largest effect will be upon those many individuals on the cusp between self-interest and benevolence, who may be inspired to be benevolent by the ethics they read: 'It is for those in whom the feelings of virtue are weak, that ethical writing is chiefly needful, and its proper office is to strengthen those feelings' (R 10.15).

Mill remained sensitive to the persuasive power of ethical rhetoric throughout his life. One of the advantages of his job at the East India Company, as he saw it, was that it practised him in the skill of putting a thought in the way that 'gives it easiest admittance into minds not prepared for it by habit' (A 1.87). People will not be converted to the right views unless those views are established in their minds through association, and sound association requires an anchoring in sentiment. That was where Bentham's writing fell so short.

This self-conscious moralization of writing by Mill raises a particular problem of interpretation. Towards the end of his life he and his wife saw themselves as leaving a 'mental pemmican' for future thinkers.[10] But on issues of particular ethical importance to him we know that he may be attempting to express himself in the way most likely to persuade us, rather than to reveal his own views most clearly. For that reason, it is a relief that *Utilitarianism*, unlike *On Liberty* and *The Subjection of Women*, was not written for widespread public consumption. Mill dedicates only a short paragraph to it in his *Autobiography*, calling it a 'little work' (A 1.265). In his earliest ethical writing, he had thought that what mattered most in practical life were the everyday, or secondary, principles by which people lived, and that most philosophers would agree on them. But he came to see that there were huge disagreements not only between philosophers but between ordinary people concerning such vital issues as the rôle of the state and the position of women

10 A pemmican is a small dried cake of meat used for emergency rations.

in society. What was important – what the greatest happiness principle itself required – was to get people straight on these secondary principles. In his writing on these contentious issues, Mill is of course attempting to state what he believes; but he is also using the skills of a rhetorician to persuade. Those skills are in the background in *Utilitarianism*, which is the largely submerged part of the iceberg of which *On Liberty* and *The Subjection of Women* are the highly visible tip.

It has to be admitted, however, that *Utilitarianism*, like most great works of philosophy, is not easy to interpret. It is indeed a 'little work', in the sense that it deals with complicated and important issues in a very short space. In this book, I shall be providing my own interpretation of Mill's views on these issues, and I do so in the hope not so much of persuading you to accept my view, but of providing a context in which Mill's words can be read carefully and reflectively, as so often they have not been. For any philosophical text, there is a range of reasonable interpretations, and as a reader your task is to develop your own.

But what is the point of interpreting a text if we can predict that there will be no single clearly correct interpretation? Certainly, the history of philosophy should not primarily be an end in itself. There is point in reading the works of past philosophers almost only in so far as their writings can help us to answer questions that matter to us independently of their rôle in history. Two questions Mill attempts to answer in *Utilitarianism* are what the good life for a human being might consist in and what the right way to live might be. Interpreting his text provides insights into these questions which may otherwise remain hidden.

I shall begin my discussion of *Utilitarianism* with two chapters on his answer to the first question (mainly in 2.3–10 and 4), concerning the good life. According to Mill, utility or happiness consists in pleasure (*hedonism*), and I shall discuss this claim and develop, in chapter 3, a view that follows a lead of Mill's but moves beyond him. Mill believes that hedonism can be proved, and this is part of his proof of utilitarianism itself in chapter 4, to be discussed in my own chapter 4. This chapter of mine will also cover some of Mill's claims about ethical theory in the first chapter of

Utilitarianism and about 'sanctions' or moral motivation in his third chapter. I shall suggest that Mill's views on sanctions – especially in the final two paragraphs of his chapter 3 – are closely tied up with his arguments for utilitarianism. Chapter 5 will discuss the different forms of utilitarianism in the light of Mill's own version, the central passages here being 2.2, 19–20, 23–5. Two important and related challenges to utilitarianism have received particular attention in the latter half of the twentieth century. One concerns 'integrity', and here the above passages from chapter 2 are again important, along with Mill's third chapter; integrity will be the subject of my chapter 6. The other challenge, as already mentioned, concerns justice, and Mill's long discussion of justice in chapter 5 of *Utilitarianism* will be analysed in chapter 7. I have shown how Mill's ethical and political writings as a whole must be understood in the context of his commitment to utilitarianism. In the final two chapters, I shall discuss two of his most well-known works in political philosophy – *On Liberty* and *The Subjection of Women* – and show how they are best seen as applications of the doctrine of *Utilitarianism*.[11]

I have chosen this order of presentation because I think it is the best way to approach Mill's text in the light of contemporary problems in ethics. The discussion of the nature of welfare leads into Mill's proof of hedonism. That proof is also a proof of utilitarianism, so my discussion of utilitarianism itself comes after the proof. Then follow the two chapters each on 'problems for utilitarianism' and 'applications of utilitarianism'. Some of Mill's book, such as the central paragraphs of chapter 2, concern issues which are no longer of great scholarly interest. I refer those who wish some discussion of these less studied parts of the text to the notes in my Oxford Philosophical Text of *Utilitarianism* (Mill

---

11 I have chosen these two works largely because contemporary interest in liberalism and feminism has meant that both receive a good deal of attention and are often set beside *Utilitarianism* in courses on Mill. Because utilitarianism was the foundation of all Mill's work, utilitarian interpretations could equally well be offered of, for example, *Considerations on Representative Government* (1861; 19.371–577) or *Three Essays on Religion* (1874; 10.369–469).

1997). I shall also be making reference to other works by Mill. Any reasonable interpretation of Mill's *Utilitarianism* must also be an interpretation of his utilitarianism. But, except in the last two chapters, it is of course *Utilitarianism* which is the focus of the book.

Utilitarianism as a doctrine remains as vibrant in philosophy as it ever was, and continues to attract spirited defenders and detractors. But even critics should be ready to give utilitarianism the respect it deserves. It is a humane and progressive doctrine, which in practice brought to an end many injustices based on conservative orthodoxy. Its proponents have been, on the whole, benevolent, and sincerely concerned to further the welfare of others; this is undoubtedly true of Mill himself. At the level of philosophical theory utilitarianism has enabled great advances to be made in the rational understanding of ethics. Utilitarianism may have some theoretical implications which are difficult to accept, but anyone whose rejection of any philosophical theory can be said to be reasonable must have given that theory impartial and serious consideration. Mill's text is well worth such consideration, and it is with the aim of encouraging it that I have written this book.

Further reading

Mill's *Autobiography* is one of the classics of English literature, and provides much insight into his character and self-understanding. The best biography is the well-written Packe 1954. Interesting also is the book by Mill's disciple Alexander Bain (1882). A useful brief historical account of Mill is Thomas 1985, though there is little discussion of *Utilitarianism*. All of the ethical essays by Mill discussed in this chapter are in vol. 10 of the *Collected Works*, and should be read with care by any serious student of *Utilitarianism*. The best accounts of Mill's philosophy as a whole are Ryan 1970; 1974 and Skorupski 1989. An excellent book dedicated to his ethics and political theory is Berger 1984.

Chapter 2

Welfare and pleasure

Welfare and ethics

Probably, at least sometimes, you think that certain aspects of your life make it good for you. These aspects are what I have in mind when I use the term *welfare*. Your own welfare consists only in those aspects of your life that are good for *you*. Your life may turn out to be good for other people, perhaps because you can help them in some way, but its being good for others is conceptually distinct from its being good for you. Welfare, then, is what makes a person's life worth living for that person. Though one could make fine distinctions here, I shall take it to be roughly equivalent to a person's good, self-interest, flourishing, well-being, prudential value or utility.

Despite the fact that this book is about utilitarianism, I decided not to employ the term *utility* in a central rôle. First, it is ambiguous, having been used in the utilitarian tradition to refer either to welfare itself or to what produces it. In the latter, instrumental sense, the banana milkshake I am now

drinking has a certain utility; in the former sense, it is the pleasure produced by the shake that constitutes utility. Secondly, and more importantly, I want to stress that the question of what makes life worth living must not be linked too closely to utilitarianism. All of us, after all, have more than a passing interest in that question, and it is one of special importance to moral philosophers, whether or not they are utilitarian. Most accounts of morality will include principles, duties or virtues of prudence and beneficence. Prudence is concerned with furthering your own welfare, beneficence with furthering that of others, and it would be pointless to advocate prudence and beneficence in isolation from any view of welfare. If you are ignorant of what makes lives go well for people, then you will be unable to make your own life or the lives of others go well.

This is not to deny that the idea of welfare is particularly important in utilitarianism. Indeed, some conception or theory of welfare is one essential component of any utilitarian theory. Another essential component is a *maximizing principle*, according to which welfare is to be brought to some maximum level. The conception of welfare at the heart of any particular utilitarian theory is prior, practically and theoretically, to the maximizing principle. You cannot maximize anything before you know what it is, and this is why I shall spend this chapter and the next on Mill's theory of welfare. Mill's proof concerns both elements of utilitarianism, so maximization will be discussed in chapter 4; but my main discussion of what maximization of utility involves will be in chapter 5.

Before reading further, it is important to appreciate that the question of what makes life worth living is largely separate from that of what the moral life consists in. Mill's theory of welfare can be seen as quite independent of his utilitarianism, his view that morally we are required to maximize welfare. Even if you end up denying utilitarianism, perhaps because it fails to make room for justice or rights, you could still accept Mill's theory of welfare.

Bentham's account

As we saw in chapter 1, Jeremy Bentham, who died twenty-nine years before the publication of *Utilitarianism*, was a great influence on Mill. Mill's account of welfare can be seen as a response to the criticisms of Bentham's own view by writers such as Thomas Carlyle. First, then, let me describe the Benthamite view which Mill later criticized and developed.

Bentham offers an *experience account* of welfare, according to which your welfare consists only in experiences that you have. Anything that happens beyond your conscious awareness and does not affect that awareness cannot affect your welfare. Imagine, for example, that someone spies on you over a period of time, learning all there is to know about the intimate details of your life. If you never find out, and your experiences are – from the inside, as it were – what they would have been had the spy never begun surveillance, your welfare, according to an experience account, has not been affected by what has happened. What you don't know, as the proverb says, can't hurt you. Someone who denies this thereby denies experience accounts.

Which of the various experiences individuals have did Bentham believe constituted welfare? Pleasures (see Bentham 1789: ch. 1, paras 1, 5). So Bentham can be called a *hedonist, hēdonē* being the ancient Greek word for 'pleasure'. Though Bentham is a hedonist, his position is far from that of the sensualist, who advocates the life of luxurious excess. For Bentham, any experience which makes me better off counts as a pleasure, whether it be drinking champagne or reading philosophy.

Of course, pleasurable experiences are not the only ones that matter. Some aspects of my life make it, in those respects, worth *not* living. The experiences of physical pain, depression, boredom, fear, embarrassment – all these make my life worse, and constitute what I shall call *harm*. According to Bentham, harm consists of *pains*, and it includes the experiences just mentioned, along with others.

The most important aspect of Bentham's account for our purposes is its allowing for the idea that pleasures and pains can be *measured*. Bentham assumes that any particular pleasure or pain has a determinate value and can be traded off against other pleasures or decreases in pains, and that what will guide such trade-offs will be a scale of measurement that attaches numbers to pleasures and

21

pains. This kind of scale is now called *cardinal*, a term not found in either Bentham or Mill themselves. Whether it would in fact be possible to develop a version of Bentham's notorious *felicific calculus* that we could really use to measure welfare should not be our first question. Rather, we must ask whether the assumptions on which the very notion is based are correct.

A cardinal scale of measurement is a scale with a zero point and units. Weight, for example, can be measured in grams. The scale begins from zero, and each unit, one gram, is equal to any other unit. Any physical object in theory can be weighed against any other, and the different weights plotted on a cardinal scale. How might this work for pleasures? Consider the pleasure of drinking Bell's blended whisky for one minute. According to Bentham, the value of any pleasure is to be determined by its duration and intensity (Bentham 1789: 4.2).[1] So let us make this pleasure – lasting one minute at its usual intensity – our standard unit of welfare value, so that two minutes of drinking will be worth two units, three minutes three units and so on (until the pleasure is dulled and it will take more than one minute's drinking to achieve one unit).[2] Now let us assume that the intensity of the pleasure of drinking an excellent single malt whisky such as Lagavulin is twice that of drinking Bell's. Having plotted these pleasures on a scale, you can begin to make judgements about your welfare. Given a choice between whiskies, if the time available for drinking each is the same, your welfare will be increased by choosing the single malt over the blend.

---

1 The other characteristics related to measurement of pleasures mentioned by Bentham – *certainty*, *propinquity*, *fecundity* and *purity* – might be relevant in practical thinking, but are not in themselves relevant to the actual welfare value of any pleasure.

2 It is worth noting that the notion of intensity can be understood either purely psychologically or evaluatively. On the first conception, intensity can be understood independently of evaluation, rather as, for example, a colour can be said to be more or less intense. On the evaluative conception, the intensity of a pleasure depends on its evaluation by the person experiencing it. Take two pleasures, one a minute long, and another two minutes long. If you value each equally, the intensity of the first must be twice that of the second. It is likely that Bentham failed to make this distinction. For more on this and related issues, see Mayerfeld 1997.

Now consider pains. Let us stipulate that one minute of standard social embarrassment is worth minus one unit. Purchasing one unit of welfare at the cost of one unit of harm will leave things where they were. Now imagine that you are offered the choice of three minutes drinking Lagavulin ($3 \times 2 = 6$ units) or three minutes drinking Bell's ($3 \times 1 = 3$ units). If you choose the Lagavulin, however, your greed in front of your host will embarrass you, at the standard intensity, for four minutes ($4 \times {}^-1 = {}^-4$). On this account, then, your welfare will be maximized if you choose the Bell's rather than the Lagavulin, since the Lagavulin overall would give you only two units of welfare as opposed to three.

The question at issue here is not whether we could in fact carry out a programme of measurement as envisaged by Bentham, but rather whether the value of every pleasure depends only on its duration and intensity, so that it could theoretically be placed on a cardinal scale with other pleasures and pains. Mill thought not, but, before we move on to his own account of welfare, consider the sort of objection to Bentham's account which Mill found troubling.

Haydn and the oyster

In 2.3, Mill says that many have taken hedonism to be a 'doctrine worthy only of swine', and he was almost certainly thinking here of Carlyle's characterization of utilitarianism as a 'pig philosophy' (Ryan 1974: 97). In one sense, as Mill notes in 2.4, this accusation misses its target once the Benthamite accepts that human capacities differ from those of pigs. As we saw, Bentham is not advocating the pursuit only of those pleasures which we experience in common with other animals. He might suggest that, even though 'quantity of pleasure being equal, push-pin is as good as poetry',[3] in reality poetry is nearly always to be preferred on the ground of its being more productive overall of pleasure.

This reply, one which Mill sees as 'taking the lower ground' (2.4) and himself puts little weight upon, is not sufficient to dispel

---

3   Misquoted from Bentham's *Rationale of Reward* in *B* 10.113. Push-pin was a simple children's game.

a serious worry one might have about full cardinal commensurability. Consider the following *thought experiment*. Like many of the imaginary cases I shall discuss in this book, it requires certain peculiar assumptions; but often a good way of deciding whether a certain philosophical view is right is to consider its application in unusual circumstances.[4]

Haydn and the oyster You are a soul in heaven waiting to be allocated a life on Earth. It is late Friday afternoon, and you watch anxiously as the supply of available lives dwindles. When your turn comes, the angel in charge offers you a choice between two lives, that of the composer Joseph Haydn and that of an oyster. Besides composing some wonderful music and influencing the evolution of the symphony, Haydn will meet with success and honour in his own lifetime, be cheerful and popular, travel and gain much enjoyment from field sports. The oyster's life is far less exciting. Though this is rather a sophisticated oyster, its life will consist only of mild sensual pleasure, rather like that experienced by humans when floating very drunk in a warm bath. When you request the life of Haydn, the angel sighs, 'I'll never get rid of this oyster life. It's been hanging around for ages. Look, I'll offer you a special deal. Haydn will die at the age of seventy-seven. But I'll make the oyster life as long as you like.'

Which life will maximize your welfare? Recall Bentham's assumptions about full commensurability. To be sure, the pleasures of Haydn are well worth having. And they are clearly far more intense than the mild sensual pleasure the oyster will experience. Eventually, however, if the oyster's life is long enough, its welfare will outweigh that of Haydn. It may be suggested that the value of the oyster's experiences to it gradually decreases as time goes on. But that is not how it seems to the oyster: it enjoys its ten millionth bask in the water as much as its first. According to Benthamite hedonism, then, your welfare will be maximized – you will lead the life best for you – if you choose the oyster life. Many people will

---

4 It should be noted that the following problem, based on extending the *duration* of a life, is a problem also for many non-hedonist theories of welfare which allow for cardinal commensurability of goods.

not accept this, thinking that it just does not matter how long the oyster's life is. It can never be better in welfare terms than the life of Haydn, since the kinds of experience Haydn had puts his life into a completely different category from that of the oyster.

In his own account of welfare, Mill tried to make room for this view. And he was doing so not just because he wanted to deflect the criticisms of Carlyle and enhance the chances of political success for utilitarianism. He himself saw the force in these criticisms, as some of his remarks in his essay on Bentham demonstrate (*B* 10.91–3, 95–7). In the first paragraph of that essay, Mill sets the poet Coleridge alongside Bentham as one of 'the two great seminal minds of England'. It was reading Wordsworth in the autumn of 1828 that assisted Mill in escaping from his depression, and in general he was heavily under the influence of romanticism, according to which emotion and feeling took priority over thought and calculation, uniqueness and creativity over mediocrity. Further, the Greek philosophers, especially Plato, Aristotle and Epicurus, with whose works Mill was familiar from his earliest days, placed philosophy and other intellectual and moral activities at the centre of their conceptions of human happiness or welfare.[5] It is no surprise, then, that Mill himself offers an account which gives special prominence to the more elevated experiences of human life.

Mill's hedonism

Before looking at that facet of Mill's argument, however, we should examine in the first place the evidence for his being a hedonist. The most important passage is 2.2. Mill outlines the greatest happiness principle (that happiness, or utility, is to be maximized), and goes on:

> By happiness is intended pleasure, and the absence of pain; by unhappiness, pain, and the privation of pleasure. To give a clear view of the moral standard set up by the theory, much

5 See Williams 1996. For a general discussion of the influence of the ancients on Mill, see Irwin 1997.

more requires to be said ... But these supplementary explanations do not affect the theory of life on which this theory of morality is grounded – namely, that pleasure, and freedom from pain, are the only things desirable as ends; and that all desirable things (which are as numerous in the utilitarian as in any other scheme) are desirable either for the pleasure inherent in themselves, or as means to the promotion of pleasure and the prevention of pain.

As we saw in the section on Bentham, a hedonist believes that welfare consists in pleasurable experiences. But this leaves open the question what it is that *makes* pleasurable experiences good. What I shall call *full hedonism* states that what makes these experiences good for someone is not, say, that God likes them to exist, or that they fulfil certain desires of that person, but solely that they are pleasurable. So there are two components in full hedonism: a substantive component, common to all forms of hedonism, which states that welfare consists in pleasurable experiences; and an explanatory component, which says that what makes these pleasurable experiences good is their being pleasurable.

Now, is Mill a hedonist, and, if so, is he a full hedonist? He tells us in the passage quoted above that pleasure is the only desirable end.[6] And elsewhere he speaks of 'pleasures' (e.g. 2.4) or 'enjoyments' (e.g. 2.10). Can we read him, then, as committed to the substantive claim that welfare consists only in pleasurable experiences?

Not immediately, for there is a sense in English of *a pleasure* where the phrase does not mean *a pleasurable experience*. Mill does not draw a clear distinction in *Utilitarianism* between the notions of *pleasure* and *a pleasure*. You might say that swimming is *a pleasure* of yours. The swimming itself is a pleasure because it gives you *pleasure*, and the pleasure is conceptually distinct from the swimming. Your swimming is not *just* a pleasurable experience,

---

6 He cannot have meant that freedom from pain in itself is a desirable end. Rather his view must be that what is desirable overall is the greatest overall balance of pleasure over pain, and that the only thing that it is desirable in itself is pleasure. See ch. 5.

going on in your head, as it were. It involves your thrashing your arms around, making a lot of waves in the pool, as well as much else. So what we might call a *pleasure-source* is an activity in which one engages with enjoyment, such as swimming, or a state which produces enjoyment, such as being massaged (remember that swimming, as a pleasure-source, *includes* the pleasurable experience). But, equally, 'pleasures' can be used to refer solely to *pleasurable experiences* themselves, that is, for example, the pleasurable experience of swimming, independently of the thrashing about and so on. Which does Mill have in mind when he speaks of pleasures: pleasure-sources or pleasurable experiences?

Mill often contrasts pleasures with 'pains' or sets them alongside the 'absence' of pain (see e.g. 2.8, 12; 4.5, 10–11; see also the contrast between the pleasures of the intellect, etc., and those of sensation in 2.4). *Pain*, in English, cannot mean quite the opposite of *pleasure-source*. If you enjoy punting, and hate housework, you may say that punting is one of your pleasures, but not that housework is one of your pains. You may say that it *is* a pain, in the sense of a trouble to you, but you may not speak of *pains* to mean activities or states you dislike in the way you can speak of pleasures as activities or states you enjoy. When Mill speaks of pains, then, I myself am tempted to think that we should understand him as speaking of 'painful' or unpleasant experiences. This might be a reason for understanding him, on grounds of consistency, to be speaking of pleasurable experiences rather than sources of pleasure in 2.2. We should remember also that the notion of pleasure, as opposed to pleasure-source, was standard in the utilitarian tradition. Bentham, for example, calls pleasures and pains 'interesting perceptions' (Bentham 1789: 5.1). But, as I said, Mill himself does not explicitly draw any sharp distinction between the notions of *a pleasure* and *pleasure*. For that reason, any attribution of hedonism to him can only be tentative; but I submit that such an attribution is not unreasonable.

Mill uses the terms *pleasures* and *enjoyments* interchangeably. To call him a 'hedonist' might therefore be said to be stretching things a little, since enjoyable experiences are not quite the same as pleasurable experiences. One can enjoy certain experiences, such as struggling painfully over the final ridge to reach the peak of a mountain, which are not well described as pleasurable. So we might call Mill an *enjoyment theorist*, rather than a hedonist. Since Bentham also stretched the notion of pleasure, he could be put into the same category. But, for ease of exposition, I shall just stipulate that enjoyment theories are versions of hedonism.

If we are to understand Mill as a hedonist, is he a full hedonist, accepting that what makes pleasurable experiences good is their being pleasurable? Again it seems that we can find this component in 2.2. Everything desirable, that is, everything good, is so because of the pleasure it contains or produces. (Remember that we might understand all this in terms of enjoyableness.)

Taking the higher ground

Let us now return to 'Haydn and the oyster', and Mill's solution. What is involved in taking the higher ground?

> It is quite compatible with the principle of utility to recognise the fact, that some *kinds* of pleasure are more desirable and more valuable than others. It would be absurd that while, in estimating all other things, quality is considered as well as quantity, the estimation of pleasures should be supposed to depend on quantity alone.

> If I am asked, what I mean by difference of quality in pleasures, or what makes one pleasure more valuable than another, merely as a pleasure, except its being greater in amount, there is but one possible answer. Of two pleasures, if there be one to which all or almost all who have experience of both give a decided preference, irrespective of any feeling of moral obligation to prefer it, that is the more desirable pleasure. If one of the two is, by those who are competently acquainted with both, placed so far above the other that they prefer it, even though knowing it to be attended with a greater amount of discontent, and would not resign it for any quantity of the other pleasure which their nature is capable of, we are

justified in ascribing to the preferred enjoyment a superiority in quality, so far outweighing quantity as to render it, in comparison, of small account.

(2.4–5)

Mill's claim, then, is that some pleasures are so valuable that they will be preferred, by those who have experienced both, to any amount of certain other pleasures. Such pleasures pass what we might call the *informed preference test*. What does this contrast between types of pleasures amount to? In the passage preceding that quoted, Mill sets up the contrast in various ways: between animal pleasures and pleasures arising from the specifically human higher faculties; between the pleasures of sensation and the pleasures of the intellect, the feelings and the imagination, and the moral sentiments; between bodily pleasures and mental pleasures. Since Mill is responding to an objection which itself rests on the sort of distinction he has in mind, he does not stop to elaborate it further. From what he says here it is difficult to find a clear criterion for placing a pleasure on one side of the divide or the other. When you savour the Lagavulin, the pleasure you take in it would seem to be quite different from that your whisky-loving dog takes in it. You can reflect on its origins and the way it is produced, comparing its flavour to other whiskies using a broad vocabulary referring to properties to which your dog is quite insensitive. But your pleasure is a bodily one, and certainly involves certain sensations.

Mill might suggest that these pleasures are mixed, and that their elements can be conceived of separately. We have here, perhaps, the gustatory sensation (a lower pleasure) and the reflection upon it (a higher pleasure). But then it is not clear how the distinction between the two kinds of pleasure on the basis of the preference of those who have experienced both will work. Does it make sense to claim that one would prefer the reflection alone to any amount of the pure pleasure of taste?

Attempts to spell out a criterion for distinguishing higher from lower pleasures on the basis of the contrasts Mill offers will, in fact, be unfruitful, not only because of the vagueness of the distinctions, but because the informed preference test will almost certainly work against any precise distinction. The pleasurable sensation of scratching an itch, for example, would seem a paradigm candidate for being placed on the lower side of the dichotomy. But there are other sensations – the sheer taste of the cappuccino at the St Giles' Café, for instance – which are such that I would prefer them to any amount of the pleasure of scratching an itch. That seems to make drinking the St Giles' cappuccino a higher pleasure. But I would not surrender the pleasure of reading philosophy for any amount of it, which turns it – in this comparison – into a lower pleasure. The lesson here is that one cannot classify a pleasure as higher or lower without saying exactly *what* it is being alleged to be higher or lower than. This is important. Mill's higher/lower distinction has usually been understood to work as a pair of mutually exclusive categories into which pleasurable experiences can be classified as 'higher' (i.e. 'high') or 'lower' (i.e. 'low'). In fact, 'higher' and 'lower' are relative terms, and whether one pleasure is higher than another depends on the circumstances of the particular comparison.

Mill's contrasts, however, are not pointless. Which pleasures are higher and which lower is indeed relative to the comparison in question. But the comparisons Mill has in mind are those between the pleasures of the intellectual, the aesthete or the morally good person, and those of the sensualist. Carlyle and others were unhappy to see the former preferred merely on the ground that they give rise to 'more pleasure'. And with respect to *these* comparisons, Mill suggests, it is quite consistent with utilitarianism to allow that the pleasures of the intellectual are so valuable that they can never be counterbalanced in value by any amount of sensual pleasure.

We can now see how Mill's distinction between higher and lower pleasures provides him with a solution to the problem posed in 'Haydn and the oyster'. That problem arose out of the full cardinal commensurability of pleasures. Pleasure so understood functions like weight. If you place an extremely heavy weight on one side of the scale, and begin placing a number of much smaller weights on the other side, there must come a moment when the sum of the smaller weights outbalances the other weight. Mill denies this for pleasures. According to him, there are *discontinuities* in value between pleasures, such that no amount of certain (lower) pleasures can ever be more valuable for the person who experiences them than some finite amount of certain (higher) pleasures (see Griffin 1986: 85). So Mill can suggest that just *one* of Haydn's pleasures – that, say, of conducting the Oxford Symphony at his own degree ceremony in 1793 – is more valuable than any amount of oyster pleasure. For him, the choice of Haydn's life would be rational however long the angel agreed to make the life of the oyster.[7]

An alleged dilemma

Mill drops full cardinality, in the sense that there is for him no single additive cardinal scale for measuring welfare. He can allow it in cases like that of the whisky-tasting I discussed in the section on Bentham, but when one pleasure is higher and another lower, the ranking can no longer be cardinal. For if it were, there would be no discontinuity, and some amount of the supposedly lower pleasure could outweigh the value of the higher. In higher/lower comparisons, the only ranking available is *ordinal* (*ordo* is Latin

---

7 Though discontinuity helps Mill here, it does raise a puzzle. If we imagine experiences on a scale from low bodily to high intellectual, there will come some point where discontinuity sets in. But why should a small change make an infinitely large difference in value? It should also be noted that there are two possible interpretations of Mill's view. On one interpretation, a competent judge will prefer any amount of the higher pleasure (e.g. intellectual insight) once they have secured a certain amount of the lower pleasure (e.g. physical comfort). On a second interpretation, the competent judge will *surrender* any amount of the lower pleasure as long as the amount of higher pleasure increases. I suggest that the second interpretation is the less problematic, since the first provides no justification for placing such importance on lower pleasures already possessed. Nor need the second have particularly unpalatable practical implications, given the importance of lower pleasures such as physical comfort as necessary conditions for pursuing higher pleasures. These points are related to another important fact: that the claim that 'quality' matters as well as intensity and duration is *not* equivalent to the claim that there are discontinuities in value. One could hold, for example, that the life of Haydn was two, three or many thousand times as good as that of the oyster. Mill runs the two claims together, but this is not particularly problematic, since what solves the 'Haydn and the oyster' problem is discontinuity.

for *ordering*). The higher pleasure is *more* valuable than the lower, but it does not make sense to ask by *how much* more, because in comparisons like these there are no units.

Mill's distinction between higher and lower pleasures attracted a great deal of critical attention, most of it hostile, from the time of its publication. By far the most common objection was that Mill faces a dilemma: either quality collapses into quantity and Mill has made no advance on Bentham, or Mill can no longer count himself a (full) hedonist.[8]

When Mill speaks of 'quantity', he almost certainly has in mind Bentham's conception of welfare, according to which the value of a pleasure depends solely upon its duration and intensity. Indeed it is probably intensity in particular which he takes to ground the notion of quantity (see, for example, the second half of 2.8). When he speaks of 'quality', he means the 'intrinsic nature' of the pleasure in question (2.4; the superiority of the higher pleasures is likewise 'intrinsic' (2.7)). Mill's claim, then, is that the intrinsic nature of a higher pleasure is such that it is more valuable for the person who enjoys it than would be the enjoyment of any amount of lower pleasure, however intense it might be.

The first horn of the dilemma allows Mill to remain a full hedonist, but at the price of dropping the higher/lower distinction. The argument is that a full hedonist must accept that what makes one experience more valuable than another can only be its pleasantness or pleasurableness (or, on our broad understanding of hedonism, its enjoyableness). If, therefore, Mill places on one balance of the scale a higher pleasure and on the other a lower pleasure, increasing the pleasurableness on the second side of the scale must eventually result in the balance tipping in favour of the lower pleasure, since each is valuable only because of its pleasurableness.

If Mill denies that pleasures are commensurable in this way, the argument continues, then he must accept that the higher pleasures are more valuable for some reason other than their being

---

8   Versions of this argument can be found in Bradley 1927: 116–20; Green 1883: 167–78; Martineau 1885: vol. 2, 305–8; Moore 1903: 77–81; Rashdall 1907: vol. 1, 25–7; Sidgwick 1907: 94–5.

more pleasant, such as their enabling those experiencing them to realize their true selves. But this will impale him on the other horn of the dilemma, on which he can no longer be a full hedonist. He might perhaps still be able to say that welfare consists in higher pleasures, but the good-making property of these pleasures will not be their pleasurableness alone. And, once he allows in, say, 'being self-realizing' as a good-making property, Mill will be unable to remain a hedonist at all, and have to admit that self-realizing experiences, even when not pleasurable, can add to a person's welfare.

All this, however, is just to beg the question against Mill. According to him, the value of a pleasurable experience depends not only on its duration and intensity, but also on its quality, its intrinsic nature.[9] Mill can suggest, then, that the higher pleasure is valuable because of its pleasurableness, and thus avoid the first horn of the dilemma. The only way in which the lower pleasure could outweigh the higher pleasure would be for its nature to be transformed so that it would no longer be a lower pleasure. Merely increasing its quantity – that is, the duration and intensity of the pleasurable experience – will not be enough. Nor need Mill flinch from claiming that higher pleasures are more pleasurable, and hence more valuable, as long as full cardinal commensurability is ruled out. This means that Mill can avoid the second horn of the dilemma, on which he could no longer be a hedonist, by postulating no good-making property other than pleasurableness in the first place. Higher pleasures are good for people purely because of their pleasurableness.

The point may, however, be pressed: *what* about the nature of higher pleasures makes them more valuable for the person experiencing them? Must it not be that they enable self-realization, or that they are, say, noble? (Mill in fact mentions nobility as a characteristic of the character of the person living a life of higher pleasures in 2.9.) Here Mill can refer to a point he stresses elsewhere in *Utilitarianism*, and which again can be found in Bentham (Bentham 1789: 1.11), viz. that ultimate ends must be

---

9 It is worth considering whether intensity is not itself part of the 'quality' of a pleasure; see Dahl 1973: 38, n. 1.

accepted as good without proof (1.5; 4.1). Why are the higher pleasures more valuable? Because their nature makes the enjoyment of them more valuable. But why does their nature make them more valuable? It just does; and, Mill and Bentham agree, any theorist of welfare must reach a point such as this. For Bentham, it is a brute fact that pleasures are valuable and that the degree of their value depends on their intensity and duration. For the self-realization theorist, it is a brute fact that self-realization is a good. Brute facts can be facts none the less.

So, to recap. Mill believes that welfare consists only in pleasurable (or enjoyable) experiences, and that these experiences are valuable only because of their pleasurableness. The longer and more intense the pleasurableness of any experience, the more valuable it is. The nature of a pleasure also affects its value, to the point where discontinuities set in. A mental pleasure, for example, is more valuable than a bodily one, however long or intense. Here, 'being mental' is not a good-making property, just as, for example, 'lasting for four minutes' is not a good-making property. Similarly, 'being noble' and, perhaps, 'being refined' or 'being deep', are just facts about experiences like their being mental, and can affect value in the same way. So Mill can remain a hedonist: only pleasurable experiences are valuable, and only pleasurableness is a good-making property.

There is nevertheless something to the criticisms of Mill. Though he can avoid the dilemma so often posed for him and remain a hedonist, there does remain something of a gap in his account. If we believe Mill, how pleasurable, and hence how valuable, an experience is depends not only on the length and intensity of the pleasure, but also on its nature as mental, noble or whatever. Length or intensity instantiated in an experience alone, independent of enjoyableness, plausibly does not increase its value at all. Indeed, in the case of pains, length and intensity make things worse as they increase, but only to the extent that the painfulness increases. According to Mill, the same must be true of, say, nobility. To the extent that an experience is merely noble, and not enjoyed (if Mill will allow this), it is not valuable.

But if nobility can increase enjoyableness and the value of

enjoyableness, we might ask why it cannot be a good-making property in its own right. Can an experience which is highly noble (or refined, or profound), but nevertheless not enjoyable, not add something of value to my life? We might also wonder what conception of pleasure or pleasurableness Mill is working with. For Bentham, pleasurableness was an introspectible property of sensations that varies in length and intensity but is otherwise common to all pleasures. The sheer nature of the experience in question could not affect pleasurableness so understood.

Mill, however, refuses to accept that nobility independent of enjoyableness can be of value (2.15). Here we see his deep commitment to the hedonistic spirit of classical utilitarianism, which can be captured in what I shall call the *enjoyment requirement*: only pleasurableness or enjoyableness makes things good (this is the explanatory component of full hedonism). As we shall see in a later chapter, Mill believed that human beings desire only pleasure. Only pleasure is good, and we desire only pleasure. This view is too narrow: there are many, many properties of our lives which add to their value independently of enjoyableness; and some of these properties are the very ones Mill claimed affected the enjoyableness of pleasures.[10]

The competent judges

Mill believes, then, that pleasurable or enjoyable experiences are what constitute welfare, and that their value for the subject of them lies in their being enjoyable. One enjoyable experience is more valuable than another if, other things being equal, it is longer or

---

10   A view similar to Mill's, and influenced by Moore 1903: ch. 6, is sometimes suggested, according to which pleasure is a *necessary condition* for something independent of pleasure's being valuable; see e.g. Parfit 1984: app. I. Knowledge alone, for example, is of no value; but knowledge enjoyed is valuable, and the value emerges from both the knowledge and the enjoyment. A version of this view will be discussed in the next chapter, but it is worth pointing out at this stage that it faces a problem similar to that I have raised for Mill. If nobility, for example, can affect value independently of pleasure but only in its presence, the reason for its being unable to add value when pleasure is absent remains obscure.

more intense. But when things are not equal, and the experiences differ radically in nature, one pleasure may be so much more valuable than another that no amount of the latter could outweigh the value of the former.

You will recall that Mill believes that when it comes to deciding which of two pleasures is more valuable, the decision of those who have experienced both is final (see 2.5, quoted above, and also 2.8). Mill is quick to point out that the introduction of the notion of competent judges is required anyway, independently of the higher/lower distinction: 'What means are there of determining which is the acutest of two pains, or the intensest of two pleasurable sensations, except the general suffrage of those who are familiar with both?' (2.8).

In the case of intensity, it would be peculiar to suggest that an experience has a certain intensity *because* someone (a competent judge) says it has that intensity. Rather, the judge says it has that intensity because it does indeed have it. Since Mill speaks of the judgement of quality as analogous to that of quantity, we should assume that a higher pleasure is not higher merely because the competent judges say that it is. Thus Mill states confidently: 'It is better to be a human being dissatisfied than a pig satisfied; better to be Socrates dissatisfied than a fool satisfied' (2.6). The judges will agree with Mill, because they are competent to assess the way things are.

The deliverances of the competent judges, then, are *evidential*. They are a tribunal to which we refer to decide what is true independently of any human judgement. Nor do they represent an *ad hoc* device, floating free from the rest of Mill's philosophical commitments. As an empiricist, Mill believes that human knowledge is based on the deliverances of our senses. This is why he is keen to base ethics on 'observation and experience' (1.3), and we shall see in my chapter 4 that his commitment to the observational method emerges again in his attempt to prove utilitarianism. Further, hedonism itself, with the stress it places on the importance of the way experiences of the individual subject appear to that subject, itself sits very easily with empiricism.

Because the views of the judges are only evidential, it is of course conceivable that they may be mistaken, and Mill implicitly accepts this in allowing for disagreement among them. One pleasure is more valuable than another if all '*or almost all*' competent judges prefer it (2.5, my italics), and, if they differ, the judgement 'of the majority among them, must be admitted as final' (2.8). Mill is claiming not that the majority *must* be right, but that it is only reasonable to respect the decision of the majority. He is correct: the chance of the majority's being right is greater than that of the minority's. It may be that Mill does not make sufficient room for the vagueness of value and the vagaries of taste. But he might well have accepted that it would be absurd to ask the judges to decide between, say, the pleasures of reading Tolstoy and those of reading Dostoyevsky. Certainly it would not threaten his main thesis, which is that some pleasures are clearly higher than others.

Another common worry about the judges is whether they can be sufficiently impartial. To be a competent judge of the relative values of, say, reading Hegelian philosophy and drinking blended whisky, it is not sufficient that one have *experienced* both; one must have *enjoyed* them. Further, though this is not in the text, we should presumably also accept that a competent judge will have enjoyed them *properly* and *to the right extent*. If you enjoy reading Hegel because, though you do not understand a word of it, you are reminded of the beautiful lecturer on Hegel you once heard, you are not a competent judge. Nor are you competent if you enjoy reading Hegel only to the extent that you prefer it to doing nothing at all (locked in a room alone with some Hegel, you would read it in preference to staring out of the window at the sky). Competence in this case requires some degree of understanding and intellectual curiosity. But here the concern about impartiality enters. It may be that the characteristics required to assess the value of higher pleasures are fundamentally opposed to those required in the case of the lower pleasures: 'The philosopher who is a half-hearted sensualist cannot estimate the attractions of a debauched existence, any more than the sensualist flicking through the pages of Hume can estimate the pleasures of philosophy' (Ryan 1974: 111).

There is something in this. Certainly it is true that some people are of such an intellectual or sensual bent that they find it hard to appreciate the kind of enjoyment to which they are not naturally attracted. But I see no reason to assume that this is true of all. Many of the philosophers I know, whose judgements of the value of the enjoyment of reading philosophy I would be ready to accept, frequently demonstrate a capacity to appreciate physical pleasures as well. Whether Mill himself was such a philosopher I shall consider shortly.

Is Mill's position not, however, objectionably élitist? This objection is to some degree misplaced: what matters is whether Mill's view is true or not, and it may be that the truth is unpalatable. But let me say one or two things about it, since reflection on this issue does in fact raise some questions about Mill's conception of welfare.

First, Mill is not going as far as did Aristotle in suggesting that individuals themselves are not the final arbiters on whether an experience they are having is pleasurable (Aristotle *c*. 330 BC: 1176a15–19). Secondly, he is not advocating that everyone should give up lower pleasures and start reading philosophy or poetry. What matters is not the experiences, but the enjoyment of them. Those who gain no enjoyment from reading philosophy cannot gain anything from it. Thirdly, and relatedly, he is not suggesting that people should be forced into such activities. This would almost certainly be counter-productive from Mill's point of view, because the coercion would remove the possibility of enjoyment, and there are anyway good utilitarian reasons for allowing people to make up their own minds (see ch. 8).

One assumption Mill is making is that some experiences are more valuable than others. This, apart from general worries about the status of value judgements, is not a particularly radical assumption. It must be accepted by anyone who believes that ecstatic pleasure is better for a person than severe pain. But Mill also assumes that the nature of certain enjoyed experiences or enjoyments is such that they are of incommensurably greater value than certain others. And he gives us some idea of what these experiences are: the pleasures of the intellect, the feelings and the moral sentiments are higher than those of sensual bodily indulgence. Here, as Mill realized, one can say little to defend one's views about relative values. But I myself am ready to accept that there are such discontinuities. Faced in a thought experiment with the choice of the pleasure of reading right through Jane Austen and any amount of the mild physical pleasure to be gained from a not very vigorous massage, I should undoubtedly choose the Austen. Among those who disagree with me and Mill will probably be those who, along with Bentham, would choose the life of the oyster in my earlier example.

What is perhaps doing some of the work behind the scenes at this point in Mill's argument is something like Aristotle's notion of 'practical wisdom' or *phronēsis* (Aristotle *c.* 330 BC: bk. 6). Those who can judge the value of experiences correctly are those who are not only sensitive to the salient features of those experiences, particularly their intensity and nature, but able to attach to those features the evaluative weight they deserve. For Aristotle, the correct judge of what is really pleasurable, and how good anything is, is the excellent or virtuous man, while for Mill it is the comptetent judge. Both must be assumed to possess some faculty which allows their judgements to be decisive.

But there remains a nagging doubt about these judges. I noted above how Bentham and Mill failed to distinguish clearly between the concepts of 'pleasure', 'a pleasure' and 'enjoyment'. Similarly, in his discussion of higher and lower pleasures, Mill does not anywhere differentiate the notion of a *kind* of pleasure, such as that of reading philosophy, from an *individual instance* of a kind, such as that particular experience which I hope you may enjoy when reading Mill.

Mill's *Utilitarianism* is intended partly as a guide to how to live. Living involves making choices, often between one individual instance of a kind of pleasure and an instance of another kind. At six o'clock, for example, I may have to choose between an individual instance of reading Hegel and an instance of drinking gin and tonic. I might decide to consult a panel of competent judges to help me make up my mind. Mill says that a competent judge must have experienced both pleasures. Clearly, the two *individual* pleasures I am contemplating, since they are both merely possible, cannot actually have been experienced by anyone. So the judges must be assumed to have enjoyed both *kinds* of pleasure, i.e. to have experienced in their own lives other individual instances of these kinds of pleasure.

But if I consistently apply the views of the panel in my decision-making, my life will be an austere one indeed. For their view is that reading philosophy is incommensurably more valuable than any lower pleasure. So it appears that my welfare will be promoted maximally if I stick at the philosophy for as long as possible – that is, for as long as I enjoy it properly to some less than trivial extent – and pursue lower pleasures, such as drinking gin and tonic, only when higher pleasures are beyond me. This is what we might call a *lexical* view of welfare maximization, according to which secondary values are to be promoted only when primary values have been promoted maximally.[11]

It would not be implausible to suggest that Mill himself, because of his upbringing, was indeed something of a 'half-hearted sensualist', who believed the lexical view correct. At the beginning of 2.7, he considers the case of people who, though capable of higher pleasures, occasionally pursue lower pleasures instead, implying quite clearly that he thinks that this is a mistake on their part, to be put down to weakness of will. And at the close of the same paragraph he claims that many people over time have 'broken down' in an attempt to combine both sorts of pleasure. This is not to say, of course, that Mill held lower pleasures to be worthless. The ultimate end, he suggests, is a life 'as rich as possible in enjoyments, both in point of quantity and quality' (2.10). Nevertheless, the best life for me will be a life in which higher pleasures are maximized; lower pleasures are to be pursued only to the extent that pursuit of a higher is not possible, because of weariness,

---

11 See Rawls 1971: 42–3, n. 23. Rawls makes reference to Mill's higher/lower distinction, and to a similar distinction in Hutcheson 1755. The idea can be found in Plato c. 380 BC: 580d–583a. It should be noted that lexicality can be introduced *within* the range of, say, intellectual pleasures. So serious appreciation of Hegel, for example, may be better than any amount of superficial skimming. And it could be that serious appreciation is best achieved by at least the occasional gin and tonic. But this view still seems excessively cerebral.

physical need or whatever. Again, there are interesting analogies here with the views of Aristotle, who believed that recreational pleasures are valuable not in themselves, but only instrumentally in providing relaxation between excellent or virtuous activities (Aristotle *c* 330 BC: 1176b27–1177a1).

Where Mill's comparisons go wrong is in their starkness. The choice is between one higher pleasure and one lower pleasure, between Jane Austen and the massage. Human life, however, as Mill himself realizes, must consist of a combination of such enjoyments. Because he accepts the lexical priority of higher pleasures, Mill does not stop to consider combinations of enjoyable experiences. But the lexical view is too extreme: this is the place, if anywhere, where Mill's élitism spoils his analysis. Given the choice, whether in the context of a thought experiment or human life itself, between reading Jane Austen right through on the one hand, and a combination of reading all of Jane Austen except *Northanger Abbey* along with a huge and varied amount of lower pleasure, it seems quite rational to prefer the combination.

Since we are looking to Mill for guidance on how to live whole lives, we should consider higher and lower pleasures in the context of whole lives. Mill does in fact allow us the material to do this, speaking of the competent judges as preferring 'the *manner of existence* which employs their higher faculties' (2.6, my italics), and of 'which of two *modes of existence* is the most grateful to the feelings' (2.8, my italics). He talks of the ultimate end as 'an existence' in 2.10, and continues to take this global view in following paragraphs. At this level, the claim about discontinuity again looks plausible. It is indeed better, in most cases, to be a human being dissatisfied than a pig satisfied, however long and however intense the porcine enjoyments might be.

There is a problem in a strict application of the competent judges test to the relative value of whole lifetimes. Here it really is true that the judge does not know what it is like to be a pig in the sense of having lived the life of a pig. Each of us can live only one life. But we should be charitable in interpreting philosophers, and Mill is no exception. A human being does most of the things a pig does: eats, drinks, has sex, sleeps, plays and so on. We certainly have more of an idea of what it is like to be a pig than the pig has of what it is like to be human. Here, then, our judgements 'must be admitted as final' (2.8).

Finally, we must consider whether Mill's views of human welfare have undemocratic implications. It is important here to remember the distinction between theories of welfare and theories of morality. One could accept Mill's distinction between higher and lower pleasures, and yet deny that this distinction ought to dominate morality, and in particular the morality of public policy-making. But Mill is a utilitarian, who believes that welfare ought to be maximized. Given the discontinuities between higher and lower pleasures, is he not committed to the view that taxation for education and the arts should be increased hugely, possibly at the expense of other areas, such as sport? This would not have been the view of the majority in his day or ours, so is Mill advocating an undemocratic political system?

In fact, despite the tensions he perceived between the views of the majority and the truth, Mill remained a democrat throughout his life. He took the longer view: over time, the best chances of bringing about a world in which large numbers of human beings led lives containing a rich mix of higher pleasures lay in democracy. Mill would anyway have accepted the French writer Alexis de Tocqueville's view that there was no longer any practical choice in Europe between democracy and other political systems (Tocqueville 1848: 'Author's preface', para. 1). The real question was what *sort* of democracy would be best for humanity, and that was a question Mill would answer in the light of his own views concerning human welfare and morality.

So we now reach the end of the first of my two chapters specifically on welfare. Remember that I have been discussing welfare independently of morality, so that you might accept Mill's views on welfare or something like them even if you do not in the end believe utilitarianism. We have seen how Mill's hedonism provides a response to a particular problem in views such as Bentham's, and how Mill's own view, with its unexplained notion of 'pleasurableness' and the rôle played by non-hedonistic properties in determining goodness (if only via pleasurableness), seems to point in a direction away from hedonism. In the following chapter we shall head in just that direction.

Further reading

On theories of welfare in general see Sumner 1981: ch. 5; Parfit 1984: app. I; Griffin 1986: chs 1–4; Kagan 1992. On hedonism see Broad 1930: ch. 6; Edwards 1979; Sprigge 1988. On Mill's conception of welfare see, as well as Broad and the critics cited in n. 5, Mitchell 1970; Martin 1972; Dahl 1973; West 1976; Berger 1984: ch. 2; Skorupski 1989: 295–307; Donner 1991: chs 1–3; Sumner 1992; Riley 1993.

Chapter 3

Experience, desire and the ideal

Veridical and non-veridical experience

In the previous chapter, I outlined Mill's hedonism. Mill believed that welfare – that is, what makes life good for the being that lives it – consists in pleasurable (or enjoyable) experiences, and that what makes these experiences good for their subject is their being pleasurable. Because both of these views can be ascribed to him, he can be called a *full hedonist*. But our experiences can be understood in two importantly different ways, each of which has various implications for any view of welfare based on them. It is important to notice, incidentally, that the distinction I am about to draw is independent of that between pleasurable experiences and the sources of pleasure drawn in chapter 2 (the distinction between the pleasurable experience of swimming, and the swimming itself). The following distinction is between two different conceptions of pleasurable experience.

We can speak of 'experiencing *something*'. If

45

I taste Chateau Latour 1970, then I experience drinking that wine. If I swim six lengths, then I experience swimming six lengths. These *veridical experiences* can be contrasted with *non-veridical experiences*, which purport to be experiences of something real, but in fact are not. Dreams consist largely of non-veridical experiences. If I dream that I am riding a horse, then I am indeed having an experience. But I am not experiencing, or having the veridical experience of, riding a horse. That I can have only by sitting on a real live horse. In my dream, it is only *as if* I am riding a horse.

But if my dream is extremely vivid, it does of course have features in common with a veridical experience. In particular, it feels the same 'from the inside': the *experience itself* is the same. Indeed, I may not be able to distinguish the veridical experience from the non-veridical, other than by using extraneous criteria (noting, for example, that after the non-veridical experience I wake up).

When Mill claims that welfare consists in experiences, does he mean veridical experiences or non-veridical experiences, or both? And, prior to that, why should it matter? Consider this case (cf. Nozick 1974: 42–5):

The dream life. Ahmed is living a life rich in higher and lower pleasures. He spends as much time as he can engaging in intellectual and moral pursuits, both of which he enjoys to the full, and the rest of the time he fills with lower pleasures. Bina is in a coma after a road accident, but her memory and imagination combine to give her roughly the same experiences as Ahmed.

Do not worry too much about the neurophysiological assumptions required by this thought experiment. I realize that people in comas almost certainly do not and could not have experiences like Bina's. What is important about the case is that it enables us to distinguish two versions of the experience account of welfare. On one version, the *veridical experience* account, Ahmed's life exhibits a high degree of welfare, while Bina's is worthless. What matters on this account are *veridical* experiences *of* certain activities, events or whatever in the world. Bina's experiences are merely *as of* visiting the National Gallery, swimming, helping a friend.

Ahmed and Bina have roughly the same experiences. On the *wide* experience account, their lives will therefore be of roughly the same welfare value. According to this account, because welfare consists in experiences, whether these experiences arise from living in the real world or from dreaming is irrelevant to their value for the subject. What matters is just experiences, how things seem to people from the inside.

To return to Mill: is his view a veridical or a wide experience account? Since he can be interpreted in either way, we should consider both accounts. I shall suggest that the problems with each, though different, lead in a similar direction towards an account of welfare not based on experience at all, a direction in which we saw Mill himself heading at the close of chapter 2.

Mill's account and the value of authenticity

The problem with the wide experience account is straightforward enough. It requires us to conclude that Bina's dream life is as valuable for her as Ahmed's life in the real world. That is something that many will not accept. The source of an experience, not just the way it appears from the inside, is relevant to how valuable it is for its subject.[1]

Before discussing the veridical experience account, let me briefly deal with one doubt about whether Mill could be taken to be advancing it. Recall the competent judges. According to Mill, one experience is more valuable than another if those who have experienced both judge it to be so. Now there is no difference from the inside between experiences like Ahmed's and experiences like Bina's. So, it might be suggested, in any comparison between a

---

1   There are at least two aspects of Mill's philosophy as a whole which might be thought to suggest a wide experience interpretation of *Utilitarianism*. One is his attraction to phenomenalism, the view that the world in some sense consists in sensations, and the other is his apparent acceptance of the view that pleasure is a sensation; see e.g., respectively, *E* 9.177–87 and *AP* 31.214, n. But phenomenalists and those who take pleasure to be a sensation are able to make at least a reasonable case for the claim that they can consistently draw a distinction between veridical and non-veridical experiences.

veridical experience and a non-veridical experience, which are introspectively indiscernible from each other, a competent judge can only value them equally.

Again, we have to be charitable in construing the informed preference test. Most of us have had non-veridical experiences, in dreams and in the real world, when what we take to be an experience of something is not such. And though the fact that these are non-veridical experiences may be unknown by us at the time, we can often later reflect upon them in the context of a mental life consisting primarily of veridical experiences. I can compare my dream experience of riding a horse *as a non-veridical experience* with my experience of riding a horse *as a veridical experience*. And that is enough for it at least to be possible for me to evaluate them differently.

So let us turn to the veridical experience account. Many people believe strongly that Ahmed's life goes much better for him than Bina's does for her, and the veridical experience account provides a basis for this belief in the stress it places on the genuineness of experiences. But remember that Mill is a full hedonist, who believes that the only good-making property of an experience is its being pleasurable or enjoyable. So if Mill accepts a veridical experience account, he must claim that the source of the value of the genuine experiences in Ahmed's life is his enjoying them. The sheer fact that they are genuine is of course important, since on this account only genuine experiences are valuable. But the genuineness cannot be a source of welfare value, or a good-making property, since that would require dropping hedonism.

Here there might seem to be a serious problem for the veridical experience account in combination with full hedonism. For Ahmed's life and Bina's life are *equally enjoyable*. If welfare consists only in enjoyment, then it seems that any version of full hedonism must allow that their lives are of equal welfare value.

We might respond to this objection on Mill's behalf. According to him, whether one experience is more valuable than another is a question to be answered by someone competent. Mill could plausibly argue that Bina's view of how enjoyable her experiences are is not that of a competent judge. For she is unaware of an important fact about her experiences, that they are non-veridical. A competent judge, however, might take a different view.

But this leads us into the same issue as that which arose at the end of the previous chapter. Recall what Mill added to Bentham's criteria of duration and intensity for assessing the value of pleasures: their nature, or quality. He can therefore, consistently with his full hedonism, claim that the value of Ahmed's pleasures to him depends partly on their being genuine, in the sense that their pleasurableness is affected by their being genuine (he would of course have also to explain exactly what conception of pleasurableness he has in mind, and how it could be affected by genuineness). But note two things. First, he would then have moved towards an Aristotelian view, according to which how pleasurable an experience is is a matter to be judged not only by the person experiencing that experience. Secondly, on this view Mill cannot say that their being genuine itself adds to their value, since that would be to leave full hedonism behind. If, however, their being genuine can affect how enjoyable they are, why cannot it be a source of value in its own right? Ahmed's experiences are genuine experiences of study, aesthetic appreciation, moral action, eating, drinking. Part of what makes these experiences valuable for him is their being enjoyable (so there is *some* welfare value in Bina's life). But another good-making property of Ahmed's experiences is that they are indeed experiences *of* study, aesthetic appreciation, and so on.

Beyond experience

So we should allow that the nature of an experience, and in particular its being genuine, can itself directly add to its value. We should move beyond hedonism to a view which allows not only for the value of enjoyment, but for that of genuineness. One version of such a view we might call, after G.E. Moore (1873–1958), the *pure organic* view (Moore 1903: 27–31). According to this view, the sheer experience of, say, helping a friend and not enjoying it is worthless; likewise, a non-veridical enjoyment of helping a friend, such as that experienced by Bina, is of no welfare value. What counts is the bringing together of the two. Experiences which are both veridical and enjoyable are valuable, and their value lies in the combination of these characteristics. On their own, neither being veridical nor being enjoyable adds anything to welfare.

The pure organic view goes too far. First, Bina gets something out of her life. It is better than an existence in which her brain is quite inactive, and she experiences nothing. Secondly, some veridical experiences can be valuable for a person even if they are not enjoyed. Consider a rather morose sort of person, who enjoys nothing very much, but who sets himself the task of cataloguing the flora and fauna of a hitherto unnoticed, but ecologically fascinating, part of Africa. He may not enjoy the experience of constructing his catalogue (though let us assume that, though he is never absorbed or engaged in it, he does not find it unenjoyable), but it does seem to make his life better for him.

So a *disjunctive* experience account, according to which welfare value arises out of veridical valuable experiences and/or the enjoyment found in such experiences begins to look more defensible. But even here there seems to be something left unexplained. According to the disjunctive view, the welfare value of any activity I engage in can arise from either the experience of that activity or my enjoyment of it or both. But consider our naturalist in Africa. According to the disjunctive view, the welfare value here consists in his experiences. But why must it be the *experience* of his accomplishment that is valuable for him? Can we not say that adding substantially to the sum of human knowledge *itself*, independently of its being an experience, is valuable for a person? In other words, might there not be yet another source of welfare value in the nature of accomplishment itself?

Creating the catalogue will of course involve certain experiences. But the naturalist's accomplishments will not be identical with his experiences. He may bring it about, for example, that another naturalist is led into discovering a link between various species of bird which had never before been noticed. This sort of accomplishment adds to the value of the first naturalist's life for him, *even if* the naturalist's own experiences remain unaffected by them, perhaps because he never hears of them, or even because he dies before the effects of his actions occur. So accomplishment is valuable for people in itself, and this helps to explain why we are ready to count the experiences involved in such accomplishments as valuable.

My conclusion, then, is that not all welfare value lies in experiences, enjoyed or otherwise, and so any experience account is to be rejected. At this point, what has become by far the most widely accepted account of welfare in modern times will be suggested as a way to alleviate many of the difficulties I have noted in experience accounts. This is the *desire* account of welfare. Consider the dream life. What makes that life worse for Bina than Ahmed's is for him, it might be claimed, is that fewer of her desires are fulfilled. Like many people, Bina probably does desire not to be living a dream life. As Robert Nozick puts it, 'we want to *do* certain things, and not just have the experience of doing them' (Nozick 1974: 43). Our naturalist presumably had a strong desire to further human understanding of the natural world. The fact that this desire is fulfilled explains why we think his life goes better for him when he does succeed, even though he may be unaware of his success. A desire account might also be taken to provide a uniform explanation of the sources of welfare, which were beginning to appear quite disparate after the rejection of the disjunctive view: what is valuable about certain experiences, about certain enjoyments, and about certain activities and states is that they fulfil people's desires for them. Mill has sometimes been interpreted as a desire theorist, partly because of the work done by the notion of preference in the informed preference test. I myself do not accept that interpretation, but my arguments in the following two sections would count against Mill so understood. Because desire accounts are likely to be suggested as alternatives to hedonism, because some grasp of them is required if one is to see Mill's view in the context of contemporary discussions of welfare, and because their flaw leads us back in the direction Mill himself was heading in, they deserve some discussion.

Desire accounts

Recall that, when beginning to discuss hedonism in the previous chapter, I pointed out that theories of welfare have both a substantive and an explanatory component. The substantive component tells you which things will make you well off. Mill, for example, believed that we would be made well off by having pleasurable experiences of various kinds, and this makes him a hedonist. The explanatory component of any theory will tell you what *makes* the things said to be of welfare value by the substantive component good for people. Mill, as we have seen, held that pleasurable intellectual, moral and other experiences contribute to my welfare in so far as they are pleasurable or enjoyable. It is their being pleasurable, in other words, that makes them valuable. That is what makes him a full hedonist.

Theorists of welfare who differ over the explanatory component can agree over the substantive component. For example, one form of desire account could be a form of hedonism, according to which welfare consists in pleasurable experiences. But the desire theorist will suggest that what makes these experiences valuable for a person is not their being pleasurable, but their fulfilling desires. On the other hand, a theorist *might* say that welfare consists in the fulfilment of desire, but that what makes this valuable for the person whose desires are fulfilled is this fulfilment's being pleasurable. This would be to accept the explanatory but not the substantive component of full hedonism. I have already discussed hedonism, and I shall later be discussing a third view of welfare with which desire accounts might overlap in some areas. So I shall now restrict myself to *full desire* accounts, according to which welfare consists in the fulfilment of desire, and what makes the presence of desired items in a life good is their fulfilling desires.

The most straightforward version of such a theory I shall call the *present desire* account, according to which a person's welfare consists in the fulfilment of their present desires. The problem with this view is that it relativizes welfare judgements to particular times. Human beings are often irrational at particular times even when we would not describe them as irrational people. Consider, for example, the case of a fairly well-balanced adolescent, with a full and varied life. One evening her mother forbids her to attend a certain nightclub. The girl is furious, and rushes up to her mother's bedroom, where she knows a revolver is kept by the bed. She holds the gun to her own head, her only desire at that time being to retaliate against her mother.

According to the present desire account, the judgement, 'It is better to die than to continue living' is true of this girl at this time, since this is her strongest desire. But before her mother forbade her to attend the nightclub, this judgement would have been false, because the girl's desires would have been different. This suggests either that the present desire view is committed to contradictions, or that it is not really a theory about welfare – about how to assess a person's life – but a theory of welfare-at-a-time. Secondly, however we understand the deliverance of the theory at the time of the girl's holding the gun to her head, it is absurd. The theory suggests that if this girl pulls the trigger, she will have advanced her own welfare.

The *comprehensive* account takes a much broader view of people's lives. According to this view, welfare consists in the maximal fulfilment of a person's desires over their life as a whole. The most obvious version of a comprehensive account will weight desires according to their intensity, and sum them. Thus, on the assumption that judgements can be made about how to trade off intensity against quantity, the best life for me will be that in which the largest number of intense desires is fulfilled. The difficulty with this *purely summative* view can be seen in the following case (taken from Parfit 1984: 497):

Addiction I offer you daily injections of a drug. Every morning, you will wake with a very strong desire for the drug, which I shall fulfil. The effects of the injection will be neither pleasant nor painful.

On the purely summative view, you should be delighted by my offer. For I am presenting you with the chance to fulfil a very large number of very intense desires. But my guess is that you would decline the offer, preferring not to have these desires in the first place. In which case, a *global* version of the comprehensive account might be more plausible. The purely summative view suffers from the same sort of fault as did the present desire view: narrowness of focus. The present desire view relativized judgements about a person's welfare to particular times in that person's life. The purely summative view allows one to make judgements about a whole life; but those judgements themselves may well in certain cases be based only on short-term desires. The global view makes allowances for the fact that people have preferences about how their lives go as a whole, suggesting that my greatest welfare consists in the fulfilment of my desire to live in the way I most prefer. And the higher up my preference order of ways of life my present way of life actually is, the better off I am. Since you would prefer not to live a life dependent on my drug, such a life will make you less well off than a life without dependence.[2]

Again, however, there is a problem with such a view. Consider the case of an orphan, brought up within a monastery, with no knowledge of the world outside. He is given a choice of three lives: monk, cook, or gardener. He chooses the life of a monk. But his personality is such that, if he were to know of the options available to him outside the monastery, he would vastly prefer many of these to the life of a monk.

We might agree with the global view that the boy's welfare in the monastery consists in the fulfilment of his desire to live the life of a monk, as opposed to no life at all or the lives of either a cook or a gardener. But this cannot be the best life for him, since he would do better outside the monastery. The preferences on which assessments of welfare are based must not be preferences formed in ignorance of available options. According to the *informed desire* account, the life that would be best for a person is the one they would desire if fully informed of the facts about the various options available to them, and their greatest welfare would consist in the

---

2 It should be noted that the global view does not rule out summation, merely that form which characterizes the purely summative view.

fulfilment of that preference or desire. The fulfilment of the desire, in other words, is what makes this life best for them.

Desire and reason

Now we come to an insurmountable problem for all desire accounts: their reliance on a view influenced by a particular interpretation of the views of the Scottish philosopher David Hume (1711–76) (see e.g. Hume 1739–40: bk 3, sect. 1; 1751: app. 1). According to this view, desires are not open to rational criticism in the light of what is good, because there are no facts about what is good.[3] In other words, what someone desires cannot be criticized for being less good for them than some alternative other than in the light of the desires that person actually has, or would have in certain conditions. Desire accounts therefore leave hostages to contingency. Consider the case, for example, of a person who, fully informed about the options available to him, judges correctly that he could become a successful politician who would do a great deal to help the oppressed. But his paedophiliac desires to be around children lead him to desire far more strongly the life of a not very successful teacher.

In this case, though the person is fully informed, he most desires a way of life which not only others but *he himself* may judge to be far less good for him than some other way of life open to him. Even under conditions of full information, one's judgements about one's own welfare may deviate from what one most desires.

At this point, a desire theorist may drop the requirement that anything that makes me better off does so in so far as it fulfils an *actual* desire I have. Rather, it may be said, welfare consists in whatever *would* fulfil the global desires I would have *if I were* (1) rational (i.e. not subject to such distractions as overpowering sexual desire) and (2) fully informed.

But, again, though these further restrictions make it more likely that such preferences will be in line with reflective judge-ments about welfare, it will not necessarily be so. We can imagine

---

3   We can put aside the question of whether the thesis that welfare consists in desire fulfilment is a factual claim about what is good, important though it is.

a case in which someone's rational and informed global preferences would be quite absurd (this case is adapted from Rawls 1971: 432):

The grass-counter In a position of rational and informed choice, Cara, who is capable of a life of great accomplishment, friendship, love and pleasure, would desire most strongly a life of counting blades of grass.

It appears that, according to the informed desire account, grass-counting must be the better life for Cara. To this example the informed desire theorist is likely to object that Cara is almost certainly suffering from some kind of neurosis. But this reply illustrates particularly clearly something that has been occurring throughout my argument above: that the selection of any particular desire account is shaped by a prior conception of what is good and bad for people.

The present desire account was rejected because we judge that a short life ending in pointless suicide is worse than a long and happy life. The summative view was rejected because there is no good to be had in the satisfaction of addictive cravings. The global view was denied because a better life was available for the orphan beyond the walls of the monastery. The first informed desire view, which did not include a rationality requirement, was dismissed on the ground that an unsuccessful teacher's existence, particularly one dominated by sexual desire for children, could not be better than that of a just politician's.

The grass-counter case is the site of the desire theorist's last stand, and surrender is now called for. A person's desires are often not for what is best for them. I might meet a stranger on a train, and strongly desire that this stranger succeed in the future. The stranger may succeed, long after I have forgotten him, thus fulfilling my desire, but not advancing my welfare in any way.[4] And, as we have seen, even those desires concerned more directly with a person's own life may not match up with that person's welfare. These

---

4   The example is from Parfit 1984: 494. The rejection of theories which allow the fulfilment of such desires to count is again guided by a prior understanding of welfare.

theories, then, fail to provide an alternative to the flawed experience accounts discussed earlier in this book.[5]

Why have desire accounts become by far the most widely held accounts of welfare? One reason is probably the attractiveness of the liberal idea that decisions about a person's welfare should be left up to them (Scanlon 1993: 187–8). Preference-ranking might also be thought to offer the possibility of interpersonal comparisons of welfare. Another reason, however, is a failure to distinguish clearly between the substantive and explanatory components in theories of welfare. It is quite plausible to suggest that, in general, the satisfaction of people's desires makes them better off. This is because desire is often for what is good. Indeed we cannot make sense of a desire, such as a desire for a saucer of mud, which cannot be understood, without a lot more explanation, as a desire for something thought good or as a desire for something which is a means to something thought good (Anscombe 1957: 70). These desires are usually described as cravings, *irrational* cravings.

It is not at all plausible, however, to suggest that what *makes* the satisfaction of desires good for people is that their desires are satisfied. If this were plausible, we would feel no puzzlement at cases such as the saucer of mud. In normal cases, we desire something because we think it will be good in some way independently of its satisfying the desire (cf. Williams 1973a: 261).[6] Being desire-satisfying is not a good-making property, so desire accounts, and the large amount of contemporary thought in welfare economics and elsewhere which rests upon them, are mistaken.

---

5 It might be said that desire theorists are permitted to seek 'coherentist' support from unreflective beliefs or 'intuitions' about welfare, and to use these beliefs in honing their theory. My point, however, is that these beliefs themselves suggest that desire fulfilment is not the sole component of welfare. I myself am readier to use unreflective belief as a guide to welfare than to morality, since there is less likelihood of ideological distortion in the case of belief about welfare. It is harder to engender false beliefs about welfare, and less necessary for social control.

6 There is a link here with the *evidential* status of the competent judges: they desire the higher pleasures more than the lower because of their (experience-based) beliefs.

The ideal

Our lives are good for us because they contain certain things which are good for us, and these things are good because they instantiate certain properties which make them good. The best way to understand welfare and its sources is to centre the discussion on certain core *values*, by which I mean abstract notions such as, for example, 'accomplishment', which are concretely instantiated in the lives of individuals. This is to return to the method of the ancient Greeks. Discussion about welfare among Greek philosophers consisted largely in the suggestion and discussion of one or more values which were alleged to constitute welfare. Aristotle followed his mentor Plato in stressing the importance of the conceptual requirement on any correct view of welfare that it be unimprovable.[7] Imagine that I suggest that welfare consists in pleasure and knowledge. You might agree that these values are certainly important, but think that friendship should be included as well. There are, then, two ways in which to attack any conception of welfare which lists goods or values in this way. The first is to argue that certain alleged values do not deserve a place on the list, the second to argue that the list is incomplete.

How is one to decide on a list? One can start only with one's beliefs, or 'intuitions' as philosophers tend to call them, and one's desires (the objects of which, because desire aims at the good, can be permitted to be candidates for inclusion on a list), and continue by subjecting them to reflection. I might start, for example, with the belief that pleasure is a constituent of welfare. When I say that pleasure is a value, I am implying that pleasurable experiences are worth having in themselves, and I may go on to stipulate that they are valuable in so far as they are pleasurable. I am suggesting that an existence which consisted only of such experiences would be good for the being whose existence it was. Here I am adding to Aristotle's completeness requirement the idea of Moore that the worth of any purported value *in itself* is best understood by

---

7   See Aristotle *c*. 330 BC: 1097b14–20, and 1172b23–34, in which reference is made to Plato *c*. 360BC: 20e–22c, 60b–61a; Crisp 1994.

considering the value 'in isolation', so that any value it has can be discerned (Moore 1903: 91). These two methodological aids – the completeness requirement and the method of isolation – are the most important tools needed to construct a theory of welfare.

I have taken the title of this section from the final chapter in Moore's book. 'The ideal' is welfare correctly understood, and any life will be good for a person to the extent that it instantiates values from this ideal. So it could be that the ideal is hedonistic; and one could even count a desire account as an ideal account which includes only the value of desire fulfilment. The point of introducing the broad notion of the ideal is to allow for theories which include values that are neither hedonistic nor constituted by the mere fulfilment of desire, and I shall call theories which move beyond hedonism and desire accounts *broad ideal* accounts. At this point, we can again refer explicitly to Mill's account of welfare. I have argued that Mill is a hedonist, so a broad ideal account obviously cannot be attributed to him. But his view is far closer to the broad ideal account I am sketching than contemporary desire accounts. This is for two reasons. First, any plausible broad ideal account will both incorporate the insights of hedonism, since pleasurable experience must be at least part of what makes life worth living, and set itself firmly against desire theory, since desire fulfilment is not good. Secondly, as we saw in chapter 2, Mill came very close to moving beyond hedonism to a broad ideal account. The only claim he would have had to drop in order to do so would be the enjoyment requirement – that nobility and so on can be said to add value to experiences only in so far as they affect the enjoyableness of those experiences. In one sense, that is a small leap, though for Mill it would have amounted to the large one of distancing himself from the hedonistic heritage bequeathed to him by Bentham and his father.

As for Moore, his own conception of the ideal was as follows: 'By far the most valuable things, which we know or can imagine, are certain states of consciousness, which may be roughly described as the pleasures of human intercourse and the enjoyment of beautiful objects' (Moore 1903: 188). I shall not stop to discuss Moore's arguments for this position. We have already seen, primarily on the basis of arguments relying on the completeness requirement in the earlier parts of this chapter, that restricting the constituents of welfare to experiences alone is undesirable. Indeed that was the point of introducing the broad notion of 'the ideal': to allow non-experiences to be included. But even if we expand on Moore's account, allowing the non-experiential side of friendship to be included (my being held in respect by my friends and so on), it is still deficient. Friendship and aesthetic enjoyment do indeed appear to be important constituents in welfare. But surely there is more to a good life than just these?

There are, for example, enjoyments other than the Bloomsbury pleasures mentioned by Moore. Pure sensual pleasure, intellectual enjoyment, delight in physical exercise are all to be included. Perhaps the more general heading 'pleasure' would serve. The next task would be to consider which kinds of pleasure are to count, and for how much, and why (this, of course, is one of the tasks Mill is undertaking in the second chapter of *Utilititarianism*). Are sadistic pleasures to be included? Or pleasures based on misunderstandings of their source? And so on.

John Finnis, in his book *Natural Law and Natural Rights*, outlines a richer conception of welfare (1980: 85–90). He lists the following as constituents of the good life: life, knowledge, play, aesthetic experience, sociability (friendship), practical reasonableness and religion. Aesthetic pleasure and friendship I have already allowed. Whether religion is a welfare value seems to depend importantly on whether or not God exists. Since that is a question I do not at present wish to discuss, I shall put that value to one side. Play could perhaps be included under my broad heading 'pleasure'. Life I do want to rule out, since it is only a condition for welfare. Mere life in itself is neither good nor bad. Consider an extremely primitive unicellular creature: can its merely being alive be said to add anything of welfare value to its existence?

That leaves knowledge and practical reasonableness. Both of these are important values. Knowledge is perhaps better construed as 'understanding', and should be taken centrally to concern understanding of things that *matter*. Mere knowledge, such as that of vast numbers of railway timetables, adds little to a person's welfare, except in so far as its acquisition, use and contemplation can give pleasure through amusement. Understanding other people, the real nature of the institutions within which one lives, the Greenhouse Effect or the work of Marx – all these can plausibly be said to constitute welfare.

'Practical reasonableness', or perhaps better 'practical reason', is also a strong candidate for inclusion in the broad ideal.[8] It is important to human beings that they be permitted and enabled to govern their own lives, in the sense of making autonomous, informed and uncoerced decisions about the shape their lives are to take. One aspect of this good is instrumental. As Mill well realized, each individual is almost always the best judge of what will be best for them; and even when any individual appears a rather poor judge of their welfare, making decisions on behalf of that person, particularly if this represents unwanted intrusion on that person's life, will often make things even worse. But practical reason is also of value in itself, as is suggested by the following example (adapted from Griffin 1986: 9; cf. *SW* 4.20):

The committee When you are 22 years old, you are approached by a committee composed of friends and family. One of the members tells you that the committee will, if you wish, take over the running of your life for you. The committee will decide which job you should take, where you should live, which hobbies you should indulge in and so on.

Your first doubt will probably concern whether the committee would in fact make the correct decisions. But let us assume that that doubt can be put aside: your own past record of decision-making is pretty bad, while the committee can produce evidence of its success with others. Nevertheless, it would be a mistake to hand over control of your life like this. Part of what makes life worth living is running one's own life for oneself, even though that might result in one's making more mistakes than would have been made by a committee such as that in the example.

---

8 Cf. at this point the title of chapter 3 of Mill's *On Liberty*: 'Of individuality, as one of the elements of well-being.' More on this in chapter 8.

Since running one's own life is in itself a good, Finnis was right to include something like practical reason on his list of welfare values. Surely, however, it also matters what one does with one's life. This is partly a matter of the success of one's practical reasoning, but that is not the whole of it. Let me call this value *'accomplishment'* (see Griffin 1986: index, s.v.; above, 50–1). As in the case of understanding, some conception of what is important must play a rôle in the elucidation of this value. Mere success is not sufficient: the grass-counter achieves that. And intention to accomplish exactly what is accomplished is not necessary. Consider a person who, by luck, discovers the cure for AIDS in the course of pure research. Accomplishment seems to have to do with the attainment of excellence, and this attainment is in many cases at least partly a matter of luck. I am thinking of spheres of life in which, for example, we may find moral, intellectual or physical capacities realized to a high degree.

Authoritarianism, awareness, pluralism and plants

After reflecting on the ideal offered by some other philosophers, I now have a provisional list of welfare values: friendship, pleasure (including aesthetic pleasure), understanding, practical reason and accomplishment. These values, I am suggesting, are what make life worth living. And, as I have said, the list is open to criticism from two directions. It may be argued that I have included something which I should not have, or that I have missed some other value. My list is extremely crude. When we consider the variety of valuable forms of life available to human beings, and the even greater variety of ways in which these lives are good (lives and their constituents can be fascinating, profound, fun, challenging, exciting, creative, fulfilling, unusual and so on and on), its crudeness becomes only more manifest. The list of properties that make lives good for people is immense, and after thousands of years of philosophy we have made little advance in understanding it. Since so much work remains to be done here, rather than defending my list further, I shall conclude by answering a few general questions about the broad ideal account of welfare I have offered.

First, authoritarianism. Broad ideal accounts have often been attacked on the grounds of élitism or paternalism. Mill's own theory, though I have characterized it as hedonistic and hence a narrow ideal account, has also been charged with the same fault, as we saw in the previous chapter, since his theory does not leave it to individuals to decide how much value various pleasurable experiences have. By removing the individual as final arbiter of the value of their own life to them, it is suggested, many ideal accounts not only ignore the individual's own perspective but can leave the way open to outside interference.

There are two initial responses to this accusation. One is to stress again the distinction between a theory of welfare and a theory of morality. It would be quite consistent to allow that others *could* run a person's life better than they themselves, but to claim also that to intervene against their will or coerce them in any way would be *wrong*. But what I said above about the welfare value of practical reason should anyway alleviate worry at this point. A person has to be quite incompetent to make important decisions about the shape of their own life before serious interference on paternalistic grounds could conceivably be justified.

The second general question about the broad ideal account concerns the rôle of awareness. Experience theorists, for instance, might try to win back support for their position by suggesting that awareness of the good in one's life makes that life, in that respect, better for one.

This I can agree with. Consider again the naturalist who, without his knowledge, made possible important advances in our understanding of the natural world. I claimed that his life was in fact improved by his success, though he never knew of it, and we can now see that this is because of the value of accomplishment. But this is quite consistent with the claim that he would have been even better off had he been informed of his success. Does this constitute the basis of a 'more is better' argument? Should I add 'awareness' to my list? I think not. For had the naturalist heard of the further research, he would have been (to some degree at least) delighted, and delight comes under the heading of 'pleasure'. He would also have had a better grasp of something extremely important, to him at least, viz. the place of his own life in the world. And that is surely one of the central aspects of understanding.

Thirdly, someone may ask how practical reason could possibly function in the light of such a plurality of welfare values. If there are six different values to take into account, how can one trade one against the other if there is no common currency? (On this issue, see Griffin 1986: 31–7, chs 5, 7.)

As I said when discussing Mill's competent judges, it is important to be aware of the distinction between welfare values as types and as tokens, that is, between, say, 'friendship' as a *kind* and 'a friendship' as an *individual instance* of a kind. It would be absurd to suggest, for example, that friendship is more valuable than understanding, since ranking of welfare values at the level of types will be quite impossible. But such ranking is not required in practical reasoning, in that what one is engaged in there concerns *particular* friendships or *particular* opportunities for understanding. If, for example, I am offered a job at a philosophy department in another country, I might believe that, because some of its members are working on topics close to my own interests, my understanding of philosophy would increase. But, I might also think, the cost to my friendships might be too great. Note how reasoning such as this does not require reduction of the values concerned to some common currency. Practical wisdom, discussed above also in the section on competent judges, is an important component of practical reason. It consists partly in a capacity to judge the contribution certain options will make to one's welfare, and is quite conceivable even on the assumption that welfare itself consists of a number of irreducible values.

Finally, plants. Most people will think that a view of welfare has been reduced to absurdity if it implies that the life of a geranium can be good *for that geranium*. But, an experience theorist may suggest, because I cut the connection between welfare and conscious experience, I am committed to this view. If the success of the naturalist can affect his welfare even though he is quite unaware of it, why should not the plant food I give to my geranium also increase its welfare?

I have to accept that we talk of plant food as 'good for' geraniums. But this is in the sense in which we might say that the economic depression of the 1930s was good for the Nazi party in Germany, or that unhygienic conditions are good for the bacterium which causes cholera. What is good for a thing in this sense is what enables it to function well or to 'flourish' as a thing of that kind.

But when I say that accomplishment is a good for a person, I am not suggesting that it is good in the same sense. There is nothing good in the life of a cholera bacterium which makes its life good for it. My claim is that accomplishment is *a welfare value*, and that the instantiation of this value in any life makes it to that extent good for the individual living the life. We can now see that I am committed to the *possibility* that the lives of plants may instantiate welfare values in the same way as our lives and the lives of many other animals. But whether this is in fact the case will depend on the list of values in question. As far as I can see, none of the values on my list could be instantiated in a geranium's life, and I conclude that the lives of plants are neither good nor bad for them.

In this chapter, I followed Mill's lead and, unlike him, moved beyond hedonism. I showed that most contemporary theories of welfare, based on desire fulfilment, fail, and that we should return to ideal accounts of welfare. Mill thought he could prove hedonism, however, as one component of utilitarianism, so our discussion of welfare will be incomplete until we have discussed that proof. This will be the subject of my next chapter.

Further reading

In addition to works mentioned at the end of chapter 2, see on experience and welfare Smart 1973: sect. 3; Nozick 1974: 42–5; Glover 1984: chs 7–8. On desire accounts, see Ayer 1965: ch. 11; Brandt 1979: ch. 13; Sen and Williams 1982: introduction; Goodin 1991; Scanlon 1993. On the broad conception of the ideal, see

Moore 1903: ch. 6; Rashdall 1907: vol. 1, ch. 7; vol. 2, ch. 2; Raz 1986: ch. 12; Hurka 1993: ch. 4. On the measurement of welfare, see Griffin 1986: chs 5–7. For suggestive attempts to combine theories of welfare from different categories, see Parfit 1984: app. I; Sen 1980–1.

Chapter 4

The proof and sanctions of utilitarianism

Moral theory and methodology

A moral theory is a systematic account of what makes actions right or wrong. Mill states his 'creed', or his moral theory, succinctly in 2.2: '[A]ctions are right in proportion as they tend to promote happiness, wrong as they tend to produce the reverse of happiness.'

What does this mean? That will require some discussion (see chapter 5), but for now I shall just state that Mill's view of what he calls in the very first paragraph of *Utilitarianism* 'the criterion of right and wrong' is that the right action is that which produces the greatest overall balance of pleasure over pain. This is utilitarianism, or, more precisely, one form of it.

What other moral theories are there? Let me mention two for the sake of illustration and comparison. The first is that of the German philosopher, Immanuel Kant (1724–1804) (see Kant 1785). Mill states Kant's moral theory as follows: '"So act, that

67

the rule on which thou actest would admit of being adopted as a law by all rational beings"' (1.4).

As it stands, this view could be made consistent in practice with utilitarianism, were the utilitarian principle said to be the only rational law. But Kant was not a utilitarian. He believed, for example, that his theory, when properly developed, showed that one should never lie, *even if* doing so would produce more happiness than telling the truth, because the law regarding telling the truth that rational beings would accept would forbid lying. It is anyway worth pointing out that utilitarianism and Kantianism would still be different *theories* even if their practical implications were identical, since the reasons they would give for acting would be quite different. A distinction similar to that I drew in chapter 2 between the explanatory and substantive elements of theories of welfare can be made here. Both a utilitarian and a Kantian might morally condemn a certain lie, but the utilitarian would say that what made the action wrong was its failing to maximize utility, while the Kantian would insist that its wrongness consisted in its failure to conform to a law which could be willed universally.

A third moral theory which has become prominent recently is 'virtue ethics'. This theory, the roots of which can be found in the writings of Aristotle, has at its heart neither the notion of the 'greatest happiness' nor that of rational moral law, but rather that of the virtuous person (see Aristotle *c*. 330 BC). One should act as the virtuous person would act. Again, strictly speaking, such a theory can be made practically equivalent to utilitarianism by stipulating that the virtuous person will act so as to produce the greatest happiness. But virtue theorists deny this, arguing that doing what virtue requires can lead to less than the greatest happiness.

Several questions spring immediately to mind about the status of these theories. An obvious one is whether any one of these theories, or any other, could be *true*. But that question is one *about* morality and moral theory, not within morality itself, and is not an issue of central interest to Mill in *Utilitarianism*; so I shall put it to one side.[1] Mill was writing in a context in which

---

1 For an interesting discussion of Mill's views on the nature and status of moral judgements, see Berger 1984: ch. 1.

people were actively disagreeing over moral theory, and his main methodological question concerned how we are to decide between these different theories. Note that there are two issues: first, *how* to decide between theories, and, secondly, *which* theory to decide upon. Mill saw these two issues as closely interwoven.

As well as moral theories, there are theories about how to decide upon moral theories. One such theory, which it might be misleading to call a theory at all, Mill contemptuously discards in 1.3. This is the thesis that we have a *moral sense* which enables us to discern what is right in each individual situation. There are no universal principles, but conscience tells us what to do when a moral dilemma arises. Mill takes the *intuitive* theory a little more seriously. This theory again states that we have a moral instinct, but adds that it enables us not to make particular judgements, but to recognize general moral principles. Mill is quick to point out in 3.7 that the intuitive view can be made consistent with utilitarianism, and that even an intuitive theorist who denies utilitarianism will 'hold that a large *portion* of morality turns upon the consideration due to the interests of our fellow-creatures'.

Mill allies himself with the *inductive* school, according to which questions of right and wrong are matters of 'observation and experience' (1.3). Mill was an empiricist, who believed that our understanding of the world must be based ultimately entirely on the evidence of our senses. That is why he is so contemptuous of the moral sense view. The moral sense would have to be quite unlike any of the other senses, which have physical correlates, and anyway the evidence of our senses themselves counts against the moral sense view, since there is widespread and deep disagreement in ethics. Mill's empiricism sat alongside his naturalism, that is, the view that the world is ultimately entirely explicable in terms of the principles of the natural sciences, among which he would probably have included psychology. Like all our knowledge, he believed, natural science is based ultimately on observation of the contents of our experiences, and so it comes as no surprise to find Mill suggesting that choices between moral theories, if they are to be respectable, are to be similarly grounded.

Mill's objection to the intuitive school is twofold. First, it is unscientific, making appeal to allegedly 'self-evident' principles, principles which can be understood as soon as one understands the words in which they are couched and which require no support from empirical observation. Secondly, Mill says, intuitive moralists rarely offer any list of these principles, and still more rarely do they systematize them by reducing them to a single first principle. Rather they offer the everyday morality of common sense as itself an authority, or some set of general principles intended to ground common sense morality which is less plausible than that morality itself.

Mill would not be content even with an intuitively founded utilitarianism. There must be a first principle in morality, he thinks, and it cannot be self-evident, since this would imply some special innate moral faculty which we do not have. But this is not to say that utilitarianism can be deductively proven. According to Millian utilitarianism, the only good or ultimate end is happiness, and ultimate ends cannot be proved.

> We are not, however, to infer that its acceptance or rejection must depend on blind impulse, or arbitrary choice. There is a larger meaning of the word proof, in which this question is as amenable to it as any other of the disputed questions of philosophy. The subject is within the cognizance of the rational faculty; and neither does that faculty deal with it solely in the way of intuition. Considerations may be presented capable of determining the intellect either to give or withhold its assent to the doctrine; and this is equivalent to proof.

(1.5)

The utilitarian principle, in other words, cannot be offered up as just obvious to those who properly understand it. Nor can it be proved deductively, in the way that one can prove that, say, medicine, a means to health, is good, *on the assumption that* health is good. Mill does believe that it would be a simple matter to demonstrate that common sense morality has been shaped largely by the utilitarian principle, though that principle has remained largely unrecognized (1.4). That would not show that the principle was correct. It can nevertheless, he suggests, be provided with arguments which place it on a rational footing as sturdy as the claim about medicine, and it is these arguments which he aims to provide in chapter 4.

Though chapter 4 of *Utilitarianism* is often referred to (quite rightly) as the chapter containing Mill's 'proof', it is in fact entitled 'Of what sort of proof the principle of utility is susceptible'. In the quotation above from 1.5, Mill does not tell us what kind of considerations may be adduced in favour of utilitarianism. To do so is one of his purposes in chapter 4, the other being actually to adduce them himself. Again, we see him working at two levels: the methodological level and the level of concrete moral theory.

Mill begins chapter 4 by referring back to the claim in his first chapter that ultimate ends cannot be proved. Nor, he says, can 'matters of fact', the first principles of knowledge. In the case of facts, however, one can make appeal to the faculties which judge them: the senses and internal consciousness. Imagine that we are in a room with the curtains closed. I cannot prove to you deductively that it is raining outside; but I can take you to the window, open the curtains and show you the rain falling. For an empiricist, if that is not proof, it is equivalent to it. In normal circumstances, you could not ask for anything more.

At the end of 4.1 Mill asks whether we can appeal to the senses or to some other faculty in the case of the first premises of our conduct. In the second paragraph of the chapter, he asks another question. Given that the utilitarian view is that happiness is the only thing desirable as an end, and so cannot be proved 'directly', what conditions must be met before utilitarianism is believed? In the rest of the chapter, Mill provides answers to these questions. The faculty to which appeal can be made is desire (4.3). And the conditions which must be met are: (1) happiness must be desired and (2) nothing else must be desired.

Mill deals with (1) in the notorious third paragraph. He discusses (2) at greater length in paragraphs 3–8. The argument is summarized in paragraph 9, and the proof itself (Mill uses the word in 4.9) comes in paragraph 10. Since the proof is an appeal to the reader to consider the arguments which have gone before, the two lines of Mill's argument – the discussion of the kinds of considerations required, and the actual presentation of them – are run in tandem. We might say, then, that the proof has three stages, the first and third of which correspond to the two considerations above. In paragraph 3, Mill attempts to show the following:

1 Happiness is desirable.
2 The general happiness is desirable.
He then endeavours to prove in the following five paragraphs that:
3 Nothing other than happiness is desirable.

These are the three stages of his proof of utilitarianism, and there are problems with each.

Stage 1: 'visible' and 'desirable'

The only proof capable of being given that an object is visible, is that people actually see it. The only proof that a sound is audible, is that people hear it: and so of the other sources of our experience. In like manner, I apprehend, the sole evidence it is possible to produce that anything is desirable is that people do actually desire it. If the end which the utilitarian doctrine proposes to itself were not, in theory and in practice, acknowledged to be an end, nothing could ever convince any person that it was so. No reason can be given why the general happiness is desirable, except that each person, so far as he believes it to be attainable, desires his own happiness. This, however, being a fact, we have not only all the proof which the case admits of, but all which it is possible to require, that happiness is a good: that each person's happiness is a good to that person, and the general happiness, therefore, a good to the aggregate of all persons. Happiness has made out its title as *one* of the ends of conduct, and consequently one of the criteria of morality.

(4.3)

It is hardly surprising that this paragraph is the most notorious in Mill's writings, for, as we shall see in the next section, it appears that Mill is attempting to prove the utilitarian principle in a single paragraph. In this section I shall restrict the discussion to his attempt to show that the happiness of each person – that is, the pleasurable experience of each person – is a good to that person. The suggestion that pleasure is desirable is hardly difficult to accept, and one might be forgiven for wondering why Mill thought he had to argue for it. The paragraphs following paragraph 3 provide the answer. Mill uses the same type of argument in an attempt to demonstrate something much less plausible, that we desire nothing other than happiness or pleasure.

The most famous and influential criticism of Mill's argument is that of G.E. Moore in *Principia Ethica* (1903). After quoting 4.3, Moore begins his spirited critique:

> There, that is enough. That is my first point. Mill has made as naïve and artless a use of the naturalistic fallacy as anybody could desire. 'Good', he tells us, means 'desirable', and you can only find out what is desirable by seeking to find out what is actually desired ... The important step for Ethics is this one just taken, the step which pretends to prove that 'good' means 'desired'. Well, the fallacy in this step is so obvious, that it is quite wonderful how Mill failed to see it. The fact is that 'desirable' does not mean 'able to be desired' as 'visible' means 'able to be seen'. The desirable means simply what *ought* to be desired or deserves to be desired; just as the detestable means not what can be but what ought to be detested and the damnable what deserves to be damned.
>
> (Moore 1903: 66–7)

'Naturalistic fallacy' is a term of art for Moore, and he seems to have meant several things by it. Here his objection to Mill is that he *defines* the word 'good' as 'desired'. The basis of Moore's disapproval of such definitions has come to be known as the 'open question argument'. An acceptable definition, Moore claims, should not leave an open question. If I define 'triangle', for example, as 'plane figure bounded by three straight sides', my definition has succeeded; for it is not an open question whether triangles are plane figures bounded by three straight sides, in so far as it would make no sense to discuss the issue. But a definition of 'good' as 'desired' fails the test, because it clearly is an open question whether what is desired is good.

Whatever the power of the open question argument, Moore's criticism of Mill misses its target. Indeed it is not clear why Moore read 4.3 as he did. It is undoubtedly a passage open to many different interpretations, and I shall endeavour to provide one at the end of this section. But Moore's own interpretation is a little peculiar. Definitions of the kind Moore discusses are usually signalled, as by Moore, using inverted commas. There are no inverted commas in chapter 4 of *Utilitarianism*; Mill is not interested in defining words.[2] He wishes to suggest that happiness is good, desirable, an end, and his project here is analogous to Moore's own in the final chapter of *Principia Ethica*, where, as I mentioned in the last chapter, Moore claims that what are good are the pleasures of friendship and aesthetic appreciation.

According to another conception of the naturalistic fallacy, it is committed when one attempts to derive an evaluative conclusion from entirely non-evaluative premises. It is almost certain that Mill is not doing this, since, first, it would constitute just the kind of 'direct' proof he is at pains to deny is possible, and, secondly, he himself had castigated this very error earlier in his career (*S* 8.949–50).

At times, it seems that Moore is concerned not so much about purported definitions of 'good' or illicit derivations as about equations of goodness, which he sees as a 'non-natural' property (i.e. beyond the scope of scientific investigation), with a natural property. Now Mill is not claiming that goodness is the same as what is desired. Not only does he not say this, but it would go against the grain of chapter 2, where he accepts that many people's desires have gone off the track and led them to seek lower rather than higher pleasures. What Mill says is that desire offers the only *evidence* for something's being good.

There is indeed a difference between Mill and Moore concern-

---

2 Mill's reference to 'synonymy' in the footnote to 5.36 can be put down to looseness of expression.

ing naturalism, and here Moore's view is preferable to Mill's. Naturalism, properly understood, must require that the world is ultimately explicable in the terms of science. But 'goodness' and 'rightness' are *not* properties dealt with by the natural sciences as we understand them, so naturalism, because of its commitment to the reduction of the evaluative to the non-evaluative, will rule out the possibility of an autonomous ethics. But this disagreement between the two philosophers need not arise in the context of the central issues of chapter 4. For empiricism, broadly understood, does not have to be naturalistic. One can appeal to people's experience as a source of knowledge without restricting oneself to the view that the only properties of which we can have experience are natural properties.

It has to be admitted, however, that 4.3 is liable to confuse. Mill makes such rhetorical use of the similarity between 'visible' and 'desirable' that some readers are bound to misunderstand the particular aspects of the analogy he was drawing. Moore is quite right, of course, to suggest that 'desirable' does not mean 'can be desired' as 'visible' means 'can be seen'. 'Desirable' means something like 'worth desiring'. But Mill surely realized this, and we should remember here not only his obvious competence as a speaker of English but also his strictures against confusing 'is' and 'ought' at the end of the *System of Logic*. The analogy on which Mill's argument depends in 4.3 is that between matters of fact and ultimate ends of conduct, with which he introduces the chapter itself.

Recall my attempt to prove to you that it is raining outside, by drawing back the curtain and appealing to your visual sense. Imagine now that we are disputing whether the Radcliffe Observatory is visible from my window. I shall not be able to persuade you using a 'direct' or deductive proof. We shall have to look out of the window, and, when you see the Observatory, that is surely sufficient to persuade you to accept that it is visible.

Just as I can appeal to your visual sense in the case of matters of fact, Mill is suggesting, I can appeal to your desiring faculty in the case of ultimate ends. Most of the objects of our desires we desire because we believe them *valuable* or *desirable* in some respect.[3] If I ask you *why* you want to go to Alaska for your holiday, you are unlikely to reply, 'I just do'. You will offer certain considerations in favour of going, considerations that you take to make such a holiday desirable, such as the enjoyment you will experience in the beauty and isolation of the place. If we consult our own desires, we shall surely find that pleasure is at least one of the things we desire, and that we view it as something desirable. As I suggested above, Mill could equally well have offered the bald claim that happiness is desirable, and few of his readers would disagree. But he wishes to use the connection between desiring and desirability in the final stage of the argument.

Someone might object at this point that our desires are not infallible. It is surely possible that what we desire is not good, or is even bad. Further, there may be desirable objects which are not desired, and this throws doubt on the final stage of Mill's proof, in which he suggests that happiness alone is desirable. Mill would probably have accepted these points. As we saw in chapter 2, he allows in 2.7 that some people desire only lower pleasures, which, if they were to accept Mill's methodology in chapter 4, would lead them to think that happiness consists only in lower pleasures. Desires can go wrong, and, as Mill suggests, a watertight proof of utilitarianism is not available. All he can offer are considerations to determine the intellects of his readers. Such determination is surely his main concern in this chapter: he speaks of 'an appeal' in 4.1, of utilitarianism's 'claim to be believed' in 4.2, and in 4.3 of *giving* proof, *producing* evidence, the *acknowledgement* of happiness as an end, and *convincing* a person that it is so. The very last sentence of chapter 4 leaves it up to the reader to make up their own mind. By appealing to the natural fact of what his readers and all other human beings desire, rather than any self-evident or intuitive proposition, Mill believes that he has provided a philosophically respectable reason for his reader to accept that happiness is desirable.

The conclusion of the first stage of the argument in chapter 4 is surely plausible: pleasure is good, desirable, an ultimate end. But

---

3   See ch. 3, 57.

we may doubt Mill's emphasis on desire. His argument requires that we *recognize* the object of our desire as good, and this recognition is not itself a desire so much as a sensitivity to the evaluative properties that make certain things good or desirable. It may be that Mill's naturalistic reticence to speak of such properties and his wish to avoid any charge of 'intuitionism' led him to exaggerate the rôle of desire in his proof of happiness as an ultimate end.

Stage 2: from the happiness of each to the happiness of all

Recall the concluding sentences of 4.3. Mill suggests that the *only* reason one can give why the general happiness – that is, maximum pleasure overall – is desirable is that each person desires his own happiness. Since it is a fact that each person *does* desire his own happiness, we have all the proof one could ask for 'that happiness is a good: that each person's happiness is a good to that person, and the general happiness, therefore, a good to the aggregate of persons'.

It is easy to see why so many interpreters over the years have been deeply concerned about this part of Mill's argument. The gap between egoistic hedonism (it is rational for you to pursue your own greatest happiness) and universalistic hedonism (the utilitarian view that you should pursue the greatest happiness overall) is vast, and Mill appears to be trying to leap it in one bound. He was certainly aware of the distinction between the two views (see e.g. *SD* 10.71), but it has to be admitted that he did not seem to recognize its importance.[4]

What Mill needs is the conclusion that the greatest happiness is an end – indeed, the end – of reasonable or rational action. His claim at the end of 4.3 is therefore particularly confusing, since the general happiness is here implied to be an end not for the individual but for the 'aggregate' of all individuals. Does Mill in

---

4   In the very first paragraph of *Utilitarianism*, for example, the Socrates of Plato's dialogue *Protagoras* is described as a utilitarian, though, as Mill well knew, he was advocating an *egoistic* version of hedonism, i.e. the view that each person has strongest reason to pursue *their own* happiness.

fact mean that the general happiness is an end for each individual? Henry Jones thought so, but Mill rebutted his suggestion in a letter of 1868:

> As to the sentence you quote from my *Utilitarianism*, when I said the general happiness is a good to the aggregate of all persons I did not mean that every human being's happiness is a good to every other human being, though I think in a good state of society and education it would be so. I merely meant in this particular sentence to argue that since A's happiness is a good, B's a good, C's a good, etc., the sum of all these goods must be a good.

(16.1414)

The phrase 'every human being's happiness is a good to every other human being' is almost certainly meant as equivalent to 'the sum of all individual happinesses (that is, the greatest happiness) is a good to each human being'. Strictly, his last sentence here may be said to be a logical fallacy, one which many readers have claimed to find in the penultimate sentence of 4.3 itself – the so-called fallacy of composition, committed when one ascribes to a set what is true of its members. Here are three large people; but a set of three people is not large.

But such claims are not always mistaken: p is an amount of butter, q is an amount of butter, r is an amount of butter; and $p + q + r$ is an amount of butter. We can, then, see what Mill means: good is additive, in that two people's (equal) goods contain twice as much goodness, other things being equal, as either of them taken alone. What Mill needs in his argument to prove utilitarianism, however, is exactly what he denies in this letter that that argument contains. For the egoist could agree with Mill's additive assumptions, but deny that goodness translates directly into the rationality of ends. That is, they can claim that, even though they could bring about the greatest good by acting in some way, this is not what is most *desirable for them* as an end. Rather, what is most desirable for them is their own greatest individual happiness. Mill needs an argument for impartiality.

Unless Mill really has made a huge mistake, it must be the

case that there are several assumptions behind his argument in chapter 4. By the end of 4.3, Mill believes he has said enough to persuade readers that the utilitarian principle is correct. But why should they be persuaded? One assumption Mill was making (the *moral assumption*, as I shall call it) is that they are already taking morality seriously. *Utilitarianism* is not addressed primarily to egoists. It was written with Mill's own opponents in moral philosophy, the intuitionists, in mind, and it is assumed that they and anyone likely to be persuaded by the book already accept that there *is* a 'criterion of right and wrong' (1.1). The controversy Mill sees himself as engaged in is not whether there is such a thing as morality, but, given that there is, what is required by it.

As moralists, then, readers might be expected to allow that, since happiness is a good, other people's happiness should matter to them. For what is morality if it does not involve some concern for others? But why should they not conclude, for example, that morality requires that happiness be distributed as *equally* as possible, even if this produces less than the maximum overall?

Mill's answer to this question is not to be found in chapter 4, but it is implicit in his discussion of impartiality in chapter 5. Mill believes that the duty of impartiality, in the allocation in our everyday judicial and moral practice of what we believe is deserved, is itself based directly on the utilitarian principle:

> It is involved in the very meaning of Utility, or the Greatest Happiness Principle. That principle is a mere form of words without rational signification, unless one person's happiness, supposed equal in degree (with the proper allowance made for kind), is counted for exactly as much as another's. Those conditions being supplied, Bentham's dictum, 'everybody to count for one, nobody for more than one,' might be written under the principle of utility as an explanatory commentary.
>
> (5.36)

In a footnote to this passage, Mill addresses the objection by Herbert Spencer that the utilitarian principle cannot be the first principle of morality if it depends on a principle of impartiality. For it would then presuppose the principle that everybody has an equal right to happiness. Mill says in response:

> It may be more correctly described as supposing that equal amounts of happiness are equally desirable, whether felt by the same or by different persons. This, however, is not a presupposition; not a premise needful to support the principle of utility, but the very principle itself; for what is the principle of utility, if it not be that 'happiness' and 'desirable' are synonymous terms?[5] If there is any anterior principle implied, it can be no other than this, that the truths of arithmetic are applicable to the valuation of happiness, as of all other measurable quantities.

So here we have two assumptions which may actually play a part in Mill's argument in chapter 4, as opposed merely to explaining its structure as does that concerning the nature of the readership. According to the *aggregative assumption*, which we have already found in 4.3, happiness is a good that can be aggregated or summed. And, on the *impartiality assumption*, when summing happiness, the distinction between persons is irrelevant. The greater the overall happiness, the greater the good.[6] This passage, in a footnote close to the end of the book, is perhaps that passage in *Utilitarianism* that might best be used as a response to egoism.[7]

Mill's conception of morality is *teleological*, in the sense that he believes that it is based ultimately on certain ends (*telos* is Greek

---

5 See n. 2.

6 I am assuming that impartiality, as understood by Mill, implies maximization. Every additional pleasure counts as much as any other, so satisficing, for example, according to which one seeks that amount of happiness that is 'good enough', would be ruled out by impartiality. For it would count for less those pleasures added above the threshold of sufficiency.

7 A particular problem arises for Mill as an empiricist in his opposition to egoism. For the egoist may say that his experience supplies him with evidence only for the existence of his own pleasures. Here Mill must supply an empiricist argument for the existence of other minds. In an addendum to *E* (9.205–6), he offers such an argument, based on the correlation between experience and bodily condition; see Skorupski 1989: 239–40.

for 'end'). In his comparison of science and morality in 1.2, he claims:

> All action is for the sake of some end, and rules of action, it seems natural to suppose, must take their whole character and colour from the end to which they are subservient. When we engage in a pursuit, a clear and precise conception of what we are pursuing would seem to be the first thing we need.[8]

The *teleological assumption*, then, is that moral rules are justified only to the extent that they promote some end or good.

With these assumptions out in the open, we can understand how Mill's proof of utilitarianism is intended to work. He sees himself, his opponents and those of his readers whom he is concerned to persuade, as engaged in the process of identifying the ultimate end which will provide a ground for all human action. Morality and concern for others are clearly something to be taken seriously (the moral assumption). Morality itself will be grounded solely on the promotion of good (the teleological assumption). The proof in chapter 4 is intended to show that happiness is such an end, indeed the only end. Now if happiness is the only end, then, given the aggregative and the impartiality assumptions, we are led to utilitarianism, the view that each agent is rationally required by morality to maximize overall happiness. And, as we shall see, the impartiality assumption dominates Mill's view of practical rationality in general, so that there are no principles, moral or otherwise, to compete with utilitarianism: it is not just *moral* rationality, but rationality *tout court*, that requires the maximization of utility by each person. That is implicit in chapter 4 itself, where the principle of utility Mill attempts to prove is not only a moral principle, but the sole principle governing human action (4.9; see 4.3).

This interpretation of Mill itself suggests that his claim in 4.3 that the *only* evidence that something is desirable is that people do actually desire it is an exaggeration even on his own terms. For the last few paragraphs have consisted in argument, not pure appeal to

---

8 The first clause in this quotation is strongly reminiscent of the first sentence of Aristotle's *Nicomachean Ethics*.

desire. But this is surely fortunate for him; for were we take this restriction seriously, he would be able to show that the general happiness was desirable only were people actually to desire the general happiness. And then his 'proof' would be a wheel spinning idly, for it would be persuasive only to those who in practice already accepted utilitarianism. A similar difficulty would arise for Mill if we were to take the restriction seriously in the case of his theory of welfare. But that theory is clearly not just an appeal to the desires of humanity as they are, so much as a critique of many of those desires, based on an appeal to 'the rational faculty' and 'the intellect' (1.5).

Each assumption, of course, raises problems for the proof which depends on it. First, the egoist may remain unimpressed by Mill's assumptions that morality matters. Secondly, it is not obvious that or how happiness can be summed. Thirdly, the assumption of pure impartiality may fail to persuade not only the egoist and those who would allow self-interest at least some rational weight, but even someone sympathetic to Mill's teleological conception of morality, who may suggest that there are ends other than happiness, such as justice, which might provide reasons not to promote the overall good in certain circumstances. Finally, Mill's teleological view of morality might be questioned by someone who believed that human conduct should be guided not only by ends, but also perhaps by self-standing moral rules such as those forbidding, say, killing or lying.

I shall suggest later in this book that the impartiality assumption is particularly problematic for Mill. He unjustifiably ignores the rationality of pursuing not only self-interest, but other distributive ends, such as fairness. But let me conclude this section by suggesting that Mill is after all an intuitionist. Spelling out the assumptions above does add to the plausibility of his argument. And each assumption is there in the text: the moral and teleological assumptions are implicit in the first two paragraphs of the book, the aggregative assumption is in 4.3 as well as in the footnote to 5.36 which includes the impartiality assumption. The moral and teleological assumptions might perhaps be seen as methodological maxims, and the aggregative assumption could be seen as a technical axiom of empiricist psychology. But the impartiality assumption, which is one of the main bones of contention between Mill and his philosophical opponents, is as '*a priori*' as any intuitive principle. As I have already noted in this chapter, Mill is quite aware that intuitionism can support utilitarianism (3.7). An 'intuition' is little more than a belief for which no further grounds can be found. As we have seen, Mill was content to admit such beliefs about matters of fact and goods. His own naturalism, and his dislike of the metaphysics and the conservatism he perceived in the philosophy of writers such as Whewell, prevented his seeing that the debate between him and his opponents was ultimately about not intuitionism itself but which intuitions we should accept.

Stage 3: nothing other than happiness is desirable

By the end of 4.3, then, if we allow the importation into this part of the text of certain assumptions from elsewhere, Mill has completed the first two stages of the proof. He has suggested that desire is evidence of desirability, and that we should therefore accept that happiness is desirable. He has also argued that maximum happiness overall should be accepted as the end of our conduct. One problem for this view is that even if happiness is acceptable as *an* end, there are in fact other ends. And, using Mill's own test for desirability, this objection might be supported with reference to desires we have for things other than happiness.

So to prove his case that happiness alone is desirable Mill must defuse this objection. One of the obvious candidates which one of Mill's intuitionist opponents would have offered as an end different from happiness is virtue. Mill accepts this, and also allows that people do desire virtue (4.4). One strategy he might then have adopted would have been to claim that people desire virtue only as a means to happiness, whereas his own criterion for desirability involves desires for ends.

It is at first rather surprising to find that Mill eschews this option in favour of accepting that people do in fact desire virtue 'as a thing desirable in itself' (4.5). As Mill notes, virtue is 'in common language . . . decidedly distinguished from happiness' (4.4), so it begins to appear that he is placing himself among that large group of philosophers who, in expressing their views, unintentionally provide perfect counterexamples to them. But Mill is clearly aware of this danger, claiming that his 'opinion is not, in the smallest degree, a departure from the Happiness principle. The ingredients of happiness are very various, and each of them is desirable in itself, and not merely when considered as swelling an aggregate' (4.5).

Recall that Mill must show that people desire nothing other than happiness as an end. By happiness, he means pleasure, or rather, enjoyable experiences. What can Mill mean by claiming that virtue is one of the 'ingredients' of happiness so construed?

One way he could get to his conclusion would be by arguing that virtue *is in fact* an enjoyable experience. His desire criterion is intended to locate which objects are desirable. If it turns out to be the case that everything we desire is in fact an enjoyable experience, then he can claim that nothing other than enjoyable experiences is desirable, even if we desire virtue for itself independently of its being enjoyable.

This interpretation cannot be right. Mill's first example of something that can be desired for itself is money, and an initial problem with applying the present interpretation to that example is that it would turn Mill's argument into the 'contemptible nonsense' Moore understood it to be:

> Does Mill mean to say that 'money', these actual coins, which he admits to be desired in and for themselves, are a part either of pleasure or of the absence of pain? Will he maintain that those coins themselves are in my mind, and actually a part of my pleasant feelings? If this is to be said, all words are useless: nothing can possibly be distinguished from anything else.
>
> (Moore 1903: 71–2)

Nor is it likely that Mill intended to suggest that each person who desires virtue *believes* virtue to be the same as happiness. For this would imply that the people whose desires are to provide evidence for his view believe something which, in the case of money at least, is absurd.

Mill might be taken more plausibly, however, to be claiming that it is the possession of money and acting virtuously which are pleasurable. Mill does not, however, think that 'virtue' is an enjoyable experience. In the penultimate paragraph of this chapter, in his discussion of habit and the will, Mill allows that acting virtuously need not be pleasurable and may even be more painful than pleasurable.

A further interpretation of Mill's view might refer to the *associationism* which lies behind much that he says in these paragraphs.[9] Associationism is the psychological theory with which Mill grew up, according to which the rôle of psychology is to describe the laws governing the succession of our mental states. The mind, according to associationists, is like a sheet of blank paper, on which experience begins to 'write' as soon as we are born. Once we see how one experience is connected with another, we shall understand the workings of the mind rather as we may understand something written on a piece of paper by comprehending what led up to it. In the *System of Logic*, Mill outlines 'the second Law of Association' as follows: '[W]hen two impressions have been frequently experienced (or even thought of), either simultaneously or in immediate succession, then whenever one of these impressions, or the idea of it, recurs, it tends to excite the idea of the other' (8.852). If you have always found that the fire you have seen feels hot, seeing a fire or thinking of a fire will tend to make you think of heat.

Mill clearly has something like this in mind in his explanation of how what are originally means to happiness come to be desired for their own sake. He speaks frequently of the association which develops between these objects and happiness, saying of virtue, for example, that 'through the association thus formed, it may be felt a good in itself' (4.7), and that those 'who desire virtue for its own sake, desire it either because the consciousness of it is a pleasure, or because the consciousness of being without it is a pain' (4.8).

This is a causal claim about the desire for virtue as an end. We begin by desiring virtue merely as a means to the satisfaction

9   See ch. 1.

of some other, perhaps 'primitive' (4.6), desire. I might desire to be generous, for example, because I know that you will reciprocate with gifts which I shall take great pleasure in. But as an association develops in my mind between virtue and pleasure, I begin to desire virtue for itself, no longer merely as a means.

This causal claim links up with another that Mill makes towards the end of his argument in this chapter, that 'to desire anything, except in proportion as the idea of it is pleasant, is a physical and metaphysical impossibility' (4.10). By 'metaphysical' Mill almost certainly means 'psychological' (see 4.9; Mandelbaum 1968: 39), and his view appears to be that the strength of any desire for any end is proportional to how pleasant the idea of it is to the desirer.[10]

Mill undoubtedly does make these causal claims in chapter 4. But, once again, they are insufficient to justify his conclusion that only happiness is desired as an end. Even if one accepts his associationist account of how virtue and money come to be desired for their own sake, it is still the case that these objects, not themselves being pleasurable experiences, provide counter-examples to the claim that only happiness is desired. And they remain as counterexamples even if it is agreed that they can be desired only in so far as the idea of them is pleasant.

There is, in fact, only one interpretation of Mill's argument which will allow him to draw his conclusion. And even then one has to admit that he speaks quite loosely in his talk of desiring virtue and other things for their own sake. But it is perhaps more charitable to interpret Mill as speaking loosely than as failing to reach his conclusion.

Since Mill accepts that there are desires for ends which 'in common language, are decidedly distinguished from happiness' (4.4), he must be read as denying the common view. If we are to be

---

10 It has been suggested to me that Mill's view of desiring as finding pleasant gives him an *a priori* route to his conclusion that only what is pleasurable is desired. But the language of 4.10 suggests that his equation of desiring and finding pleasant is in fact *a posteriori*, to be arrived at after reflection on one's experience. In other words, it is, according to Mill, *conceivable* that we should desire something non-pleasurable; but in fact we do not.

said to desire only happiness, it must be the case that when we desire virtue as part of happiness, we are desiring the *enjoyable experiences* of being virtuous or acting virtuously. Given human psychology, desire cannot 'be directed to anything ultimately except pleasure and exemption from pain' (4.11). Mill's expectation must be that, when we examine the contents of our own minds, we shall find that we agree with him in rejecting the common view, since in desiring virtue what we really desire is in fact happiness.

This interpretation is borne out by the way that Mill spells out the notion of 'ingredients of happiness' in 4.5:

> The principle of utility does not mean that any given pleasure, as music, for instance, or any given exemption from pain, as for example health, are to be looked upon as means to a collective something termed happiness, and to be desired on that account. They are desired and desirable in and for themselves; besides being means, they are a part of the end.
>
> (4.5)

In speaking of music, then, Mill means the pleasure of music, and in speaking of virtue, the pleasure of virtue. By 'happiness' Mill understands whatever experiences a person finds enjoyable, and, as we would expect from his discussion of higher pleasures, these can be very various. Associationism still plays its part in the account. It is indeed through its original association with lower pleasures that generosity comes to be desired as an end (4.6). But it is important to see that the object of my desire is not strictly generosity, but the enjoyable experience of being generous, the 'pleasure' of generosity. It becomes not only a means to my happiness, but a constituent of it. My happiness is not some 'collective something' (4.5); rather it is nothing over and above those enjoyable experiences that constitute it.

It is very likely that this is another aspect of Mill's view of welfare and ethics in which he was influenced by Aristotle. We saw in chapter 2 how Aristotle required that any conception of human happiness must be 'complete'. That is, any list of human goods must include all the non-instrumental goods that feature in human lives. According to Aristotle, the happiness of any one person is made up of those goods that constitute happiness. Happiness just is those goods, not some 'abstract idea' (4.6) over and above them. We should not forget either that Aristotle believed that happiness consisted only in the exercise of the virtues. Mill did not go this far, but he did follow ancient tradition in allowing that virtue can be one ingredient of happiness.

Recall that full hedonism involved both the claim that welfare is constituted by pleasurable or enjoyable experiences, and the claim that these experiences are valuable because they are pleasurable. Mill needs only the first claim in this argument, since all he wishes to suggest here is that it is only pleasurable experiences which are desired. But he could easily be understood as committing himself to full hedonism in his claim that thinking of an object as desirable and thinking of it as pleasant are the same (4.10).

Psychology and ethics

Mill's proof is clearly closely bound up with his views of human psychology. Two particular psychological views are sometimes ascribed to him: psychological hedonism and psychological egoism.

Psychological hedonism is usually taken to be the view that human beings act only for the sake of pleasure. Mill certainly did not hold this view: he allows in 4.11 that the *will* may prompt action independently of any perceived pleasure. But he does seem to be committed to a rather technical, revised version of psychological hedonism, according to which human beings ultimately *desire* only pleasure. So any action prompted by desire will aim at pleasure.[11]

Psychological egoism is usually understood as the purely descriptive view that human beings act only to further what they take to be their own good. Again, Mill is clearly not a psychological egoist in this sense. He allows that a person can genuinely sacrifice their happiness for the sake of others (2.15–16). But he does accept

---

11   Mill's view on the relation of will and desire changed during his lifetime (see Berger 1984: 16–17; esp. 302–3, n. 20). But he does here explicitly distinguish will, the active phenomenon, from desire, the passive sensibility. Further, the distinction as I understand it here is required for his argument.

a version of psychological egoism limited to the scope of desire in the same way as his psychological hedonism. Humans *desire* not what is pleasurable, but only what is pleasurable *to them* (4.10).

A classic alleged counterexample to psychological egoism is the soldier who throws himself on a grenade to preserve his comrades. How can this be explained if each person desires only their own happiness? Does this soldier not sacrifice his own happiness for the sake of that of others?

As I have said, Mill allows for such cases, and states indeed that utilitarianism requires an agent to be strictly impartial between their own happiness and that of others. In Mill's ideal society, there would be no gap between my own good and the maximum overall good I could bring about. Doing what utilitarian morality required of me would in fact be what I most wanted to do in my own interests. Grenade examples would still be problematic, but there would at least be a coherent account to be given. Like Aristotle's virtuous man, the soldier 'chooses extreme pleasure for a short time rather than mild pleasure for a long time' (Aristotle *c.* 330 BC: 1169a22–3). But how should we explain the behaviour of the hero in the less than ideal world who is 'capable of resigning entirely . . . [his] own portion of happiness'? We have to say that such people are acting not from desire, but out of will engendered by habit (4.11). A large question remains, however, about how much sense it makes on psychological egoist assumptions to recommend utilitarianism to someone who has neither the desire nor the habitual willpower to be a utilitarian in practice. I shall say a little more about this in the closing section of this chapter.

There are equally serious problems with psychological hedonism. Even in the case of simple desires for enjoyable experiences such as eating, as Henry Sidgwick noted, 'hunger is frequently and naturally accompanied with anticipation of the pleasure of eating: but careful introspection seems to show that the two are by no means inseparable' (Sidgwick 1907: 45).[12] It does seem, in other

---

12 Sidgwick finds the view that desires for pleasurable objects are not always desires for pleasure in Joseph Butler (1692–1752), Francis Hutcheson (1694–1746/7) and David Hume.

words, that I can distinguish my desire for the pie in front of me from any desire for the pleasure of eating it. And there is no good reason for relegating my desire for the pie to the status of a desire for a means to the end of pleasurable eating.

Further, as we saw in my chapter 3, there do appear to be goods which are independent of experience and are desired as such. Consider a woman who is given a choice: either her children can succeed, but she will have the distress of thinking that they have failed, or they will fail, but she will have the pleasure of thinking that they have succeeded (this case is adapted from Parfit 1984: app. I). Such a woman may well choose success for her children.

This is a stumbling block for Mill's proof. We might reconstruct stage 3 without psychological egoism so that humans are said just to desire happiness, their own or others'. But the problem remains that there appear to be goods independent of happiness which are desired as such. Most of chapter 4 of Mill's book is concerned with the proof not of utilitarianism, but of a particular conception of utility. That proof is not ultimately successful. In addition, Mill's proof of the utilitarian principle as I have reconstructed it relies on an appeal to the intuitive plausibility of utilitarian impartiality in a footnote in chapter 5. Further discussion of whether that appeal is sufficient to justify utilitarianism I shall postpone for the present.

Sanctions

The third chapter of *Utilitarianism* – 'Of the ultimate sanction of the principle of utility' – has been less studied, coming as it does between the discussions of higher and lower pleasures and of secondary principles in chapter 2, and of the proof in chapter 4. This is regrettable, since chapter 3 contains much of interest, some of it relevant to our present discussion.

In the previous section, I raised the question of what Mill thought might motivate those reading his text to act on utilitarian principles. This, as 3.1 notes, was a question asked of Mill in his own day. Customary morality is already felt to be binding. If I remind you that you have promised to help me this afternoon, your sense of obligation will often be sufficient to motivate you to help me. But that sense of obligation is not attached to the utilitarian principle. Mill's question here is not purely psychological: he is asking not only what might in fact motivate people to be utilitarians, but why anyone *should* feel obliged to act in accordance with utilitarianism.

Mill notes that this problem arises for any moral theory which is not in line with customary morality, and goes on to suggest that it will remain a practical problem for utilitarianism until moral education is improved to the point that utilitarianism can avail itself of the various 'sanctions' of morality (3.1–2).

'Sanction' was a technical term in eighteenth and nineteenth-century ethics, defined by Bentham as a source of the pleasures and pains that motivate people to act (Bentham 1789: ch. 3; cf. *B* 10.97). If I do not eat, I shall suffer the pain of hunger, the source of which is in the *physical* sanction. What, for Mill, were the moral sanctions?

He divides them into two classes: external and internal (3.3–5). The external sanctions are not literally external to the individual, since they include the *hope* of favour from others, *fear* of their anger and *sympathy* for them. But they do depend on others directly in a way that the internal sanction does not. The internal sanction is the individual's own conscience, or their sense of duty. Here Mill shows the influence of Kant and Butler (see Butler 1726: sermons 2–3; Kant 1785: 12–14). The internal sanction has its origins in the influence of others, through education and so on, but then takes on a life of its own, providing moral motivation and concern which are independent of any other-regarding motivation and concern. Whether the conscience is innate (which Mill thought it was not) or acquired (which he thought it was), it can be attached to utilitarianism (3.6–8).

But again we are left asking *why* we should so arrange moral education that the external and internal sanctions favour utilitarianism. Mill's answer to this question comes in two vitally important, and moving, paragraphs at the end of chapter 3. Mill argues that human beings are naturally social creatures, who desire to be in accord with one another. This basis of natural sentiment provides an answer to the psychological question of how people can be motivated to act on the basis of utilitarianism. The external and the internal sanctions can both be grounded on a secure basis. Indeed 3.10 suggests that utilitarianism could become a *religion*, under which each person saw their own happiness as being only as important as that of any other. But, still, why *should* we seek to ground utilitarianism in this way? Because, being the creatures we are, we shall find the greatest happiness in living lives in accordance with utilitarianism. We have a strong desire for harmony between our own interests and those of others, and a natural dislike of discordance (3.11). And those who have this desire for harmony believe it to be something 'which it would not be well for them to be without'.

There is a direct link here with the discussion of higher pleasures, since the pleasures of the moral sentiments Mill speaks of in 2.4 and elsewhere are clearly those to which he is referring at the end of chapter 3. The implication of his argument is that as people are educated to become more and more impartial, they will see – paradoxically – that their lives are getting better and better *for them*.

Mill therefore has two arguments for utilitarianism. One is the argument of chapter 4, supported by assumptions from elsewhere in the text. This argument rests largely on the impartiality assumption, and it undoubtedly has some power. But he also argues for utilitarianism on the basis of self-interest, believing that the more one can extend one's sympathies and move beyond self-concern, the better one's life will be. As I shall suggest in chapters 6 and 7, Mill goes too far in the direction of impartiality in both arguments. First, as regards the argument of chapter 4, it matters not only how much welfare there is, but who gets it. Secondly, regarding the argument of chapter 3, there may well come a point at which adhering to the demands of impartiality will be highly costly in terms of self-interest.

It may perhaps be possible to bring about a society in which the sense of duty is so strong that it really is in each person's interest to be entirely impartial. But it is not plausible to suggest that each person brought up in such a society would have the best life possible for them. In which case, Mill's argument for bringing about a utilitarian society cannot rest entirely on self-interest alone, but must appeal to the proof in chapter 4. And there are problems with that proof.

Nevertheless, the argument of the final two paragraphs of chapter 3 is at least partly persuasive. The lives of many of us would, I suggest, have been improved had we been brought up to be less self-concerned and more strongly motivated to advance the interests of others. This has implications regarding the direction in which we should attempt to steer own own characters, and indeed those of our children.

This chapter has straddled the two that come before it, and those that succeed it. Chapters 2 and 3 concerned welfare in particular, and we have seen how Mill's argument in the fourth chapter of *Utilitarianism* is partly an attempt to prove hedonism. But he also attempts to prove utilitarianism, the theory that utility should be maximized. The basic shape of utilitarianism is easy to grasp, as soon as one distinguishes between welfare and morality and recognizes that utilitarianism morally requires one to maximize welfare. But the importance of utilitarianism, and any plausibility it might have, depend on a grasp of its details. So the following chapter will concern itself with spelling out these details, and in particular the details of Mill's own version of utilitarianism.

Further reading

There is a vast literature on Mill's proof. An excellent early analysis and defence is Seth 1908. Other important works include Moore 1903: ch. 3; Hall 1949; Prior 1949: ch.1; Raphael 1955; Atkinson 1957; Mandelbaum 1968; Cooper 1969; Dryer 1969; West 1982; Berger 1984: chs 1–2; Skorupski 1989: ch. 9. On the naturalistic fallacy, in addition to Moore, see Putnam 1981: ch. 9. On Mill's associationism, see Spence 1968. In Crisp 1996a I defend my interpretation of stage 3 of the proof against those of Berger and Skorupski. On sanctions, see primarily some of the works that influenced Mill: Plato *c*. 380 BC: bks 1, 2, 4; Aristotle *c*. 330 BC: bk 1; Butler 1726: sermons 2–3; Hume 1751: sect. 9; Smith 1759: pt 1, sect. 1; Kant 1785. See also Prichard 1912; Williams 1973a.

Chapter 5

What
utilitarianism
is

Rightness and focus

> The creed which accepts as the foundation
> of morals, Utility, or the Greatest Happiness
> Principle, holds that actions are right in pro-
> portion as they tend to promote happiness,
> wrong as they tend to produce the reverse of
> happiness.
>
> (2.2)

This passage is the clearest statement in *Utilitarianism* of Mill's moral theory. He has already, in
1.5, mentioned his two main aims in *Utilitarianism*:
to offer an account of utilitarianism, and, so far as is
possible, to prove it. The second chapter is entitled
'What utilitarianism is', and the quotation above
encapsulates Mill's own view of it. The word 'right'
here must mean 'morally right', since Mill is speaking of a 'creed' or theory concerned with 'the
foundation of morals'. Mill believes, then, that

actions are right in so far as they increase happiness, and wrong in so far as they decrease it, by increasing unhappiness.

One oddity should be noticed immediately. Mill appears to believe that rightness and wrongness can be matters of degree, and that both qualities can exist simultaneously in the same action. An action which promotes both happiness and unhappiness will be right to the extent that it promotes the former, and wrong to the extent that it promotes the latter.

There is enough leeway in our ordinary understanding of right and wrong to make sense of Mill here. Imagine that I find a purse containing thousands of pounds. The right thing to do, most of us would think, would be to hand it in at the police station. Imagine, however, that I decide to take a few hundred pounds for myself. This is wrong indeed, but not *morally as bad* as taking the whole lot. *The* right action can be understood as, or stipulated to be, the *morally best* action.[1] Any other action will be wrong, but we can speak of degrees of rightness and wrongness without confusion by using the notion of moral badness.[2]

Immediately after the above quotation, Mill continues: 'By happiness is intended pleasure, and the absence of pain; by unhappiness, pain, and the privation of pleasure.' This qualification is important. Without it, we might be tempted to think that the right action is that which produces the most happiness or pleasure overall. But of course it might also produce a very great deal of suffering, so that an alternative action which produced less pleasure, but a higher *balance* of pleasure over pain would be preferable. The right (morally best) action will be that which produces the greatest balance of pleasure over pain, or, if this is not possible, the least balance of pain over pleasure. Imagine that the following are my only options, and for the sake of argument assume that pleasure and pain can be measured:

---

1 Note that 'morally best' here need not mean 'morally best in utilitarian terms'. I am claiming that ordinary or 'customary' morality allows us to compare actions morally.
2 One might also use here a distinction between *pro tanto* rightness and wrongness, and overall rightness and wrongness.

Action A: 20 units of pleasure + 6 units of pain.
Action B: 15 units of pleasure + 2 units of pain.
Action C: 15 units of pleasure + 0 units of pain.

The balance of pleasure over pain is calculated by subtracting the number of units of pain from the units of pleasure. So action *A* is morally preferable to action *B*, since its total is 14 rather than 13. But action *C* is superior to action *A*, since its total is 15. So *the* right action is *C*.

It is often said that one attraction of utilitarianism is its simplicity. Certainly what Mill says here seems straightforward: you should act so as to maximize welfare or happiness, that is, the balance of pleasure over pain. But in fact there are many variations, some of them subtle, others quite radical, between different forms of utilitarianism.

Consider first the *focus* of Mill's theory, that is, what it is ultimately *about* (see Crisp 1992). Mill, like most utilitarians and indeed most modern moral theorists, focuses on *actions*. He is attempting primarily to answer the question, 'What is the right thing to do?' But he could have focused on some other notion, such as, say, character. Then his first question would have been, 'What sort of character should I have?'

Mill's answer to this question might have been that one should have that character which results in one's performing those actions which maximize happiness. This view would have been consistent with the view he expresses in *Utilitarianism*. He might, however, have suggested that one should have that character which (itself) maximizes happiness. This view would be subtly different from that in *Utilitarianism*, since it may be that there are special features of possessing a certain character (the happiness it produces in its possessor, for example) which mean that the character which maximizes happiness is not that which produces those actions which maximize happiness (see Adams 1976). But, since characters are themselves brought about by the actions either of others or of ourselves, these theories will not diverge in their practical advice. For if having a certain character does produce happiness in its possessor, that happiness will be a consequence of the actions of those who cause the possessor to have that character.

This does suggest, however, that Mill exaggerates the importance of actions. For if you act so as to produce in me a character which causes me to do actions which are less productive of happiness than those I should have performed with a different character, but the possession of which character does in fact lead to happiness's being maximized, you will have acted rightly. My life, from the broad utilitarian perspective, will be lived better if I have this character than were I to perform the most useful actions. Focusing on actions might lead one to miss this point. Should utilitarians therefore focus on character? No, for this would run into the same problem. The focus of moral theories should be as broad as possible, encompassing acts, character, motives, rule-following or whatever – life as a whole. In other words, the primary question for any utilitarian should be that which exercised Socrates: how should one live (Plato *c.* 390 BC: 500c2–4)? Nor should we forget the importance of questions concerning groups and institutions, questions about how *we* should live. Nevertheless, whether I am asking questions from the practical point of view about how I or we should live, I shall always be ultimately interested in what to *do* – which actions to perform – in the light of the correct theory.

This can be put another way, in terms of histories of the world. Behind forms of utilitarianism such as Mill's might be said to be working something like the following principle:

> *P1:* The best possible history of the world is that in which the balance of pleasure over pain is greatest.

When it comes to our lives, this principle has the following analogue:

> *P2:* The best lives for us, including the best life for me, are those which feature in the best possible history.

And as regards actions:

> *P3:* The best actions are those which feature in the best possible history.

So, from my present point of view, looking forward in time, the best possible history from now will be that in which the balance of pleasure over pain is greatest overall, and I should act now so as to bring that history about, whether the history is brought about directly by my action, or through the mediation of character, rule-following or whatever.

Actualism and probabilism

Let me return to Mill's own version of utilitarianism. So far I have taken him to mean that the right action is the one which *in fact* produces the greatest balance of pleasure over pain. But consider the following case:

The rash doctor You have a serious medical condition, for which two treatments are available. One will leave you with a high welfare level of 50, the other with a fairly low level of 25. There is, however, only a 1% chance of success with the first treatment, and if it fails, you will die. The second treatment will undoubtedly succeed. Your doctor chooses the first treatment, and it is success-ful.

Assume just for the sake of this example that welfare can be at least roughly measured. According to Mill's version of utilit-arianism in 2.2, your doctor has not, strictly speaking, done anything wrong, since the action she took was in fact that which produced the greatest balance of pleasure over pain. And, though we would usually not know which they are, there will be similar cases where cautious doctors who employ the safe treatment would have succeeded with the risky treatment. These doctors, according to Mill, will have acted wrongly.

Mill's view may be called *actualism*, since it takes into account only what actually would happen. The right action in any circumstance is the one which will actually turn out to produce the greatest possible balance of pleasure over pain.

An alternative would be a version of utilitarianism which takes probabilities into account. This version is just one of a large number of moral theories which offer an account of rightness in terms of what the agent is justified in believing at the time of action. Remember that in the case above, the chances of one treatment's bringing about a good outcome were very low. The probabilist will suggest that such facts are extremely relevant in assessing rightness and wrongness, and will claim that the rash doctor did the wrong thing, since in assessing the rightness or wrongness of courses of action the numbers representing the welfare levels are to be multiplied by the probabilities of their succeeding. The calculations come out as follows:

Risky treatment: $50 \times 0.01 = 0.5$.
Safe treatment: $25 \times 1.000 = 25$.

Here the safer treatment is clearly preferable from the probabilist point of view.

The difference between actualism and probabilism appears not greatly to have concerned Mill. In 2.2, he offers an actualist view, while at other times he is prepared to speak of the morality of an action's depending on its 'foreseeable consequences' (*B* 10.112). This latter claim is equivalent to that in the footnote to 2.19, in which Mill says that the morality of an action depends upon the intention of the agent. For Mill believed intention to be the foresight of consequences (*AP* 31.253). We may be helped here by adapting a distinction of Henry Sidgwick's between 'objective' and 'subjective' rightness (Sidgwick 1907: 207–8). From the objective point of view, the doctor in the example did the right thing, since her action was the one that maximized overall happiness. But she had no good reason for thinking that her action would succeed, and thus she is open to criticism from the perspective of subjective rightness. Objective rightness, then, consists in the maximization of overall happiness, while subjective rightness consists in the maximization of expected overall happiness. The objective/subjective distinction enables one to accept both actualism at the objective level, and probabilism at the subjective level.

It is important to note that these are both theories about *rightness*. Neither has any immediate implication regarding how we should *think* about doing the right act in any particular case. For example, someone might accept the accounts just given of objective and subjective rightness, but suggest that doctors should not think seriously in terms of subjective or objective rightness when they are treating patients. Rather they should follow the canons of good treatment they learned in medical school, with their rough-and-ready ways of assessing probabilities. According to utilitarianism, praising and blaming themselves are also subject to the principles of rightness, so that they are objectively right if they maximize happiness, and subjectively right if they maximize expected happiness. Blame, for example, is not necessarily applicable in a case where a person has done what is objectively or subjectively wrong. More of this later in the chapter.

The notion of subjective rightness would allow Mill to offer an answer to an apparently devastating objection to utilitarianism. Since they stretch indefinitely into the future, we can never know for sure what the consequences of any action we perform will be. So we can never know how to act on the actualist interpretation of utilitarianism. But if we adopt probabilism in practice, unexpected good consequences and unexpected bad consequences cancel one another out in our calculations. So if I pointlessly punch you in the nose, I cannot defend myself by saying that my attacking you *may* turn out to have been the best thing to do, in that, for example, you may begin a campaign which makes the streets much safer. For the probabilities here are almost entirely unknown. What I did know was that hitting you had pretty much a 100% chance of causing you substantial suffering. So, according to probabilism, I should not have done it, and I can be blamed without any waiting to see whether the campaign does come about or not.[3]

---

3   Mill must assume that the consequences of our actions, from the point of view of their production of welfare or happiness, will end somewhere. For otherwise he would be faced by an infinity of time in which to maximize, and anything would be acceptable, since no action could ever be said to be that which maximizes happiness or indeed expected happiness overall (see on this issue Nelson 1991 and Vallentyne 1993). But since our sun will eventually die, and we shall probably have made no impact on life forms elsewhere in the universe, this is not a serious practical difficulty for Mill if he is permitted to assume that morality is to govern life on earth. Why is he entitled to that restriction? Surely the welfare of all beings in the universe should be our concern, in which case utilitarianism does have to assume that life with a capacity for welfare is finite? Again, probabilism provides the answer: utilitarians have to assume that such life *may* be finite, so that the notion of welfare maximization *may* have application.

Acts and rules

I shall now turn to another important distinction between types of utilitarianism, one which has received a great deal of attention in the literature on Mill. I have shown that, according to Mill, the right action is that which maximizes happiness.[4] This is *act utilitarianism*. Act utilitarianism is what philosophers have called a *direct* moral theory, since the notion at the heart of the theory – the maximizing principle – applies directly to acts.

In recent years, some writers have interpreted Mill's view as *indirect*, in particular as a version of *rule utilitarianism*. Rule utilitarians also focus their theories on actions. But the rightness or wrongness of actions depends not directly on whether they maximize happiness, but rather on certain rules, viz. those which will maximize happiness were most or all people to accept them. The most influential rule utilitarian interpretation of Mill has been that of J.O. Urmson (Urmson 1953). Because this article has received so much attention, I shall now discuss it, in the hope that my points will carry across to other rule utilitarian interpretations.

The most important of the views Urmson ascribes to Mill are as follows:

A. A particular action is justified as being right by showing that it is in accord with some moral rule. It is shown to be wrong by showing that it transgresses some moral rule.

B. A moral rule is shown to be correct by showing that the recognition of that rule promotes the ultimate end.

What is the difference between Mill's view so interpreted and act utilitarianism? Consider promising. If I make a promise to you, and a situation arises in which breaking that promise will maximize utility, act utilitarianism requires me to break the promise. This, as Urmson points out, goes against what we ordinarily believe, for we

---

4   I shall not draw the objective/subjective or actualist/probabilist distinctions unless required by the argument. So 'happiness' here can be understood to refer to happiness (at the objective level) and expected happiness (at the subjective level).

tend to think that one has a duty to do what one has promised *just because* one has promised. On the revised view, Mill can agree with this. He can claim that a rule which requires people to keep their promises would, if generally accepted, promote happiness to the greatest possible degree. For it would allow all sorts of valuable contracts and arrangements to be entered into which would be impossible were people not to trust one another. So, since it would be forbidden by a morally justified rule, my breaking the promise in this particular case would not be justified.

Let me now outline and briefly consider some of Urmson's arguments for his interpretation. Discussing some of them properly will have to wait until later in this chapter.

(1) Urmson cites Mill's claim in 1.3 that both the intuitive and inductive schools agree that the morality of an action is a matter of the application of a general law to a particular case.

Mill does indeed see himself as a member of the inductive school, that is, that group of philosophers who base their moral philosophy on 'observation and experience'. So we must assume that he himself thinks that the morality of an action involves applying general laws or rules to particular cases. But the general law he goes on to argue for is the act utilitarian principle.

(2) Urmson accepts that 2.2 might be taken in an act utilitarian way, but claims that to do so would be to ignore Mill's reference to the 'tendencies' of actions to promote happiness or unhappiness:

> *[N]ote that strictly one can say that a certain action tends to produce a certain result only if one is speaking of type- rather than token-actions. Drinking alcohol may tend to promote exhilaration, but my drinking this particular glass either does or does not produce it. It seems, then, that Mill can well be interpreted here as regarding moral rules as forbidding or enjoining types of action, in fact as saying that the right moral rules are the ones which promote the ultimate end (my proposition B).*

> *(Urmson 1953: 37)*

Urmson uses 2.2 to support his ascription of B to Mill. I accept that Mill believed B; but this passage does not show that he did. It was standard in the utilitarian tradition to refer to the tendencies of individual acts. In only the second paragraph, for example, of Jeremy Bentham's *Introduction to the Principles of Morals and Legislation* (1789), a work with which Mill would have been all too familiar, we find the following:

> By the principle of utility is meant that principle which approves or disapproves of every action whatsoever, according to the tendency which it appears to have to augment or diminish the happiness of the party whose interest is in question: or, what is the same thing in other words, to promote or oppose that happiness.

It might be said that by 'every action' here, Bentham means 'every *type* of action'. But there is no need to take this less-than-straightforward view of the passage, for elsewhere Bentham is happy to speak of an act's having tendencies as an *event's* having tendencies (1789: 4.3), and it seems particularly unlikely that in such a passage he must be understood to be speaking of *types* of event.[5]

A tendency, then, need not be a property only of types of action. If my now drinking alcohol promotes my happiness, then to that extent it has a tendency to promote my happiness. And to the extent that it promotes unhappiness, through providing me with a splitting headache hours later, it has a tendency to promote unhappiness. Its overall tendency will then be the balance of happiness over unhappiness, or vice versa. Mill is taking over this usage, and the notion of 'tendency' plays no special rôle in his definition of utilitarianism. His claim that actions are right in

---

5   Those unpersuaded should read Bentham's discussion of how to assess 'the general tendency of any act' in 4.5. This is clearly intended to be a discussion of how to assess the moral quality of individual acts. To think otherwise would require Bentham's references to 'any one person', 'that individual person' and so on to be taken as references to types of person. For another clear use of the technical sense of 'tendency' by Mill, see the letter to John Venn, discussed on p. 117. Nor is this technical use of the word by Bentham and Mill a misuse. In ordinary language, an individual item can have a tendency, as in, for example, 'That ship has a marked tendency to starboard'.

proportion as they tend to promote happiness is equivalent to the claim that they are right to the extent that they promote happiness.

(3) *In 2.24, Mill allows that there may be secondary moral principles. Urmson takes it that these principles play the rôle he describes in A, so that an action is right if it accords with such a rule. Urmson accepts that claims such as those in 2.24 may have led some to see rules as mere aids to maximizing. But, he says, admitting that rules have been arrived at by learning the usual effects of certain types of action 'does not require us to interpret them as being anything but rules when once made' (Urmson 1953: 38).*

This final claim is correct, but the question remains of the status of these rules. I shall show in the following section of this chapter that Urmson's understanding of their status is mistaken, and that his ascription of A to Mill is therefore mistaken. The same response can be made to Urmson's quotation of the final two sentences of chapter 2, in which Mill states that one should refer to the first principle only in cases of conflict between secondary principles.

(4) *Urmson argues that in 5.14 Mill makes it clear that he takes right and wrong to be 'derived from' moral rules.*

This difficult paragraph, which has been used widely by other non-act utilitarian interpreters in recent years, will be discussed in the final section of this chapter, and in chapter 7.

So far I have dealt with only some of Urmson's arguments against the ascription of act utilitarianism and in favour of the ascription of rule utilitarianism to Mill. In the following section, I shall consider the question of what the passages cited by Urmson tell us about how Mill did in fact view moral rules. This discussion, I hope, will be sufficient to show that Mill is not a rule utilitarian.

Levels of moral thinking

Since Mill thinks that the right act is the one that maximizes welfare, one might expect him to advise us always consciously and deliberately to *try* to maximize welfare, to make this our only goal in acting. But to expect this is to ignore another important distinction between different types of utilitarianism.

The act utilitarian says that what makes an action right is its maximizing welfare. This, as we saw in chapter 4, is what Mill calls the *criterion* of right action in 1.1. Note that act utilitarianism should be understood *only* to be a theory about the criterion of right action. Nothing follows from it alone concerning exactly how we should *think about* how to act in our everyday lives.

There is, however, nothing to prevent an act utilitarian from claiming that we should always consciously try to maximize welfare at every possible opportunity. This is what we might call a *single-level* act utilitarianism, since the theorist is recommending that moral agents think only at one 'level', that is, allow their thinking to be dominated constantly by act utilitarianism itself.

Imagine what life in a society of single-level act utilitarians would be like. Though presumably you could, being human, not help *enjoying* certain experiences, such as eating tasty food, you and everybody else would *adopt* no aim other than to maximize welfare. You would have no qualms about such actions as killing, hurting or lying to others.

I doubt whether such a society is even a possibility for human beings. Act utilitarianism as a single-level decision procedure requires both that one be entirely impartial between people (or, rather, their utilities), and that one be educated to the point where the theory can be rationally applied. These requirements are in tension. Children are brought up within traditions and cultures, and all the traditions and cultures that have yet developed among human beings have embodied partiality. Parents, teachers and others in society establish special relationships with children which make it possible to bring them up to be rational. It is hard to imagine a system of education which did not rest on such partialities, or to imagine partialities and attachments which could be shed once the capability to think rationally were achieved.[6]

---

6 This is perhaps a particular problem for associationists, who believe that later experiences are likely to be linked to earlier; see ch. 1. It is such associations, Mill would have believed, that made customary morality possible.

A single-level act utilitarian might accept this point, and argue that one should be *as impartial as possible* within the psychological constraints of the partialities which have arisen during one's upbringing. 'Ought', as philosophers say, implies 'can'. This raises the question whether such a view is entitled to be called 'single-level'. The single-level theorist might suggest that all the *moral* thinking agents will have to do will be of an act utilitarian kind. But this misses the point that the development of partialities is itself moralized. Human upbringings have always been intricately interwoven with non-utilitarian practical moralities. Children feel non-utilitarian moral indignation from a very early age at unfairness to themselves, their siblings or friends. It is not at all clear whether these and the multitude of similar apparently natural reactions which play such an important rôle in the upbringing of children are purely culturally engendered. If they are not, then single-level act utilitarianism collapses. For it will not be psychologically possible in the moral sphere of one's life to be a pure utilitarian. This suggests that single-level act utilitarianism is an impossibility not only for societies, but for any individual within any society.

This is an empirical matter, of course, and it is hard to imagine how it might be resolved without the most appalling experiments. There is in fact a stronger argument, one offered by Mill, against single-level act utilitarianism. When we ask single-level act utilitarians why they advocate constant attempts to maximize utility, they must, because they are act utilitarians, reply that this method of doing one's moral thinking is the most conducive to overall welfare. But this appears extremely unlikely to be the case.

Consider first how much time people in a single-level act utilitarian society will have to spend calculating the welfare values of the various courses of action open to them at any time. Indeed, unless there are *some* rules to guide their practical thinking, they will never cease calculating, and nothing will be achieved. It is not a large step from rules about how long to spend calculating to the rules of what Mill calls 'customary morality' (3.1). Mill recognizes clearly that there is no need to think that act utilitarianism as a moral theory requires adoption of act utilitarianism as a single-level decision procedure. In response to the objection to utilitarianism that there is not time to calculate all the effects of any course of action on the general happiness, he writes:

> [T]here has been ample time, namely, the whole past duration of the human species. During all that time, mankind have been learning by experience the tendencies of actions;[7] on which experience all the prudence, as well as all the morality of life, is dependent ... It is truly a whimsical supposition that, if mankind were agreed in considering utility to be the test of morality, they would remain without any agreement as to what *is* useful, and would take no measures for having their notions on the subject taught to the young, and enforced by law and opinion ... [M]ankind must by this time have acquired positive beliefs as to the effects of some actions on their happiness; and the beliefs which have thus come down are the rules of morality for the multitude, and for the philosopher until he has succeeded in finding better.
>
> (2.24)

Mill thinks that customary morality, that set of moral principles which most of us are brought up to accept and which forbid, for example, murder and theft, has emerged 'due to the tacit influence of a standard not recognised' (1.4). Human beings are by nature concerned with their own happiness, and this concern, extended to others, has led, without our fully being aware of it, to the development of a customary morality founded in large part on the principle of utility. The rules of morality are like the 'landmarks and direction-posts' used by a traveller who has already been told his ultimate destination, or the Nautical Almanack employed by sailors in navigating (2.24). There is no point in heading for a landmark or consulting an Almanack unless it brings one closer to arriving at one's destination, and that such consultations ordinarily do just that is what justifies them. Mill recognizes that it would be as impossible to be a single-level act utilitarian and succeed as it would be to negotiate a complex voyage without navigational aids (2.24).

---

7   Here Mill uses 'tendencies' in the ordinary non-technical sense, applying it to the class of actions.

So the rules of customary morality are, to put it crudely and thus possibly misleadingly, 'rules of thumb'. They save time, and are reliably based on the experience of humankind over the ages, but they are irrelevant to the *ultimate* justification of any action, which depends solely on the extent to which that action promotes happiness. They do not, as Urmson suggests, play any rôle in Mill's theory of the criterion of moral action. But now a question arises. Mill is not a single-level act utilitarian, and admits the rules of customary morality into our moral thinking. So is he saying that utilitarianism, though it is the correct theory about the rightness of actions, should *never* play any part in the moral thinking of actual moral agents? Is he offering, in other words, a *self-effacing* version of act utilitarianism, according to which there are good act utilitarian reasons for never consulting the act utilitarian theory in our decision procedures (see Parfit 1984: 40–3)?

In fact Mill is neither a single-level nor a self-effacing theorist; his is a *multi-level* view, of a particularly subtle kind (see Hare 1981: 25–8). Sometimes we should just follow the ordinary customary morality most of us have been brought up with, that is, not murder, not steal and so on. Reflection on the nature of that customary morality shows, incidentally, why speaking of it as consisting in 'rules of thumb' can be slightly misleading. We can imagine an act utilitarian who took customary morality as a set of rules of thumb thinking as follows: 'Should I kill my boss? Well, customary morality contains a rule of thumb that one shouldn't kill, because killing in the past has been shown to be unproductive of utility. So I suppose I shouldn't kill him.' This train of thought is quite alien to us, and would have been so to Mill. Part of the function of customary morality is to shape what we think about, how we think and which options we even take seriously. Customary morality is inculcated deep within us, so that we would not even ask the question of whether to kill others in most circumstances. In other words, Mill was suggesting that we go on with much of customary morality as it now is: sincerely urging children not to steal, resisting the temptation to lie and feeling compunction at so doing, and so on. In that sense, he is something of a moral conservative. But this is perhaps the one place where conservatism is the only plausible option.

But customary morality *itself* also contains – or rather, Mill believes, *should* also contain – the act utilitarian principle of impartial benevolence, which should be used when, for example, one comes across irresoluble conflicts between non-act utilitarian principles within customary morality. You have promised to meet a friend for tea at four, for instance, but then your boss asks to see you urgently to discuss the welfare of another employee. If the non-utilitarian parts of customary morality cannot resolve this dilemma, then you can employ the act utilitarian principle:

> We must remember that only in . . . cases of conflict between secondary principles is it requisite that first principles should be appealed to. There is no case of moral obligation in which some secondary principle is not involved; and if only one, there can seldom be any real doubt which one it is, in the mind of any person by whom the principle itself is recognised.
>
> (2.25)

Mill is claiming here, then, that in your everyday life, you should not consult the principle of utility except when two non-utilitarian principles conflict.[8] Customary morality works, or should be made to work, at two levels: the non-act utilitarian, and the act utilitarian. I say 'should be made to work' because Mill, as we would expect, given his claim that customary morality rests on the principle of utility without our realizing it, admits that that principle does not *feel* obligatory to us *now* (3.1). This is in contrast to the present customary morality, which is underpinned by a sense of moral obligation. Our present customary moral rules are such that we feel morally bound to obey them, and in this respect of course they differ from those found in navigation. Mill argues, however, that education and opinion should be employed to ensure not only that each individual

---

8 As we shall see shortly, this is something of an exaggeration on Mill's part, since he believed that the ideal customary morality would also allow pure motivation by the act utilitarian principle to promote overall happiness.

may be unable to conceive the possibility of happiness to himself, consistently with conduct opposed to the general good, but also that a direct impulse to promote the general good may be in every individual *one of* the habitual motives of action, and the sentiments connected therewith may fill a large and prominent place in every human being's sentient existence.

(2.18; my italics; see also 3.1–5, 10–11)

Mill allows that a 'desire to be in unity with our fellow-creatures' is strong in human nature, and has been strengthened by the evolution of culture; and he envisages the teaching of this feeling of unity as a religion, as a way of grounding a sense of utilitarian obligation (3.10; see ch. 4).

But for Mill there is yet another level of moral thinking independent of either the non-act utilitarian or the act utilitarian levels of everyday moral thinking, a level beyond customary morality: philosophy itself.

Mill is prepared, in other words, to engage in several forms of discourse, and advocates that we do the same. If one heard Mill using moral language, he might have been operating at one of three levels: (1) the non-act utilitarian level of customary morality: for example, 'That was courageous'; (2) the act utilitarian level of customary morality: for example, a dilemma such as the 'tea' case; (3) the philosophical act utilitarian level, as in 2.2 of *Utilitarianism*.[9] It would not have been surprising to hear him telling a child that it is wrong to steal. The evidence of Mill's writings shows that he was clearly prepared to speak and to think in the terms of customary morality. But when he was engaged in doing serious moral philosophy, that is, in making claims about what *really* makes actions right or wrong, he would have denied that actions are wrong *just because* they are actions in contravention of customary

---

9 This makes interpretation of Mill's writings particularly difficult. For if he makes claims apparently inconsistent with utilitarianism, such as his suggestion in a letter to Arthur Helps of 1847 that inequality is bad *in itself* (17.2002), it is not clear whether he is operating at the level of philosophical theory, or that of customary morality. See ch. 1.

morality. Actions are right or wrong solely in so far as they promote happiness or unhappiness.

This is why one should not assume that Mill's restriction of the use of the act utilitarian principle to conflict resolution *within* customary morality is conservative to the point of forbidding reflection *on*, and consequent change in, customary morality itself. He attaches no intrinsic weight to customary morality: '[T]hat the received code of ethics is by no means of divine right; and that mankind have still much to learn as to the effects of actions on the general happiness, I admit, or rather, earnestly maintain' (2.24). He does not rule out reference to the principle of utility during philosophical reflection, carried out as an enterprise detached from the life of customary moral practice. Mill is keen that philosophers hold customary morality up to the light and improve it so far as they can. This is part of what he sees himself doing in *Utilitarianism*. In later chapters, we shall see how Mill's reflection on the customary morality of his time regarding the liberty of the individual and the relations between the sexes led him to advocate various important changes in the customary moral principles governing these areas.

Demandingness and rule-worship

Let me summarize the distinctions between moral theories and between types of utilitarianism I have been drawing in this chapter, since they are very easy to confuse. First, theories differ in their *focus*. Most focus on actions, but others may focus on characters, or whole lives. Secondly, utilitarian theories can be *actualist* or *probabilist* concerning the outcomes of actions. I suggested that Mill seems to be attracted to both views, and that he is best interpreted in the light of two conceptions of rightness: *objective rightness*, according to which rightness is determined by factors extraneous to the agent's beliefs and expectations, and *subjective rightness*, according to which rightness does depend on the agent's beliefs, or rather the beliefs an ordinary human agent could have in the situation in question. The third distinction I drew involved the notion of the *criterion* of right action, that is, what makes actions right or wrong. Some theories are *direct*, applying the notion at the heart of their criterion directly to their focus without mediation. According to *act utilitarianism*, what makes an action right is that it maximizes welfare or expected welfare. Whether an action is right depends directly on whether it maximizes. According to *rule utilitarianism*, an *indirect* theory, what makes an action right is its conforming to that set of rules the general acceptance of which would maximize welfare or expected welfare. Mill is an act utilitarian. Finally, utilitarian theorists differ over the kind of decision-procedures agents should adopt. *Single-level* utilitarians advocate decision-making's being dominated by the utilitarian principle, while *self-effacing* utilitarians recommend against any reference to the principle. *Multi-level* theorists recommend that reference be made to it sometimes. I showed how Mill's is a multi-level view, and that he believes both that we should consult the utilitarian principle in cases where conflict arises between two or more non-utilitarian principles, and that utilitarian philosophical reflection can support changes in customary morality. It is very important to keep these various distinctions apart when trying to understand utilitarianism. Perhaps the most common confusion, and one still found in much contemporary writing in ethics, is between a version of multi-level act utilitarianism, such as Mill's, which advocates adherence to ordinary moral rules, and rule utilitarianism.

I want now to continue discussing Mill's views in the light of these distinctions, and to concentrate in particular on some issues that arise in one of the most complex paragraphs in *Utilitarianism*, 2.19, with its long footnote. These issues concern the demandingness of morality and its scope of concern, the possibility that Mill is not after all an act utilitarian, and the so-called 'rule-worship' objection to certain forms of multi-level utilitarianism.

In paragraph 2.19, Mill brings up the objection to act utilitarianism that it is too demanding. This objection can perhaps be understood through further reflection on the single-level act utilitarian society I described in the previous section. According to that theory, you are permitted to make no time for your own personal concerns or projects, or for developing friends or relationships, except in so far as doing these things maximizes utility impartially. Your own welfare is to be put in the balance in your practical reasoning along with that of everyone else, and your welfare counts only as much as anyone else's. Surely such a theory will be impossibly demanding? Mill responds to the objection, as we might by now expect, by drawing the distinction between the criterion of rightness and the everyday thinking of moral agents, claiming that such an objection is

> to mistake the very meaning of a standard of morals, and to confound the rule of action with the motive of it. It is the business of ethics to tell us what are our duties, or by what test we may know them; but no system of ethics requires that the sole motive of all we do shall be a feeling of duty; on the contrary, ninety-nine hundredths of all our actions are done from other motives, and rightly so done, if the rule of duty does not condemn them.

Mill believes that customary morality is solidly grounded on the principle of utility. Indeed this perhaps offers a particularly strong rationale for his claims that customary morality should be assessed and reformed in the light of philosophical utilitarian reflection. Since customary morality allows us much leeway to act on motives other than those of duty, such as self-interest or love of others, Mill himself wishes to permit this, presumably thinking that our so acting will in the end lead to the maximization of happiness. He does think that customary morality ought to demand a little more of us than it does at present, as we have seen in this and the previous chapter. Utilitarianism – pure impartiality – should play a greater rôle in customary morality than it now does. Morality's becoming more demanding, and the scope of duty's expanding, is indeed a sign of moral progress in a society (AC 10.338). But Mill is a gradualist, who recognizes that reforms in customary morality can only be piecemeal.

As we saw in the previous section, Mill does allow some place for utilitarian and purely benevolent motivation in his ideal customary morality. But even when we do act from duty and from the principle of utility, he suggests, we have to take into account the interests of only those particular people concerned, such as, in the example in the previous section, your friend, your boss, the other employee and of course yourself. The reason for this is as follows:

> The multiplication of happiness is, according to the utilitarian ethics, the object of virtue: the occasions on which any person (except one in a thousand) has it in his power to do this on an extended scale . . . are but exceptional; and on these occasions alone is he called on to consider public utility.

This passage again shows, incidentally, that Mill was exaggerating when he said that conflict between secondary principles was the only time at which the principle of utility should be consulted. The main thrust of the passage was as false when Mill wrote it as it is now. Because of large inequalities in the distribution of property, many people in Mill's day, especially those with the leisure to read *Utilitarianism*, had the opportunity, as we do now, to promote utility 'on an extended scale', by contributing to worthwhile charitable projects or themselves taking part in projects to alleviate severe suffering. Utilitarianism is almost certainly much more demanding than Mill allows. It is tempting to think, in fact, that Mill is deliberately being disingenuous here. He was quite aware of how much further there was to go before customary morality became ideal, and that the route to that ideal would seem demanding to many. The rhetoric to encourage people on that road comes in chapter 3 of *Utilitarianism*, especially in the closing paragraphs. Here, he may be more concerned to allay doubts. Better to persuade a reader to become a feeble utilitarian than put them off entirely by stressing the demandingness of utilitarian morality. I shall say more about the theoretical implications of the demandingness of morality in the following chapter.

Mill continues his discussion of how far moral thinking should range:

> In the case of abstinences indeed – of things which people forbear to do, from moral considerations, though the consequences in the particular case might be beneficial – it would be unworthy of an intelligent agent not to be consciously aware that the action is of a class which, if practised generally, would be generally injurious, and that this is the ground of the obligation to abstain from it. The amount of regard for the public interest implied in this recognition, is no greater than

is demanded by every system of morals; for they all enjoin to abstain from whatever is manifestly pernicious to society.

(2.19)

So at times, Mill is ready to admit, you should be prepared to think of society as a whole, rather than just particular individuals. This passage throws up a problem of interpretation which returns us to the issue of whether Mill is an act or rule utilitarian. I claimed above that Mill was not a rule utilitarian. Another version of indirect utilitarianism, which one might call *utilitarian generalization*, makes no essential reference to rules, but is structurally very similar to rule utilitarianism. It requires that we perform no action which is such that, if people were generally to perform it, welfare would not be maximized. Mill's statement here, which Urmson does not discuss, appears to come very close to such a theory. It would mean that if I were to break a promise, I would have done wrong *even if* I had maximized welfare. For breaking promises, if practised generally, would almost certainly be 'generally injurious'.

We need to notice two things. First, the passage concerns the moral thinking of agents, and not the criterion of morality. It is likely that by 'obligation' here, Mill means the *sense* of obligation which prevents our killing, stealing and so on. Our having this sense is, as we have seen, justified by the principle of utility. Secondly, Mill does not say that the consequences in the case he imagines *are* beneficial, only that they might be. So he is conceiving of a case in which a moral agent is confronted by a situation in which customary morality requires something of them, perhaps not to lie. They see that ignoring customary morality here *might* – perhaps might well – produce the best consequences. But they should, Mill is suggesting, at least be prepared to recognize that one should abstain from the sorts of activities that are likely to be very harmful to others. He himself can provide an act utilitarian justification for this, but, as he says, this view is likely to be accepted by any moral theorist, not just an act utilitarian.

Why should they respect their sense of obligation in such a case? Mill offers two arguments a few pages later (2.23). The first is that our inclination to tell the truth is extremely valuable in utilitarian terms, and lying on any occasion will weaken that inclination. The second is that when we lie we lessen the trustworthiness of human assertion, which again has many good effects on the general happiness. So Mill's advocacy of respect for the principles of customary morality is consistently act utilitarian. Respecting those principles will in fact turn out, on the whole, to maximize welfare or happiness.

This explains why the quotation ends with Mill's claiming that the action in question would in fact be 'manifestly pernicious' to society. He also thought that we would be well advised, when considering the consequences of any possible course of action, to consider the consequences of the whole class of actions of which this is a member. In an 1872 letter to John Venn, he says:

> I agree with you that the right way of testing actions by their consequences, is to test them by the natural consequences of the particular action, and not by those which would follow if every one did the same. But, for the most part, the consideration of what would happen if every one did the same, is the only means we have of discovering the tendency of the act in the particular case.[10]
>
> ('Letter to John Venn' (1872) 17.1881)

One of the consequences of my and others' habitually lying which are likely to become salient will be the weakening of dispositions to tell the truth and to trust what others say, and there will be many others. There may be exceptional cases, however, in which following customary morality turns out not to maximize happiness, and in these cases Mill, as an actualist, must accept that customary morality should not have been followed. But we cannot predict the future, so his suggestion that we usually adhere to customary morality is likely to be justified over the long term.

This explains why Mill cannot justly be convicted of what philosophers have come to call 'rule-worship' (Smart 1956: 348–9). Consider the following case (adapted from McCloskey 1957):

---

10 This is one of the clearest examples of Mill's use of the technical sense of 'tendency'.

The sheriff A town in the Wild West has been plagued by a series of violent crimes. The sheriff is confronted by a deputation led by the mayor. The deputation tells him that, unless he hangs the vagrant he has in his jail, whom the whole town believes to be the criminal, there will without doubt be a terrible riot, in which many people will almost certainly be killed or maimed. This vagrant has no friends or family. The sheriff knows he is innocent.

What should the sheriff do? He could just allow the riot to take place; but that would be to allow a lot of preventable suffering, since he could punish the innocent vagrant, and thus appease the mob. By breaking the normal rules of justice that people should be given fair trial, and that those known to be innocent should not be punished, he could produce the best outcome.

What would be Mill's view of such a situation? As an act utilitarian, he must accept that punishing the innocent man would indeed be the right action, if we assume that this would indeed bring about the best results in utilitarian terms. But, a single-level act utilitarian objector might say, Mill advises that we follow rules pretty well without exception. So Mill will claim that the sheriff should abide by the rules and not hang the innocent man. This is, from the utilitarian point of view, rule-worship, since Mill is advocating keeping to a rule for no good reason.

But, once one is clear about the distinction between the criterion of right action and the decision-procedures of real moral agents, one can see this objection to be mistaken. Were Mill present during the sheriff's ordeal, he would advise keeping to the rule. But this would be because keeping to the rule *on the whole* maximizes happiness. Breaking rules can have all sorts of bad consequences. In this case, for example, the sheriff's ploy may be discovered, or, if not, he may become tempted to punish innocent people in future, when it would be quite unjustified even on utilitarian terms. It is just not clear in practice whether, in any particular case, one might maximize by breaking the rule; and, because it can be assumed that it usually will not maximize to break the rule, breaking the rule should not usually be considered. Mill is not advising that one abide by customary morality for its own sake, but rather because so doing is the strategy which will, he predicts, maximize welfare in the long run. Given our ignorance of the future, the course of action that act utilitarianism requires is nearly always adherence to customary morality.

Mill allows, however, that there are some clear exceptions to customary rules, such as that against lying. You should lie, for example, to the axe-wielding maniac who asks you which way your friend went (2.23). Mill believes that the limits of the principle of veracity ought to be defined, in order that unjustified exceptions to it be prevented. These limits will be decided through philosophical use of the act utilitarian principle, guided by empirical knowledge of the kinds of cases under discussion. The same goes for the rules of justice (5.37), and I suggest (though of course the work remains to be done) that sound act utilitarian arguments could be constructed for lying to the maniac but not hanging the innocent man.

Split psyches and different discourses

Mill's act utilitarianism states that the right action is the action that maximizes welfare. It is usually assumed that any theory about what the right action is commits its holder to the view that what we are required rationally to do is to perform that action; in other words, that our strongest reason (perhaps our only reason) at any time when the theory applies is to act in accordance with that theory. But this is not so. It is quite consistent to argue, for example, that the right action is always that which maximizes happiness, but that there are reasons, perhaps grounded on self-interest, which may weigh against performing that action. The rationality or reasonableness of self-interest, in other words, may sometimes outweigh the demands of morality.

It might be argued that Mill himself is not committed to giving an act utilitarian answer to the more general question, 'What should I do?' (as opposed to the specific question, 'What ought I to do morally?'). For in the *System of Logic*, Mill argues that there is an 'Art of Life', of which there are three 'departments': 'Morality', 'Prudence' or 'Policy', and 'Aesthetics' (8.949–50). Further, he implies in *Utilitarianism*, at the conclusion of the proof in 4.9, as well as at the end of 4.3, that moral action is just one sphere of human conduct among others. Could it not be that reasons grounded in prudence or in aesthetics will compete with and perhaps override the reason to maximize happiness?

The answer here appears to be 'No', for the principle of utility provides us with a test for 'all human conduct' (4.9). In other words, 'Prudence' and 'Aesthetics' are also governed by the principle that one should maximize happiness overall. We know from 1.3 that Mill believes there must be a single fundamental principle within morality. In the *Logic*, Mill makes it clear that there can be only one ultimate standard of conduct *per se*, since admitting several principles is to allow for the possiblity of conflict between them (*S* 8.951). He continues:

> Without attempting in this place to justify my opinion . . .
> I merely declare my conviction, that the general principle to
> which all rules of practice ought to conform, and the test by
> which they should be tried, is that of conduciveness to the
> happiness of mankind, or rather, of all sentient beings: in
> other words, that the promotion of happiness is the ultimate
> principle of Teleology.

A footnote to this passage in the 1865 edition referring to *Utilitarianism* shows that this general principle is indeed that proved in the fourth chapter.

Mill mentions several specific 'arts' in this discussion. Each has its own first principle, according to which something is desirable or 'should be'. The art of building has as its first principle that buildings are desirable, the art of architecture that beautiful buildings are desirable, the art of hygiene that the preservation of health is desirable, and the art of medicine that the cure of disease is desirable. Taken independently, of course, each of these ends is acceptable enough. But what happens when a conflict arises? Imagine, for example, that a certain amount of money is available to spend at a hospital, and a representative of each of the four arts mentioned above is pressing for the money to be spent on functional buildings, beautiful buildings, preventative care and new medical equipment, respectively.

Mill claims that conflicts should be resolved using the 'Art of Life', divided into its three departments. Just as his distinction between customary and philosophical levels of moral thinking can be understood in the light of a distinction between discourses, so the departments of the 'Art of Life' can be seen in terms of the concepts that feature in the discourse central to each department. In the department of the 'Art of Life' concerned with 'Morality' or 'the Right', our four representatives should assess the various proposals in the light of customary morality, using the utilitarian principle to resolve any conflicts that arise. In the department of 'Prudence', 'Policy' or 'Expediency', they will judge the suggestions according to whether they approve of them generally, in a way that is not strictly moral, that is, in Mill's sense, not concerned with duty. Is it *sensible* to cure ill health, for example, rather than prevent its arising in the first place? Would it not be *admirable* to secure a permanent position in the hospital for a certain world-class surgeon by supplying the equipment she needs? And so on. Finally, there is the department of 'Aesthetics' or 'the Beautiful or Noble', or, as Mill seems to call it in 5.15, 'Worthiness'. Here enter aesthetic considerations concerning the proposed buildings, the effect that the installing new equipment would have on the appearance of the local environment, and so on.[11]

---

11 The tripartite distinction between departments can be found before the *System of Logic*, in the later essay on Bentham (*B* 10.112–13). In that essay, the distinction is between various aspects of actions: the moral (that of which we approve or disapprove: right and wrong), the sympathetic or loveable (that which we admire or despise), and the aesthetic (that which appeals to our imagination, and gives rise to love, pity, or dislike). The only department which receives roughly the same title across the essay on Bentham, the *Logic*, and *Utilitarianism* is that of morality. But 5.14 and 5.15 do suggest that the expedient is equivalent to what we admire or despise. The admiration Mill has in mind here is at least partly what we might call moral. Likewise, the aesthetic department, described as 'Worthiness' in 5.14, is probably at least partly concerned with what we might count as moral: 'That was an ugly thing to do.' The various divisions are set out below:

	'Bentham'	
Moral aspect	Sympathetic aspect/	Aesthetic aspect/
Right and wrong	Loveableness	Beauty
	System of Logic	
Morality/	Prudence/Policy/	Aesthetics/The beautiful/
The right	The expedient	The noble/Taste
	Utilitarianism	
Morality	Expediency	Worthiness

Within each area of these three discourses, we should expect to find the same division we have already found within morality. What underlies customary morality is the utilitarian principle that the right action is that which maximizes happiness. This principle can be used to decide conflicts between other, lower-level principles. We should expect there to be a first principle likewise to decide between conflicts in the other two departments of the 'Art of Life'. We have already seen that Mill believed that there must be only one supreme and ultimate principle in the 'Art of Life', and that this is the principle of utility, the principle that happiness should be maximized.[12] The utilitarian moral principle is just this principle applied to morality. So it seems that the foundations of Prudence and Aesthetics will be analogues of the principle of utility applied in each discourse.

Mill accepts that the 'Art of Life' is 'in the main . . . unfortunately still to be created' (S 8.949). But the outline he gives is a good demonstration of the reductive nature of his utilitarian views, and in particular his *welfarism*. Mill believes that the only valuable thing in the world is happiness or pleasure (this is part of the point of chapter 4 of *Utilitarianism*), and he is thus forced to conclude that practical disputes in the department of 'Aesthetics' are ultimately to be resolved in terms of human happiness, rather than purely aesthetic values such as beauty. This reductive welfarism also results in his distinctions between departments in the 'Art of Life' appearing somewhat vague and artificial. For, *in the end*, what grounds what we should do, the right

---

12 Mill does not use the word 'maximization'. But he does say in the quotation in the text above that 'the general principle to which all rules of practice ought to conform . . . is that of *conduciveness* to the happiness . . . of all sentient beings' (my italics). He goes on to say that encouraging virtuous dispositions which will in certain cases produce more pain than pleasure can be justified only if 'it can be shown that on the whole more happiness will exist in the world if feelings are cultivated which will make people, in certain cases, regardless of happiness'. The reference to quantity of happiness strongly suggests that his principle here is that happiness should be maximized. And, of course, he speaks in *Utilitarianism* not of the happiness principle, but the *greatest* happiness principle.

thing to do, the prudent thing to do, the aesthetic thing to do is the same: the maximization of happiness. The various departments are merely ways of referring to different discourses, which can only roughly be distinguished from one another by the concepts they involve. In our dispute at the hospital, it would perhaps not be long before our disputants were compelled, if they were following Mill, to carry on their disagreement in straightforwardly utilitarian terms. But that itself may be inadvisable for utilitarian reasons, as we saw in our discussion of single-level utilitarianism. There are serious questions, for all utilitarians who allow different discourses, about when we are to engage in discourse at a particular level, and how we are to know when to move from one level to another.

This throws up an even more serious question about whether the notion of different discourses and levels of moral thinking, as used by utilitarians, makes coherent sense (see esp. Williams 1985: ch. 6). According to Mill, customary morality has no ultimate validity. Our engagement in it is justified only by the utilitarian principle. Now consider that part of customary morality which concerns relationships, in particular, loyalty to close friends. According to customary morality, loyalty to friends is morally right, admirable and to be encouraged, and consequently most of us have strong moral dispositions to be loyal. Imagine a case in which your loyalty to your closest friend is being put to the test, and is in competition with some other customary moral principle, such as fairness. According to Mill, nothing justifies your disposition to be loyal other than the impartial utilitarian principle. The problem is that this is not how it 'feels'. You will feel motivated by loyalty to your friend for reasons quite independent of the principle of utility: 'I have known her for years; she's been so good to me; she's a decent person; I like her a lot.'

The problem for Mill is that reflection on the utilitarian principle appears to undermine dispositions like these. How can I go on *in the same way* being loyal, being kind, not stealing, not lying and so on, when I reflect fully upon the fact that I really have no ultimate reason for doing any of these things? The difficulty, then, is that theoretical discourse, dominated in Mill as it is by the act utilitarian principle, will seep into practical discourse and cause havoc.

There is also a problem of seepage in the other direction. As Mill is fully aware, customary morality is deeply ingrained in people, to the extent that they will act in accordance with it almost without thought in most cases. But Mill's advocacy of appeal to the utilitarian principle in cases of conflict within customary morality seems to assume that we can, when engaging in theoretical discourse, somehow 'rise above' our customary moral dispositions and survey them for what they are, that is, mere aids to utility maximization, from the utilitarian point of view. But how can this be possible? How can I shift from my everyday deep attachment to friends, for example, to a point of view where nobody matters any more than anyone else?

I shall say more about these issues in the next chapter, but for the time being let me briefly mention some possible Millian responses. The first requires us to note that he does not see the rules of customary morality as *mere* rules of thumb, as one might use such rules in, say, navigation or carpentry. He is not advocating radical change, or claiming its possibility. Secondly, Mill might point out that human beings are in fact quite good at shifting from one discourse to another. My own utilitarian friends do not seem worse friends for the fact that they claim, when speaking theoretically, that my interests should be given by them no special priority. Thirdly, Mill may suggest that there will be some seepage between discourses, but that this is only to be expected. Mill advocates engagement in customary morality because of human frailty: we cannot predict the future, we know too little about the past and we are anyway insufficiently benevolent. So an attempt by any individual deliberately and consciously, independently of customary morality, to maximize happiness would almost certainly be disastrously self-defeating. Mill's multi-level view is a messy compromise between a single-level view and a self-effacing view. But, he may argue, since his theory about moral thinking will in fact produce the most happiness overall, messy as the theory is, it is justified by the supreme principle of practical reason, the principle of utility.

Supererogation

In 5.14, Mill distinguishes the sphere of duty from what we might admire or like someone for doing. Customary morality allows that people deserve praise for going beyond the call of duty, as in, for example, heroic actions, or actions of kindness not required by morality. Philosophers have called these actions *supererogatory* (the Latin *erogo* means 'to demand'). This 'practice' itself, according to Mill, has a utilitarian justification, since not demanding too much from people will encourage them to do what they are asked to do, and so promote utility overall (*AC* 10.337–8; *TL* 5.650–1).

In 5.15, to be discussed further below, Mill distinguishes *within* morality, between perfect and imperfect obligations, the former corresponding to rights. If I have a duty to repay a debt to you, that is a perfect obligation, since you have a right to repayment. But my duty to be generous is imperfect, since no particular person has a right to my generosity.

Is the principle of utility, considered as the first principle of morality, a perfect obligation or duty? I suspect that Mill would answer 'No', since the language of rights need not enter into moral discussion at the fundamental level (5.36, n.). The perfect/imperfect distinction is one that operates rather at the level of secondary principles, that is, at the level of customary morality alone. Again, this way of talking can be seen to have a utilitarian justification.

Mill speaks of 'duty' in two ways. First, when he is thinking reflectively *about* customary morality, that is, about what it should contain: *x* is a duty if making it a duty would maximize utility (cf. 'Letter to Brandreth' (1867) 16.1234). But there is an independent question to be asked when one is operating *within* morality: what *really is* the fundamental moral duty? Here Mill's answer is: to maximize overall happiness.

It has to be admitted that there is something of an instability at the heart of Mill's project, arising out of his unwillingness to accept the 'intuitive' basis of any moral system, his own included. If morality is what he seems to think it is – a practice of social coercion that has evolved naturally and largely unreflectively over time in order to protect important sources of human welfare – then

Mill's own claim that utility should be maximized can be seen as merely another attempt at coercion, with no moral justification in itself. But, of course, Mill does believe that the principle of utility is a justifying principle. This is the place where his intuitionism enters, and morality seems to be more than a natural coercive practice.

Punishment and the origin of moral language

In chapter 5, Mill enquires into justice. I shall deal in detail with his argument in a later chapter, but a brief sketch is called for now. Mill is concerned that, because of the power of the sentiment of justice, justice may be seen as a principle opposed to the principle of utility. It may maximize utility, for example, to commit an injustice such as punishing an innocent person, as in the sheriff case we discussed above. Mill aims therefore to probe the sentiment, in order to explain it and to see whether it can itself be made consistent with the principle of utility (5.1–3). His first step is to consider the various types of action described as unjust, such as depriving a person of his liberty, property or legal rights (5.4–10).

In search of the 'mental link' which holds these attributions of justice together, Mill turns to the etymology of the word 'justice' itself (5.12). He claims that the original element in the development of the notion of justice was conformity to law. The sentiment of injustice then came successively to be felt at violations of laws that *ought* to exist.

Mill is quite aware that people speak of justice in contexts where regulation by law would not be appropriate (5.13). But he claims that the idea of the breaking of a law that should exist remains: 'It would always give us pleasure, and chime in with our feelings of fitness, that acts which we deem unjust should be punished, though we do not always think it expedient that this should be done by tribunals' (5.13). Where enforcement by law is out of place, Mill suggests, we substitute for it expressed disapproval of the offence.

So Mill claims to have explained the origin and development of the sentiment of justice. But then, in a paragraph which has received a great deal of attention from recent commentators, Mill says of his account:

> [I]t contains, as yet, nothing to distinguish that obligation from moral obligation in general. For the truth is, that the idea of penal sanction, which is the essence of law, enters not only into the conception of injustice, but into that of any kind of wrong. We do not call anything wrong, unless we mean to imply that a person ought to be punished in some way or other for doing it; if not by law, by the opinion of his fellow-creatures; if not by opinion, by the reproaches of his own conscience. This seems the real turning point of the distinction between morality and simple expediency.
>
> (5.14)

In recent years, several writers have used this paragraph to argue that Mill is not a utilitarian. Recall the act utilitarian criterion of right action: an action is right if and only if it maximizes welfare. Its rightness consists in its having the property of being welfare-maximizing. But here Mill might be taken to be suggesting that the notion of appropriate punishment enters the criterion in such a way that it becomes non-act-utilitarian.

Here are some of the interpretations which have been offered:

D.P. Dryer An act *a* is wrong if and only if (1) some alternative would have more desirable consequences, (2) it would be contrary to a rule the observance of which would in general have more desirable consequences than would failure to observe it and (3) it is an action of a kind the condemnation of which would in general have more desirable consequences than the absence of such general condemnation (Dryer 1969: cv).

David Lyons An act *a* is wrong if and only if a coercive social rule against doing acts of kind *a* would be justified by increasing overall welfare (Lyons 1976: 109).

David Copp An act *a* is wrong if and only if (1) there is a maximal alternative to *a* open to the agent and (2) it would be maximally expedient that, if the agent did *a*, they would feel regret for this to some degree (Copp 1979: 84).

John Gray An act *a* is wrong if and only if punishing it would have the best consequences (Gray 1983: 31).

All these writers assume that we can use 5.14 as evidence for Mill's view on the criterion of morality. I have shown how 2.2 is best interpreted as a commitment to an act utilitarian criterion of rightness. Some of these writers argue that Mill saw the principle of utility as a principle not of rightness, but of goodness. What makes things *good* can then be said to be utility-maximization, leaving the way open for a non-act utilitarian conception of rightness. However, 2.2 is explicitly about the rightness of actions. So this provides one good reason against interpreting 5.14 in a non-act utilitarian way: it would commit Mill to an internal contradiction.

What, then, are we to make of these lines? In paragraph 5.14 and those surrounding it, Mill is engaged in what philosophers call 'metaethics'. He is considering what is happening when people make moral judgements, and is not primarily concerned with offering any ethical judgements himself. When we call an action wrong, Mill is suggesting, we mean to imply that it ought to be punished, by law, opinion or conscience. His phrase 'mean to imply' here is best taken as equivalent to 'mean', since in 5.14 he explicitly says he is analysing the 'notions' of right and wrong. Thus he is not including the notion of justified punishability in his own criterion of rightness and wrongness, but rather analysing the notion of wrongness itself. According to Mill, when one says that an action *a* is 'wrong' one means that *a* ought to be punished by law, opinion or conscience.

Mill himself has earlier claimed that what makes an action wrong is its failing to maximize happiness. This appears to commit to him to the following:

1 An action is wrong if and only if it fails to maximize happiness.
2 Any wrong action ought to be punished by law, opinion or conscience.
3 Actions which fail to maximize happiness ought therefore to be punished by law, opinion or conscience.

This gives rise to a serious problem for Mill. He is committed to saying that an act which fails to maximize welfare is wrong, and that wrong acts are acts which ought to be punished. But what will he say about a case in which a certain act fails to maximize utility and yet punishment of it would also fail to maximize utility? In this case, it might seem that he is committed to recommending an action – punishment – that his own theory says is wrong.

Mill allows that punishment by law might fail to maximize happiness (5.13). Why should punishment by opinion not be the same? Can we not imagine a case in which a person has failed to maximize happiness, and yet expressing disapproval of his conduct would serve only to annoy him and perhaps spur him on to more of the same? Here again Mill would have to admit that he should not be punished by opinion.

But Mill allows in a third kind of punishment in his account of wrongness: punishment by one's own conscience. In cases where the agent has failed to maximize happiness, and this third kind of punishment would not maximize utility, Mill does *not* have to retract his claim that the action is wrong. For it is consistent with his act utilitarian version of the principle of utility to claim that such conduct ought to be punished by conscience. The principle of utility, as a practical principle, applies to human conduct. It does not *govern* consciences directly, since, unlike legal punishment or blaming others, conscience is not something over which we have control. Thus there is no imaginable case of an agent's failing to maximize happiness to which Mill would be forced to retract any attribution of wrongness. For he can always claim that the non-maximizing agent should be punished by the reproaches of their conscience.

There is no doubt that this position has some peculiar implications. First, it appears that Mill's view of the best possible world does not map onto his view of the world which he believes should occur. For the best possible world, according to his welfarism, will be that in which welfare is maximized, whereas in some cases he must say that some people should be punished by their consciences even if this does not result in welfare's being maximized. Secondly, and relatedly, because of the gap that has opened up between acts and the history of the world, he must allow that there may be cases where something ought to be the case and yet one should not act to bring it about. Imagine that you could, by reminding a certain agent of what they have done, bring about the reproaches of the conscience which they ought to feel, but which would not maximize welfare. Because you yourself would thereby be failing to maximize welfare, you should not remind them. Indeed, there may even be cases where you should *prevent* a punishment by conscience, even if it is something that ought to happen, if this prevention will maximize utility.

Thirdly, there is something distinctly odd about Mill's practical advice on this interpretation. Mill thinks that an agent who fails to maximize happiness should be punished, at least by their own conscience, if not by law and opinion. There are several difficulties with this, the first two practical, the third more profound.

1 We cannot know for sure whether any action of ours was or was not the maximizing action, so it is not clear how we are to decide when to feel guilty.
2 By recommending that we follow customary morality most of the time, Mill makes it difficult for us to feel guilty about doing what is really wrong. If I lie, for example, and it is indeed a failure to maximize utility, I shall feel guilty about lying. My conscience is likely to be unaffected by my failure to maximize.
3 Let us imagine a world in which guilt is experienced always and only at a failure to maximize. Recall the case of the rash doctor above. Imagine a similar situation, in which the risky treatment would have succeeded, but the doctor is not rash, employing the less risky treatment. According to Mill, this doctor should feel guilty for this, though in fact most of us feel that this is quite unjustifiable.

Let me mention a few possible Millian responses. First of all, given the important connection between wrongness and actual punishment by others, Mill probably has subjective rightness and wrongness in mind in 5.13–14. That deals with 3, concerning the foreseeability of the future. In Mill's ideal world, as implied in chapter 3 of *Utilitarianism*, people will have become largely impartial. They will have a pretty good idea of when happiness has been maximized or not, and will no longer need much or any of customary morality, having moved beyond it. This notion of the ideal world provides some material for dealing with 1 and 2 above.[13]

This raises the vital question, however, of how we should praise and blame others in our world as it is. Mill's advice, I think, would be that one should largely go on praising and blaming as one has always done, in line with customary morality, but also begin to use praise and blame to exert gradual pressure on others to move closer to the ideal act utilitarian world. This advice itself, of course, would be grounded in its likelihood of bringing about the greatest happiness overall.

So there are responses available for some of the objections that might be made to Mill on my interpretation. Nevertheless it cannot in the end be denied that Mill's position is not helped by the addition of quite the analysis of ascriptions of wrongness that he gives. His is a brave attempt to offer an account of the natural origin of morality, but ultimately he appears to run into an open question argument which falsifies his suggestion.[14] According to Mill, when I say '*a* is wrong', I *mean* '*a* is such that its performance ought to be punished by law, opinion or conscience'. But this is certainly mistaken, since when I say that *a* is wrong, I can leave it an open question whether *a* should be punished.

Perhaps Mill would have done better to allow that moral language, even if it has its origin in social coercion, takes on a life of its own, so that talk of wrongness need not directly imply anything regarding punishment. Often, when we speak of wrongness, we are indeed attempting directly to punish someone, seeking the application of legal sanctions, or the punishment of the offender through the sheer unpleasantness of our disapproval or the pangs of conscience to which it might give rise. But this is not always the case, as for example when we are discussing utilitarianism itself as

---

13 Though it does of course lead Mill into the problems concerning the single-level view discussed earlier in this chapter.

14 Open question arguments were discussed in ch. 4.

a moral view. If there is nothing to morality but social coercion, then it makes little sense to discuss it philosophically, unless in some obscure way this is itself an attempt to coerce others. If, however, there are independent principles of rightness and wrongness, then these must be conceptually independent of praise, blame and punishment. For praise, blame and punishment are themselves social practices which morality can assess. It was again Mill's reticence to accept what he saw as the intuitionist view that there could be moral principles independent of real social practices that led him into this analysis of moral language. If he had recognized the intuitionism at the heart of his own view, he would not have been tempted to offer a reductive account of morality which is in danger of undermining it as a rational practice.

This has been a long and complex chapter, but only because Mill's own views, as recent commentators have seen, are far more sophisticated than had previously been recognized. We have seen that Mill's utilitarianism focuses on actions and is an act, not a rule, utilitarian version, that he speaks both in actualist and probabilist terms about rightness, and that he allows for different levels of moral thinking, one being customary morality, this itself being justified by utilitarianism. His account of utilitarianism must be understood in the light of his views about practical reasoning as a whole, and this I attempted by looking at his discussion of the 'Art of Life' in the *System of Logic*. Finally, I suggested that his metaethical discussion in chapter 5 can be made consistent with his act utilitarianism, but still faces the problem of the open question argument. In the next chapter, I shall discuss some of the difficulties which arise out of the strict impartiality of act utilitarianism.

Further reading

Many famous articles were written concerning act and rule utilitarianism, the advantages of each, and Mill's position. The literature in this area must be treated with care, since terminology is not consistent and some writers run together the distinctions drawn in this chapter. Among the most important pieces are Harrod 1936;

Urmson 1953; Rawls 1955; Mabbott 1956; Smart 1956; Lyons 1965; Singer 1972; Berger 1984: ch. 3; Parfit 1984: chs 1–5. The most well-worked-out multi-level utilitarianism is that of Hare 1981: esp. chs 1–3. A clear account of rule utilitarianism can be found in Hooker 1995. A good short account of the 'Art of Life' is Ryan 1965. Several of the revisionary non-utilitarian interpretations of Mill are well discussed in Sumner 1979 and Berger 1984. In addition to those cited in the text above, the following papers are important: Brown 1972; Brown 1973; Harrison 1975; Lyons 1976.

Chapter 6

Integrity

Integrity and the separateness of persons

> I must again repeat, what the assailants of utilitarianism seldom have the justice to acknowledge, that the happiness which forms the utilitarian standard of what is right in conduct, is not the agent's own happiness, but that of all concerned. As between his own happiness and that of others, utilitarianism requires him to be as strictly impartial as a disinterested and benevolent spectator.
>
> (2.18; cf. 5.36, including n.)

It is ironic that Mill's defence of utilitarianism against the charge that it is egoistic encapsulates particularly well what many modern writers think is mistaken about utilitarianism. According to utilitarianism, all that matters is welfare and its maximization: *whose* welfare is irrelevant. That is to say, utilitarianism is concerned primarily not with the *distribution* of welfare, but with its *aggregation*.

135

I shall argue in this chapter and the following that a serious flaw in utilitarianism is that it ignores what has come to be known as 'the separateness of persons'.[1] From your own point of view, it can matter a great deal whether a certain good accrues to you, to someone close to you or to a stranger. That is the thought I shall be attempting to develop in this chapter. But how welfare is distributed also matters independently of any special concern individual agents might have for themselves or those with whom they have some personal relationship. When goods are to be shared between individuals, how well off those individuals are in itself makes an important difference. Fairness, or justice, requires us to give some priority to those who are worse off. I shall discuss fairness and justice in the following chapter.

In this chapter, then, I intend to argue that utilitarianism fails to capture the importance to each agent of their each having their own life to live and their own personal attachments to others. My discussion will revolve around a famous critique of utilitarianism by Bernard Williams, which has come to be known as the 'integrity objection'. I discuss it in this book since it is one side of the most serious objection to the ethical view Mill is defending in *Utilitarianism*. The other side – justice – Mill discusses explicitly in his final chapter, but he also says in various places much that is relevant to integrity.

Talk of 'the integrity objection' can be misleading. First, Williams does not have in mind anything like the virtue of uprightness or honesty. He uses the term in a sense more like that in which we speak of the integrity of a work of art. Secondly, there is not just one integrity objection. Williams can be understood to be making several, related, points about utilitarianism under the heading of 'integrity'.

Most of these points are made, or at least clearly foreshadowed, in his 'A critique of utilitarianism' (Williams 1973b), so

---

1   See Rawls 1971: 27 and *passim*. The phrase originates, I believe, from J.N. Findlay. Rawls uses it in relation to justice, whereas I use it also to cover the reasonableness of giving priority to the interests of oneself and those close to one.

it is on that text that I shall mainly concentrate. In this chapter, I shall not so much be attempting a straightforward exegesis of Williams, as trying to bring out some lines of argument suggested by his text. Williams himself says that his claim was primarily that utilitarianism leaves no room for integrity in the sense of the value to be found in a 'person's sticking by what that person regards as ethically necessary or worthwhile' (Williams 1995: 213). This chapter could perhaps be read as an attempt to spell out my own understanding of that value, though it is important to note, first, that I put less stress than does Williams on what is *ethically* worthwhile as opposed to what is worthwhile from the agent's own point of view; secondly, that I shall couch my conclusion in the language of reasons rather than in that of values; and finally, that Williams, when discussing utilitarianism, often seems to have in mind single-level utilitarianism, whereas I shall be suggesting that a version of the integrity objection applies to all forms of utilitarianism.

The first 'aspect' of the integrity objection concerns morality itself. Does it not matter morally in certain situations that it is *you* in particular who are acting in a certain way? Are there not what philosophers have called *constraints* on what *you* can do? Having defended act utilitarianism against this charge, and discussed the notion of responsibility underlying utilitarianism, I shall then examine the integrity objection in connection with the nature of actual moral thinking itself. Does utilitarianism not require us to employ an unrealistic notion of a self that can float free of specific commitments and concern itself solely with welfare maximization? Here I shall argue that utilitarianism, because it need not be single-level, can again provide a response. But thoughts about motivation will lead us into thoughts about justification, and in particular about whether utilitarianism can justify its strict impartiality. I shall conclude, after a brief discussion of the moral emotions, that it cannot.

Moral agency and responsibility

Williams's critique centres on two cases which have now entered philosophical folklore (Williams 1973b: 97–9):

George George, a qualified chemist with wife and young children to support, is finding it hard to get a job. An older colleague tells George that he can get George a reasonably well-paid job in a laboratory where research is done on chemical and biological warfare. George turns down the job because of his opposition to such warfare. His colleague points out that the work is going to be done anyway, and that, were George not to take the post, the person appointed would probably be more zealous in advancing research than George.

Jim Jim, a botanist travelling in South America, comes upon a public execution in a small town. A military captain has lined up twenty Indians. He explains to Jim that they have been chosen at random from the local population, which has recently been protesting against the government. The captain offers Jim a guest's privilege. If Jim wishes, he can select one of the Indians and shoot him; the other nineteen will then go free. Otherwise, the execution by the captain's henchman, Pedro, will go ahead as planned.

Williams suggests that utilitarians – act utilitarians, that is – would say not only that George should take the job and that Jim should shoot the Indian, but that it is *obvious* that this is so.[2] This is supposed to give us pause. Where have the utilitarians gone wrong? What are they missing out?

Two important preliminary points about these cases must be noted. First, they are not meant to be 'counterexamples' to utilitarianism. Williams does indeed object to the utilitarian conclusion in George's case, but he agrees with it in that of Jim. It is not in the end what utilitarians say that worries him, but how they reach their conclusions: 'The first question for philosophy is not "do you agree with utilitarianism's answer?" but "do you really accept utilitarianism's way of looking at the question?"' (Williams 1973b: 78).

The second point is that integrity – whatever it is – is not to be seen as a *motive*. George and Jim are not to be understood as

2   Mill is an act utilitarian, and Williams's critique is directed primarily at act utilitarianism. So 'utilitarianism' in this chapter – as indeed is usually the case in this book as a whole – can be taken to refer to act utilitarianism.

themselves moved by concern with their own integrity. Rather, George will be moved by his abhorrence of chemical warfare, and Jim by his moral repugnance to killing. And being moved in these ways is at least part of what is meant by integrity itself.

An immediate utilitarian response to these cases might be that they are underdescribed. How sure is George that the zealous researcher will indeed take the job if offered it? Does George have the psychological stamina to do a job he finds appalling? How does Jim know that the captain will keep his promises? Another related response would be that only a very unsophisticated utilitarian will find it obvious what George and Jim should do. It is after all notoriously difficult to predict the future consequences of one's actions.

These responses are not entirely out of place; but they are largely, at this stage, distractions. The general point of the examples is clear, and making them or utilitarianism more complex merely delays confronting Williams's doubts. Utilitarianism does require the impartial maximization of utility, and it may well be that we can see what, if anything, is wrong with this requirement by concentrating on the stark cases of George and Jim.

There is a common idea, central to common sense morality and to many non-utilitarian ethical theories, 'that each of us is specially responsible for what *he* does' (Williams 1973b: 99). Consider Jim. If Jim kills an Indian, there will be one killing. If he refuses, there will be twenty. But is simple arithmetic applied to the number of killings all that matters here? Jim might say that morality requires *him* not to kill, and that it does not require him to act so that killings overall are minimized. There are, he might suggest, what philosophers have called 'moral constraints' on action directed at bringing about good states of affairs.

There is, however, a serious difficulty with the claim that there are moral constraints (see Scheffler 1982: ch. 4). Clearly, the wrongness of killing has something to do with the badness of the death it brings about. But if one death is bad, and this provides the main ground for a restriction on killing, then arithmetic should apply in cases like that of Jim. Twenty deaths might plausibly be said to be twenty times as bad as a single death, and this thought counts strongly against the postulation of moral constraints. At the very least, the ball is not in the utilitarian court, but in that of the defenders of constraints.

But there remains a related problem for utilitarianism. Return to the idea that each of us is specially responsible for what he or she does, and put the stress, this time, on *does*. According to act utilitarianism, what matters is how well the world goes. It is irrelevant whether I directly *cause* the world to go a particular way by *acting* (as Jim, for example, might cause the death of an Indian by shooting him), or whether the world happens to turn out as it does through my *omitting* to act or *allowing* certain events to take place (as Jim may allow the killings of the twenty Indians to take place). This is what Williams calls utilitarianism's doctrine of *negative responsibility*: 'if I am ever responsible for anything, then I must be just as responsible for things that I allow or fail to prevent, as I am for things that I myself, in the more everyday restricted sense, bring about' (Williams 1973b: 95).

This seems a more plausible identification of the root problem. Imagine that Jim decides that the prospect of his killing the one Indian is too appalling, and so chooses not to do so. If the execution of the twenty goes ahead, we should say that Pedro or the army captain killed them, not Jim. And yet, according to utilitarianism, which states that the moral value of any action depends on the welfare value of the history of the world, Jim is equally answerable. For he could have prevented the killing, and so played as important a rôle in bringing it about as Pedro or the captain.

The cases of George and Jim provide particularly clear examples of cases in which our ordinary intuitions about responsibility come apart from those which utilitarianism appears to assume. For in these cases the parties who would ordinarily be said to be primarily responsible are other people. But even where other agents are not involved, responsibility need not always devolve on the agent in the way utilitarianism seems to require. Ordinarily, for example, we should not hold a person in the developed world morally responsible for the death of a particular individual in the developing world which could in fact have been prevented by a donation. The death will be put down to, say, malnutrition. And yet, according to the utilitarian doctrine of negative responsibility, allowing someone to die in this way is as bad as killing them.

What answer can the utilitarian make to this criticism? One possible response would be to draw our attention to the relation between blame and moral responsibility. When we hold someone responsible for something, we normally take that person to be a candidate for praise or blame. We should obviously want to hold the army captain responsible for the death of the Indians, and it is because he is responsible that we should want to blame him for what he has done. According to act utilitarianism, however, blame is just a human practice, itself to be assessed by the utilitarian criterion. Often it will be justified on the ground that it helps to deter future actions of a similar kind. So we are justified in condemning the army captain, as we may put enough pressure on his conscience to prevent his committing similar atrocities in future. But there would seem little point in blaming Jim, if he chooses, after much agonizing, not to shoot. So, even if Jim is responsible, in the sense that what happens occurs as a result of what he does (his action is, one might say, a *causal condition* of the twenty deaths, and he is thus morally responsible), he is not to be blamed for what happens.

This response, however, is probably insufficient to deal with Williams's charge, because it is the claim that Jim is indeed morally responsible that is primarily in question, not that of whether he should be blamed. Williams is suggesting that our ordinary sense of what we are and what we are not responsible for cannot be swept away so easily. It is important to notice that Williams has common sense, and common sense morality, on his side.[3] Mill offers an account of the origin of common sense, or customary, morality, and of its place within the utilitarian framework. Customary morality, with its talk of particular agents being responsible for what they themselves do, has come about as a system of social coercion the justification for which rests on the promotion of welfare overall. This system itself developed out of legal restrictions on actions, so

---

3 There is in fact something of a tension in Williams's work between appeals to common sense morality on the one hand, and criticism of it on the other (see e.g. Williams 1985: ch. 10).

that our common sense idea of moral responsibility could be said to be a relic of such restrictions, with no rationale in itself independently of the promotion of welfare. Mill, then, has the resources to defuse the problem of negative responsibility. In the case of constraints, the ball ended up in the court of its defenders. Likewise, in the case of negative responsibility, the ball is in the court of those who wish to defend common sense morality. And they must not only provide a defence, but show what is wrong with the analysis provided by Mill that removes from customary morality any justificatory force independent of welfare maximization.

The self and motivation

Williams believes that one reason why utilitarianism cannot make sense of integrity is that 'it can make only the most superficial sense of human desire and action at all' (Williams 1973b: 82). It might seem that utilitarianism requires of George and Jim that, when they are thinking about their respective dilemmas, they ignore their own characters, desires, goals, projects and commitments, and ask not 'What should I do?' but 'What does utilitarianism require of any person so situated in this position in order that the history of the world go as well as possible?' '[A]s a Utilitarian agent, I am just the representative of the satisfaction system who happens to be near certain causal levers at a certain time' (Williams 1976a: 4). When I am deciding what I should do, the 'I' here refers to me in a full-blooded way, with all my commitments, and not to some abstract, etiolated, purely rational calculator of welfare. The utilitarian self is too thin. How could George just drop his opposition to chemical warfare and take the job? How could Jim, unless he is some kind of psychopath, size up the situation and immediately shoot an Indian?

How problematic for act utilitarianism are these claims about motivation and the self? In fact, utilitarianism does not require any particularly special conception of the self. In the cases of George and Jim, the most that is required is that each of them distance themselves from a single commitment, albeit an important one. So utilitarianism does not require a conception of a self which can be understood as independent from all its commitments, able to float free from them during moral deliberation. Nor need it be thought that utilitarianism requires agents to attempt to do this. As we saw in the previous chapter, the decision-procedure required by act utilitarianism is whichever one will maximize welfare. As Mill says, to deny this is 'to mistake the very meaning of a standard of morals, and to confound the rule of action with the motive of it' (2.19). Multi-level act utilitarians may draw analogies here between the sheriff case and those of George and Jim. Just as it can plausibly be said to maximize welfare overall to educate law-enforcers so that they will never seriously consider framing an innocent person, even if that leads to short-term losses of welfare in special cases, so it can be claimed that bringing people up to care for humanity or to be strongly disposed against killing can also be beneficial. In other words, the kind of moral thinking Williams holds George and Jim will, and indeed should, engage in may be roughly what the act utilitarian would recommend.

Alienation and demandingness

These charges concerning motivation and the self are related to another common accusation against utilitarianism and indeed modern ethical theory in general, that it is *alienating*. Utilitarianism may be charged, for example, with alienating George from his moral commitment to oppose chemical warfare. We have seen how the possibility of multi-level utilitarianism means that this need not be the case. The charge of alienation is now commonly made in connection with personal relationships. Consider the following example, adapted from an important article by Michael Stocker (Stocker 1976: 462):

The hospital visit You are in hospital, recovering from an operation and yearning for company. Your old friend Jones arrives, with gifts, news and bonhomie. After he has fully refreshed your spirit, and is about to leave, you thank him for coming. 'Oh, don't mention it', he says. 'I could see that utilitarianism required it of me.'

If this mode of thought is typical of Jones, then he will be alienated not only from you but from any possibility of a rich personal relationship. Utilitarianism, the charge goes, is an assault on what we really value. But, once again, the charge fails to hit home. The standard of morals, or the rule of action, is, as Mill puts it, again being confused with the motive to obey it. Friendship is a significant source of welfare value, and it is clear that people such as Jones are cutting themselves off from that. For this reason, utilitarianism is best expressed in a multi-level version, which allows Jones to visit friends in hospital with much the same intentions and thoughts in mind as anyone else.

But does there not still remain a problem of alienation here? Imagine that Smith, a multi-level act utilitarian, comes to visit you in the hospital. Unlike Jones, the single-level utilitarian, Smith has allowed herself to develop a genuine liking and concern for you. But still, she believes that the only value your friendship has is that which all human welfare has. Is this not in tension with her belief that there is something special about you and the relationship the two of you have which gives her special reason to concern herself with you? Think also about George and his family. If he accepts the utilitarian principle, can that principle sit alongside his love for his wife and children?

There is something missing from utilitarianism here, but the problem is probably best not stated in terms of alienation. What Smith is supposedly alienated from are her emotional attachments to you. But the mere thought that your mutual relationship has only the value that all human welfare has should not undermine this attachment. Indeed it would seem odd to think otherwise. Why should Smith believe that there is anything *particularly* valuable about that relationship? Other similar relationships are surely equally valuable. Nor, as we saw above, does multi-level utilitarianism require Smith to attempt to distance herself from her commitment to you. In fact, the theory approves of such commitment, because of the welfare it produces. Smith, *as an agent*, when she visits you need not have what Williams calls 'one thought too many' (1976a: 18). That is, she does not have to think, 'Well, at one level I do have concern for this sick friend of mine; but what really moves me is reflection on the fact that it maximizes welfare for people to show special concern for their friends'. She can just make the visit, without thinking of utilitarianism at all.

At the level of philosophical theory, however, there is one thought too few in utilitarianism. According to utilitarian theory, Smith's only reason for visiting you in hospital is that welfare will be maximized. But this seems to miss the plausibility of Smith's own view that she has a special reason to visit you *just* because you are *her* friend. There is indeed a 'magic . . . in the pronoun "my"' (Godwin 1798: bk 2, ch. 2). Imagine that Smith finds herself in a strange position in which by not visiting me she can bring about another hospital visit between two friends which will be of *slightly* more welfare value overall. Does she nevertheless not have a special reason to visit me?

There is a difference, then, between the notion of moral constraints, and that of what we might call the *rationality of personal concern*.[4] In the case of constraints, it was left to the defender to explain what matters so much about the fact that *I* act to bring about a certain outcome rather than others. If Jim were to choose not to kill the Indian, allowing all twenty to be killed, any defence he might offer which put particular stress on the fact that it was *he* who was going to have to pull the trigger would not look powerful when set against the deaths of so many others. 'What is so important about the fact that it is *you* who would have been the killer?', we might ask. But in the case of personal concern, where what is at stake are values to be instantiated in the life of the agent or in the lives of distant others, the appeal to the importance of one's having one's own life to lead is much more powerful. Here, claims such as 'She's my friend', or 'This is my life', can play a powerful rôle in plausible justification of non-maximizing courses of action.

Our emotional attachments to others, and indeed to ourselves, do then reveal to us certain reasons which impartial utilitarianism does not capture. We might call these 'agent-relative' reasons, since

---

4 Some philosophers speak here of options, but because I am suspicious of the idea that morality is like a divine lawgiver who can permit (or demand) I prefer to avoid this term.

they make essential reference in their formulation to the agent who has them (see Nagel 1986: 164–75).

Jones has a reason to visit you because you are *her* friend. In the same way, you can be said to have a reason to concern yourself especially with your life purely because it is *yours*. This point is related to the issue of the demandingness of morality discussed in the previous chapter. Act utilitarianism is an extremely demanding moral view, since it requires you to live that life which will bring about the best history of the world. For most of us, with the wealth and leisure to write and to read books such as this one, this will involve sacrificing large amounts of money and time to development charities. This is because of the hugely unequal distribution of wealth in the world today: one fifth of the population receives 1% of the world's income, while another fifth receives 90%. You and I are almost certainly in the latter fifth, and if we begin to surrender our resources to those in the former fifth, these resources will do a great deal more good overall.

Nor are the common responses to this suggestion likely to impress a utilitarian. Responsibility cannot be shifted onto governments. The situation is as much to do with you as was the killing of the Indians to do with Jim. Even though governments certainly ought to do more than they do at present, you can do much yourself. A few pounds or dollars can save somebody's eyesight, even somebody's life, and this will surely produce more utility than your spending it on yourself. Nor can you appeal to the harsh argument that the problem is overpopulation. There is enough wealth, and enough food, in the world to allow everyone to live well above the level of absolute poverty. It might be suggested that aid money is better spent on long-term projects. If so, then that is where your money should go. Nor can you appeal to the fact that much aid money has been used to prop up undesirable regimes and for other corrupt purposes. Some schemes to which you could contribute involve very little such risk, and even if there is such a risk, you will maximize expected utility by sacrificing time and money rather than by devoting them to yourself.

I believe that nearly of us should do more to help the poor. But the idea that I have no self-interested reason, in conflict with the reason to promote welfare overall, to retain goods for myself seems highly unrealistic. Certainly very few, if any, human beings live their lives as if they seriously believed this. As Williams says, 'It is absurd to demand of . . . a man, when the sums come in from the utility network . . . that he should just step aside from his own project and decision and acknowledge the decision which utilitarian calculation requires' (Williams 1973b: 116).

Nor is it just the level of demandingness which Williams finds objectionable in utilitarianism. It is the fact that utilitarianism rules obsessively on every part of your life. There is always something you should be doing, some way that you should be acting or living. The scope of morality is all-encompassing. 'There is, at the end of that, no life of one's own, except perhaps for some small area, hygienically allotted, of meaningless privacy' (Williams 1976b: 38).

It is important to note in passing that the cases of George and Jim both involve the agent's being required to act in a certain way by utilitarianism because of circumstances importantly shaped by *other people's* projects, projects of which George and Jim, and indeed most of us, disapprove:

> [H]ow can a man, as a utilitarian agent, come to regard as one satisfaction among others, and a dispensable one, a project or attitude round which he has built his life, just because someone else's projects have so structured the causal scene that that is how the utilitarian sum comes out?
>
> (Williams 1973b: 116)

Part of what is at stake here is the importance of *autonomy* (see Harris 1974; Davis 1980). It is offensive enough to autonomy to make the way I live my life depend entirely on the circumstances in which I find myself and not at all on my projects, decisions or judgements. But when these circumstances are seen to include the projects and decisions of others, control over my own life seems to have been shifted from me to those others whose decisions I have to take into account. Nevertheless, it should not be forgotten that the demandingness of utilitarianism does not depend on the actions of other agents. The theory may be equally demanding in situations brought about entirely by natural events, such as earthquakes or floods.

How might a utilitarian respond to these related charges concerning the excessive demandingness of utilitarian morality? In the previous chapter, we saw that Mill used the distinction between levels of moral thinking to ward off a demandingness charge. Making morality less demanding, and allowing people to pursue their own personal concerns, may well lead to welfare's being maximized overall. But we saw also how Mill failed explicitly to face up to the fact that act utilitarianism is likely to be a lot more demanding than many people will think reasonable.

There is another tack he might take, based on various claims he makes in *Utilitarianism*. Mill believes that what he calls 'nobility' is itself a good for the noble person (2.9; 2.14). He suggests indeed that selfishness is the principal cause of people's lives being unsatisfactory (2.13). Virtue is one of the higher pleasures, a part of happiness (3.10; 4.5). An optimistic utilitarian might take a leaf out of the book of Greek moralists such as Plato and Aristotle and argue that morality does not in fact involve genuine sacrifice. Though it is indeed the case that utilitarianism requires me to change my lifestyle radically and to sacrifice far more time and money to development charities, this is not a genuine sacrifice of my own welfare. Such a life will be the best for me.

This response to the problems concerning demandingness does not seem immediately implausible. There are powerful ancient and modern arguments in favour of the position that the moral life is always the best life for the agent (see e.g. Aristotle *c*. 330 BC). But ultimately they are unpersuasive. Though it may well be true that many people would improve their own lives were they to dedicate more of their resources to others, there surely comes a point where genuine self-sacrifice becomes a possibility. Mill certainly accepts it as a possibility (2.15), and his argument that in the world as it is at present the readiness to sacrifice one's own happiness gives one the greatest chance of attaining happiness for oneself is not convincing (2.16). Mill takes a Stoic line, suggesting that being prepared to sacrifice one's happiness offers freedom from anxiety about fortune and hence tranquillity in which to cultivate 'sources of satisfaction'. But the utilitarian who is ready to sacrifice their happiness *will*, we may presume, do so, and they will then be far from tranquillity and private concerns, living in poverty and working desperately hard for development charities. Perhaps Mill is right to suggest at the end of chapter 3 that in a much improved utilitarian world, moral education could shape human beings so that their own welfare overlapped entirely with the impartial maximization of welfare overall. But our present world is very unlike this.

At this point, as in the case of responsibility, one utilitarian option is just to bite the bullet. Jim is responsible for the death of the Indians, so we must face up to the fact that morality is extremely demanding. Why should we assume that morality will not be difficult to live up to? If utilitarianism is correct, then morality is extremely demanding. If it is not, then the matter lapses. The issue of demandingness itself is a side-issue.

This hard-nosed view fails, however, to deal with the rationality of personal concern. We saw in the previous chapter how Mill allowed practical reason – the 'Art of Life' – to be dominated by the greatest happiness principle, the principle that overall welfare is to be maximized. Though one 'department' of the Art of Life is constituted by prudence, prudence has no weight against the demands of the greatest happiness principle. According to that principle, practical reason is entirely impartial. The fact that a certain good or harm is going to accrue to you, to your partner or to a stranger, is not in itself relevant to the content or strength of reason you have to act. But it is implausible to suggest that practical reason is completely impartial. It makes little sense of the way all of us actually live our lives.

Moral emotions

Many of the disagreements between Williams and the utilitarian concerning integrity ultimately concern moral emotions. Emotions enter at two levels. The first is that of the moral agent. Consider the account of the ideal moral agent implied by a single-level form of utilitarianism: a cool and rational calculator of welfare, with no personal attachments, affections or concerns which might distract from impartial maximization. This ideal, embodied by Charles Dickens in *Hard Times* in the character of Gradgrind, strikes many people as obnoxious, or even dangerous.

Against it, Williams offers us his account of the emotionally engaged agent, who allows themselves to develop deep partial attachments to others, and who lives by or at least consults emotions in moral situations. Such a person might, for example, make a special place in their moral universe for the *unthinkable* (Williams 1973b: 92–3). There are just certain things, killing the innocent, perhaps, which their emotions will not allow them to consider. Rather than constantly stepping back from their emotions in order to view the universe from as abstract and impersonal a position as possible, they allow their emotions to influence their actions directly. In Jim's case, for example:

> Instead of thinking in a rational and systematic way either about utilities or about the value of human life, the relevance of the people at risk being present, and so forth, the presence of the people at risk may just have its effect. The significance of the immediate should not be underestimated ... [W]e are not primarily janitors of any system of values, even our own: very often, we just act, as a possibly confused result of the situation in which we are engaged. That, I suspect, is very often an exceedingly good thing. To what extent utilitarians regard it as a good thing is an obscure question.
>
> (Williams 1973b: 118)

I hope that the previous chapter, and indeed this one, have shed some light on this obscure question. Utilitarians – multi-level utilitarians like Mill, that is – can accept that it is a good thing to act on the basis of immediate emotional reactions, if that leads to the best outcome. The debate, in other words, is not primarily over an ideal of actual moral agency, since the utilitarian may find Williams's ideal agent far more appealing than the cold calculator. The issue is rather over what counts as 'a good thing'.

This issue can be resolved only at the level of moral theory, taking 'theory' in a weak sense to mean any kind of reflection on moral practice.[5] Here the dispute between Williams and utilitarians regarding the status of moral emotions (or the moral sentiments) becomes more foundational:

> There cannot be any very interesting, tidy or self-contained theory of what morality is, nor ... can there be an ethical theory, in the sense of a philosophical structure which, together with some degree of empirical fact, will yield a decision procedure for moral reasoning. This latter undertaking has never succeeded, and could not succeed, in answering the question, *by what right* does it legislate to the moral sentiments?
>
> (Williams 1981: preface, x)

To some extent, this charge of Williams is unfair. First, it fails to distinguish between utilitarianism as an ethical theory and as a decision-procedure. Utilitarians can restrict their claims to the theoretical level, remaining agnostic on what will be the best decision-procedure. Secondly, even at the level of theory, it is not as if an act utilitarian must treat ethical theory as grounded on a foundational rational intuition, entirely independent of moral sentiment or emotion. It is open to the utilitarian to argue that utilitarianism fits best both with beliefs based on reason and with those based on emotion or sentiment. Indeed, Mill's proof can be understood as just this kind of argument.

It is nevertheless true, as we saw in the previous section, that utilitarians fail to give *sufficient* weight to the moral emotions and the reasons that they reveal. Utilitarians can allow that much that is of value can be understood only through emotional engagement. Consider, for example, deep personal relationships. These will be quite alien to the cool and perfectly rational maximizer. But this response uncovers a tension in the utilitarian position. On the one hand, utilitarians permit emotion to play a rôle in understanding welfare values; but on the other they deny that the emotional pull everyone feels in cases analagous to those of George and Jim is to

---

5 Some level of reflection is countenanced by Williams; see e.g. Williams 1985: 112.

be given any weight of its own in an account of reasons for action. There are reasons, revealed to us in our emotional reactions to imaginary cases and to circumstances in the lives we live, that run counter to impartial maximization. This is what is true in the integrity objection.

As a final illustration of this point, let me describe two cases based on that of the original Jim:

Jim2 Because the captain suspects him of involvement, Jim2 is asked to commit suicide to save the Indians

Even if we decide that, overall, Jim2 should commit suicide, it is surely not *obvious*. Jim2 has a reason, even if not an overriding one, to preserve his own life *because it is his*, and this reason is revealed in the deep emotional attachment each of us has to our own life, and the emotionally informed concern we feel for its shape and content.

Jim3 Jim3 has lived in the area for some time and has developed a deep and lasting personal relationship with one of the Indians. The captain, knowing of this, sadistically offers Jim a choice: either he shoots that Indian and the other nineteen will go free, or the other nineteen will be shot and his friend will be freed.

Of course, utilitarians might be able to encompass Jim3's feelings in their theory. But do we not think, putting ourselves in Jim3's position, that he has a reason not to shoot his loved one which is quite independent of the reason to maximize utility?

Further reading

In addition to the works of Williams discussed in this chapter (Williams 1973b; 1976a; 1976b; preface to 1981; 1985; 1995), see the following responses to his arguments: Harris 1974; Davis 1980; Conly 1983; Barry 1995: ch. 9; Hollis 1995. Integrity is interestingly discussed in connection with 'agent-centred restrictions' on killing, etc., in Harris 1989. Alienation and modern ethical theory are discussed in Stocker 1976; Railton 1984. Good discussions of impartiality and partiality in ethics are Cottingham 1983; 1996. An excellent discussion of agent-relative attachments is Oldenquist 1982. For further defence of the critique of utilitarianism based on integrity and the separateness of persons, see Crisp 1996b. The most sophisticated attempt to combine an impartial maximizing morality with agent-relative reasons to give priority to oneself is Scheffler 1982.

Chapter 7

Justice

Justice

Consider this modern version of the sheriff case I discussed first in chapter 5:

Jean The East Midlands Serious Crime Squad has been investigating a series of terrorist bombings in shopping centres. So far no one has been arrested. The Chief Constable in charge of the Squad knows that if there is no arrest within a week, funding for the Squad will be drastically cut. He has a reasonable belief, which happens to be true, that if funding continues the bombers will be caught and that otherwise they will remain undetected. Because of the increased level of terrorist activity on the British mainland, he has been given special powers of arrest under an emergency law. This law is widely considered to be unjust, but the Chief Constable decides to make use of it. Looking through his files, he comes across the name of a person – Jean – who has made trouble for the Squad several times by exposing some

of its more unpalatable methods to the press. He invites Jean to visit him. While there, she is arrested. The Chief Constable promises her that her legal rights will be respected, but the promise is not kept. Jean is quickly charged with terrorist involvement, the judge in court being particularly ready to convict her because she is black. Funding for the Squad continues, and the real bombers are caught and sentenced within a few months. Jean's innocence remains undisclosed, and she serves a long prison sentence.

The problem for act utilitarianism, to put it simply, is that on various plausible assumptions about the bad effects of bombing campaigns the theory appears not only to exonerate the Chief Constable and others involved in this story, but to require them to act as they do. The unjust piece of emergency legislation, the violation of Jean's legal rights, the broken promise, the evil visited on a campaigner for justice and the unfair discrimination against her in court – all seem quite unjust. Surely, any moral theory that permits or recommends these injustices must be rejected?

Mill's debunking argument

Mill's argument in the final chapter of *Utilitarianism* was originally intended to be published as a separate treatise. It is the longest and most complex chapter in the book, so in this section I shall do little more than outline its structure.

5.1–2 Mill does not deny the existence or even the respectability of the 'sentiment' of moral outrage we feel in response to cases such as Jean's. He stresses, however, that despite its intensity we are not forced to see our sentiment of justice as a 'revelation of some objective reality'. It might be natural enough, but essentially an 'animal' as opposed to an 'intellectual' response, the origin of which can be explained consistently with utilitarianism. That is, it may be a mere feeling or emotion, and not a response to some genuine principle in conflict with utilitarianism. It is worth recalling that Mill believes that the ultimate principle of practical rationality, the principle of utility, is not at present attached to any strong sentiment (3.1). Indeed, according to Mill, his own nervous breakdown at the age of 20 was brought on by his being quite unmoved by the prospect of the principle of utility's being put into practice (*A* 1.139).

5.3–10 Mill begins his argument by seeking the common characteristic of the things we describe as just or unjust. He identifies five (or perhaps six) different 'spheres' of justice, i.e. areas of human life in which we speak of justice and injustice:

1 *Legal rights.* We think it unjust to deprive anyone of what they possess by legal right.
2 *Moral rights.* Some laws, such as that under which Jean was arrested, are thought to be unjust. Such laws seem to violate people's moral rights, so we may say that a second type of injustice consists in withholding from a person that to which he or she has a moral right, such as freedom from arbitrary arrest.
3 *Desert.* People are thought to deserve good if they do right, evil if they do wrong. Violations of this principle are thought to be unjust.
4 *Contracts.* Breaking faith with anyone or disappointing expectations we have voluntarily engendered is regarded as unjust.
5 *Impartiality.* Allowing one's judgement to be influenced by irrelevant considerations, such as a person's race or sex, is, as all will admit, often unjust.
6 *Equality.* This notion, says Mill, is close to that of impartiality. Some communists, for example, think that goods should be distributed according to need: equal needs give rise to equal claims to goods. The link with impartiality is obvious: the only relevant characteristic to be used when distributing goods is need, while attention to other characteristics will count, for these communists, as partiality and injustice.

The case of Jean illustrates each kind of injustice, if we allow that her trial involved the violation of a principle of equality before the law.

5.11–13 What is the link between these different spheres of justice? Mill turns to etymology. He argues, plausibly enough, that the notion of justice has its origin in the idea of conformity to law. Originally, injustice consisted in violation of actual laws, thought to have divine origin. Later, particularly among the Greeks and Romans, the sentiment of justice came to be attached to the violation of laws that *ought* to exist. Even now, though often we should wish that certain unjust conduct, such as minor unfairness within families, not be punished by law, it would 'always give us pleasure, and chime in with our feelings of fitness, that acts which we deem unjust should be punished' by public moral disapproval.

5.14–15 Mill's argument now takes a confusing turn, as it reaches the point which I began to discuss in chapter 6. It transpires that the appeal to etymology, and the consequent claim about conformity to law, were not the full story. Mill argues that the idea of punishment lies behind not merely obligations of justice, but moral obligation in general. What, then, distinguishes justice from other areas of morality?

Mill now introduces the distinction between *perfect* and *imperfect* obligations. Some ethical writers, he says, characterize imperfect obligations as actions that are required, but not at any particular time. So, I have an obligation to be charitable, but not on any specific occasion; when and to whom I am charitable are up to me. Mill considers it more precise to spell out the distinction with the idea of rights. If I have a perfect obligation, then some other person has a correlative right. In the case of charity, no person has a right to my assistance.

In this way, Mill ties the notion of justice closely to that of rights. Any case of injustice always involves both 'a wrong done, and some assignable person who is wronged', and justice 'implies something which is not only right to do and wrong not to do, but which some individual person can claim from us as his moral right'. In the case of Jean, we may describe the injustices as follows: the application of the emergency law violated her moral rights; her legal rights were violated; she had a right to what the Chief Constable promised her; because of her good work, she had a right to good treatment from the state; she had a right that her race not count against her in court, and to be treated equally before the law in being given a fair trial.

5.16–25   Now that we have an understanding of the origin and nature of the sentiment of justice, we may ask whether it can be made consistent with utilitarianism. Mill has argued that there are two 'elements' in the idea of justice: a belief that some particular individual has been harmed, and a desire to punish the person who caused the harm. He now claims that the desire to punish also has a dual origin, in the natural impulse to defend oneself and in the feeling of sympathy. Like other animals, human beings try to hurt those who hurt them or their young. Human sympathies are, however, wider than those of animals, extending to concern for all sentient beings, and human sentiments are more sophisticated than the sentiments of animals. These are the only differences.

So far, this sentiment features in the argument as a mere natural fact. Mill next claims that what is moral is 'the subordination of it to the social sympathies, so as to wait on and obey their call'. Just people, that is to say, resent only harms 'of the kind which society has a common interest with them in the repression of'. Certain conduct will be forbidden by rules of customary morality grounded on the promotion of utility. The sentiment of justice is aroused against those who disobey such rules. These rules protect the rights of individuals: 'When we call anything a person's right, we mean that he has a valid claim on society to protect him in the possession of it, either by the force of law, or by that of education and opinion.'

Why should society so protect individuals? Mill can give 'no other reason than general utility'. And we should not think this answer lacking in that it cannot explain the strength of the sentiment of justice. This is accounted for both by its animal origin and by its connection with an essential source of utility: security. The rules of justice in customary morality enable us to live with one another without continual fear of domination by those stronger than us. They thus protect 'the very groundwork of our existence'.

5.26–31   Mill returns later to the question of what is protected by the rules of justice, but before that he includes, in a digression, a separate argument that justice is not an independent moral standard. This is based on the ambiguity of the deliverances of our sense of justice. Not only do different individuals hold varying views of what is just in particular areas, but the same person can accept conflicting principles of justice.

Take punishment, for example. Some people believe that punishment is justified only for the good of the punished, others that it should be carried out only to deter other potential wrong-doers, yet others that because we do not have free will no one should be punished. Each of these views 'builds upon rules of justice confessedly true', viz. that it is unjust to sacrifice a person for the sake of others, that self-defence is justified and that no one should be punished for what he cannot help.

Similarly intractable disagreements arise in the area of apportioning punishments to particular offences, and in the issues of reward for labour, and taxation. How are we to resolve these disputes? 'Social utility alone can decide the preference.' We have already seen that Mill allows room for secondary principles in morality. The principles of justice are among these principles, and conflicts between them are to be decided in the way Mill recommends for any conflict between secondary principles, that is, by reference to the principle of utility.

5.32–6 Mill now returns to his original line of argument, to stress the importance of the source of welfare protected by the rules of justice. He shows here the influence of Thomas Hobbes (1588–1679) (see Hobbes 1651: chs. 13–17).[1] Without the rules of justice, Mill argues, each would see everyone else as an enemy. And it is these moral rules, therefore, that each person has the strongest interest in enforcing. Direct harms, either through aggression or the

---

1   It is worth pointing out the combination in Mill of Hobbesian conservatism (both here and in *On Liberty*) with Tocquevillian fear of stagnation (in *On Liberty*) and with radicalism (at points in *Utilitarianism*, *On Liberty* and *The Subjection of Women*, the clearest example perhaps being Mill's feminist understanding of marriage). This is only to be expected in a writer who accepts both that much of customary morality is well grounded, and that certain aspects of it require complete uprooting.

withholding from people of benefits they are expecting, are the clearest examples of injustice.

The sentiment of justice becomes enmeshed with the notion of desert through its connection with punishment, that is, with a return of evil for evil. And the idea of returning good for good is related to the infliction of harm via the notion of breach of faith. If you do good, you have a right to expect good in return, and if I fail to reciprocate, I harm you.

Most of the more specific principles of justice, Mill suggests, we shall find to be merely instrumental to the satisfaction of those principles already discussed. That a person should be punished only for voluntary wrongdoing, for example, is instrumental to the return of evil for evil. As for impartiality, that also is instrumental. Further, the principles of impartiality and equality are corollaries of the other principles. People who deserve *equally* well of us, for example, should be treated equally well. And this duty itself emanates from utilitarianism, according to which everybody is 'to count for one, nobody for more than one'.[2]

5.37–8   Mill ends by noting that none of the general principles of justice is absolute. Rights, for him, are not basic 'trumps' over the demands of utility (see Dworkin 1984). Mill allows that, though the sources of utility protected by justice are more important as a *class* than other sources, in particular cases the interest in security can be overridden. One should not steal; but there may be unusual occasions on which stealing is justified.[3] In such extraordinary cases, we shall deny that stealing is unjust.

Mill ends *Utilitarianism* with the claim that justice is not in fact a stumbling-block for utilitarianism:

---

2   There are other relationships between the different spheres which Mill does not mention. Many moral rights, for example, are based on desert or contract.
3   Mill's example is a case in which a life is at stake; but as the person whose life is at stake might claim to have a right to be saved, this is an unfortunate choice. What he requires is a conflict between a justice-based obligation and a non-justice-based obligation. The following example might serve. I have promised to repay a small debt to you this evening. On the way to your house, I come across a very poor beggar. He has no right to the money I am carrying, but perhaps I should give it to him anyway.

> Justice remains the appropriate name for certain social utilities which are vastly more important, and therefore more absolute and imperative, than any others are as a class . . . and which, therefore, ought to be, as well as naturally are, guarded by a sentiment not only different in degree, but also in kind; distinguished from the milder feeling which attaches to the mere idea of promoting human pleasure or convenience, at once by the more definite nature of its commands, and by the sterner character of its sanctions.

To summarize, then, Mill believes he has defused the problem of justice in the following way. First, we can understand why we feel so strongly about it once we recognize its natural origins as a device for protecting important interests. Secondly, since these interests are so important, utilitarianism itself recommends that we continue speaking of justice and injustice, even though such talk is merely instrumental to the maximization of welfare overall.

Duties, rights and obligations

Mill spreads the net of justice wide. According to him, any moral duty I have to any other specific person not only gives rise to a correlative right possessed by that other person, but is an obligation of justice. Some philosophers have argued that Mill's notion of justice is too broad.

First, it is claimed, there can be duties to specific persons, which do indeed give rise to correlative rights, but are not cases of injustice. A rapist, for example, can plausibly be said to violate the rights of the person raped, and he has of course done something very wrong. But rape is not a case of injustice (Dryer 1969: ciii; Quinton 1973: 74; Harrison 1975: 102). It is to be understood as downright viciousness, not something that goes against principles concerning the correct distribution of goods.

The second suggestion is that a failure to meet certain duties to specific persons is unjust but does not violate rights. If I nurse you through your old age, it is plausible enough to say that you have some kind of duty to leave me at least something in your will. Your not doing so will be unjust, but I have no right to any inheritance (Miller 1976: 57).

Finally, it has been said that there can be duties to specific persons that not only are not matters of justice, but do not give rise to correlative rights. If you invite me to a large informal party, and I accept, then I have at least a weak duty to turn up. But it is too much to call this a duty of justice, and you could not plausibly say that you have a right to my attendance. I am quite entitled to stay at home and paint my front gate, should I so wish (Harrison 1975: 105; Lyons 1978: 16).

There is, however, some room for disagreement in all these cases. Customary morality and ordinary language are not precise enough to rule decisively on whether rape is a form of injustice, whether deservingness of reward gives rise to a right, or whether you have a right (presumably it could be only a weak one) based on considerations of justice to my attendance at the party. Justice need not, in other words, be restricted to the distribution of benefits and burdens. Further, there are sound philosophical precedents for employing the notion of justice in a broad sense. Aristotle, for example, speaks of justice as, in one sense, 'complete virtue', and his usage here probably reflects that of fourth-century Athens.[4] Mill uses the term in an attempt to cover all those cases in which objectors would charge utilitarianism with sanctioning the violation of rights or with a general failure to make sense of certain important but apparently non-utilitarian moral obligations.[5]

What about Mill's reductive view of a right, which rests on the notion of harm to assignable individuals? Alan Ryan believes that it is easy to think of counterexamples (Ryan 1993: 12). If I am begging, and you do not give me food, then I shall suffer. I am an assignable individual, and my suffering is direct, but I had no *right* to the food.

Here Mill might claim that you have not in fact directly

---

4   Aristotle *c* 330 BC: 1129b25–6.
5   Mill seems not always to remember in *Utilitarianism* the breadth of his notion of justice. See e.g. the implication in 5.37 that the duty to save a life is not one of the general maxims of justice, discussed in n. 3.

harmed me.[6] This claim fits common sense, since we do not usually say that particular beggars are harmed by the failure of particular individuals to give them money. What if you are the *only* person who can help, and I really am starving? Then it becomes more plausible to say that the beggar does have a moral right, grounded in justice, to assistance.

Mill's analysis looks most shaky in its account of deserved 'evil for evil'.[7] We can easily use the notion of rights to make sense of deserved good: if you deserve some benefit for a service you have done me, you have a right to that benefit, and I have a duty to supply it. In the case of convicted criminals, we say that they deserve punishment. Desert, according to Mill, must involve the notion of a right. But it makes little sense to claim that a convicted criminal has a 'right' to his punishment, if only because we tend to think that rights can be waived! If a judge allows someone convicted of a serious crime to go free, whose rights are violated? The victim of the crime? But some serious crimes, such as insider dealing, are 'victimless'. In the case of deserved good, the person with the right can *claim* a benefit. Who can claim that a criminal be punished? The only answer can be society at large. Thus, society has a right that criminals be given what they deserve, judges have a duty to respect that right and criminals have a duty to accept their punishment.[8]

There is a danger here of all morality's being merged in justice (5.15). For society has a right not only to demand the punishment of particular individuals for particular crimes, but itself, through moral disapprobation, to punish those who fail to meet allegedly imperfect obligations, such as that of charity. If you give nothing whatsoever to charity, I can justifiably blame you for

---

6 Mill's conception of harm will be analysed in ch. 8.

7 See Lyons 1978: 18. Lyons suggests that Mill could employ the notion of *forfeiting* rights. So I have a right to freedom *until* I do wrong, when I must be punished. But this account seems to concern a necessary condition for desert rather than desert itself.

8 In *L* 4.3, Mill claims that 'society is justified in enforcing' certain conditions owed by each member to others in return for the protection offered by society. Talk of collective rights also allows us to talk of society's collective duties, such as that to care for the very poor.

being mean. But if duties to society can be understood as perfect obligations in the case of deserved evil, why not also in the case of charity? Why do I not have a perfect obligation to society to be charitable?

Mill can perhaps allow us to speak in this way, as long as we are clear that there is still an important difference between the obligations to administer or to accept punishment, and the obligation to be charitable. In the first case, there is little or no discretion. You must, as judge, punish this person, here and now, unless there is a strong case for mercy or amnesty. And, as a criminal, I must accept this particular punishment, and not seek, say, a period of grace so that I can finish making my model boat. When it comes to being charitable, however, I do have discretion about when and to whom to be charitable. This discretion is enough to mark off imperfect from perfect obligations.

It might be alleged that according to Mill's account of imperfect obligations we can never say that a person has acted wrongly or breached a moral obligation by not being charitable. For *in any particular case* no one has a right to charity. But Mill wants to leave open the possibility of a person's acting wrongly by breaching a moral obligation without acting unjustly (Lyons 1982: 47).

Mill can argue, however, that it makes sense to claim that a mean person acts wrongly in never giving to charity, and breaches an imperfect obligation in the process. There are several ways in which the person might meet this obligation – that is what makes it imperfect. But the claim that someone has acted wrongly does not imply that we must be able to identify a particular time when a wrong action was performed. Rather, it can be understood to refer to a course of action which is immoral overall. In this way, we can see how Mill can argue both that imperfect duties do not give rise to rights, and that they can be 'exacted' using moral sanctions (see Berger 1984: 214–22).

Customary morality is loose and unsystematic, so a philosopher can do no more than offer a particular interpretation or conception of it, in the hope that others will agree with it. Mill's conception in *Utilitarianism*, in terms of perfect and imperfect obligations, seems to me sophisticated and coherent. But certain problems do begin to arise when the account in *Utilitarianism* is compared with that in other central works of Mill, *On Liberty* in particular. I shall argue in a later chapter that there are good reasons for seeking consistency between these two books. What are we to make, then, of Mill's claim that 'selfish abstinence from defending [others] against injury' is a moral wrong? (*L* 4.6; cf. *L* 1.11; see Lyons 1982: 52). In 5.15, Mill characterizes beneficence as an imperfect obligation, whereas here it appears to be perfect, since presumably the requirement is to defend a particular person or persons in particular circumstances.

Mill might argue that some duties of beneficence are indeed duties of justice, in his broad sense. If I am required to protect you from some particular harm, you do have a right that I do so. This does not prevent Mill from allowing that there is also an imperfect duty of beneficence, which requires me to act beneficently on some, but on no particular, occasions.

This analysis also enables us to understand Mill's claim that each person in a society should 'bear his fair share in the common defence' (*L* 1.11). Just as each of us has a right that criminals be given their just deserts, so we each have a right that everyone with the capacity to do so should make a contribution towards the cost of defence.[9]

There are some passages where Mill's usage does seem loose; but even here his position is clear enough. In *On Liberty* 4.7, he distinguishes between imprudent acts and acts which consist in offences 'against the rights of others'. It is clear that the distinction

---

9 When Mill mentions this duty in *L* 4.3, he might be taken to imply that there is no correlative right, rights being restricted to negative prohibitions against injury. I suggest that we read this passage as, admittedly unclearly, drawing a distinction between negative and positive rights. I have a negative right not to be assaulted, and a positive right to your contribution to the costs of defence. This explains why Mill distinguishes a third class of acts, which are 'hurtful to others . . . without going to the length of violating any of their constituted rights'. These are acts – or rather courses of action – which violate imperfect obligations. In *L* 1.11, Mill speaks of acts such as taking a share in defence as 'positive', implying that he would be prepared to speak of 'negative acts', and consequently negative and positive duties and rights.

Mill has in mind here is that between action which is, and action which is not, subject to moral blame or punishment. Is he not, then, doing exactly what he objects to in 5.15, viz. merging 'all morality in justice'? Strictly, yes. But since Mill makes it clear later in *L* 4.7 that he is thinking of moral rules in general, we can understand him to be referring to any immoral action as an offence against the rights of others.[10] But here we might be ready to accept that my being immoral, even if does not violate the rights of particular others, does violate certain rights of society at large (see ch. 8).

Retaliation, fairness and desert

So Mill's conception of justice based on the distinction between perfect and imperfect obligations can be allowed to stand. That leaves the more important question of the success of his overall argument. Remember that Mill's aim was to debunk any claim that justice provides a moral standard independent of utility. He attempts to explain our sentiment of justice in a naturalistic way, making it consistent with utilitarianism. As I argued in my chapter on the proof, naturalism cannot be said to favour utilitarianism over any other theory. Mill is as committed – or as uncommitted – to any notion of an 'objective [moral] reality' (5.2) as any non-utilitarian. So the weight of his argument must rest on a principle of parsimony. Is Mill's account of the origin of our sense of justice so persuasive that there is no need to postulate any independent principle of justice to which it might be seen as a response?

The best way to begin to locate any weak points in an argument against a particular position is to ask how much of the argument the holder of the position under attack can accept. How much of Mill's argument could a proponent of non-utilitarian justice accept? The answer is, perhaps surprisingly, 'Most of it'.

---

10   Mill seems indeed to have different conceptions of rights and morality in mind at different times in *On Liberty*. In *L* 4.7, respecting rights appears to be equivalent to being moral, and this might include fulfilling imperfect duties (see *L* 3.9). *L* 4.3 involves a subtle distinction between negative duties (with correlative rights), positive duties (with correlative rights) and duties which do not violate rights (which may perhaps be understood to be imperfect duties).

Certainly there is no need to deny Mill's metaethical account of morality in 5.14. The phenomenon of morality is rather poorly understood. Nevertheless, Mill's suggestion that morality is essentially legalistic is plausible enough as a hypothesis. Nor is there any reason for Mill's opponent to reject the account of customary morality. They may, perhaps, find unacceptable the extension of justice to cover all perfect obligations. But this is at root a semantic issue, and the opponent can either agree to Mill's account, if only for the sake of argument, or make semantic changes to which Mill would be unlikely to object very strongly.

The opponent can even accept Mill's account of the *origin* of the sentiment of justice in the desire to punish wrongdoers, which itself emerges out of the impulse of self-defence extended by sympathy. For this would not require them to agree that this is all the sentiment of justice in fact amounts to. Believing that this would be required would be to commit a genetic fallacy as mistaken as that from which Mill seeks to distance himself in 5.12.[11]

It is here, on the issue of the very nature of the sentiment of justice, that Mill's opponents should stand their ground. As we saw, Mill attempts to establish a continuum between the sentiment of justice and the animal desire to retaliate in defence of self or offspring (5.20). The only differences between animal retaliation and the sentiment of justice are, first, that humans respond to attacks on all sentient beings, and, secondly, that the human response is more sophisticated, has a 'wider range'.

Because morality is so poorly understood, I am ready to take Mill's view here extremely seriously. Obviously his view of the origin of our sentiment of justice is too crude as it stands, but it may be that many of its operations can be explained, or 'naturalized', in something like the way he describes. Likewise, his argument that act utilitarianism will recommend the employment of secondary principles of justice is very powerful. Rights can indeed be said to protect important sources and elements of human welfare, and that in itself might be thought sufficient grounding for

---

11   A genetic fallacy is committed when one identifies what something is now with what it originally was.

respecting rights. Consider, for example, negative rights against assault, and rights to agreed payment for work performed. If these rights were not generally respected and upheld, no one would venture out of their home, let alone go to work.

But I am inclined to think that our beliefs about justice and equality in very abstract cases, where sympathy for those involved would find it hard to get a grip, suggest that the utilitarian principle is again – as we saw in the case of integrity – lacking in its failure to recognize the separateness of persons.[12] Imagine that you can bring about only one of the following outcomes:

Equality		Inequality	
Group 1	Group 2	Group 1	Group 2
50	50	90	20

Assume that each group contains the same number of people (say, a thousand). The numbers are meant roughly to represent welfare. So all those in *Equality* will have equally good lives, while those in *Inequality* will have lives either much better or much worse than the lives in *Equality*. The utilitarian is committed to the view that *Inequality* is preferable, but this seems to ignore the fact that welfare is distributed equally between people in *Equality*. Fairness, it seems, requires us to give some priority to those who would otherwise be worse off, and speaks in favour of choosing *Equality*. I find it hard to believe that my reaction here is to be discounted as a naturalistic response of extended sympathy, with no basis in rationality or reasonableness.

Nor need a principle of fairness be seen as a mere sub-principle in the department of morality within the Art of Life, governed by the single ultimate utilitarian principle of reasonableness. The utilitarian principle is plausible. But there is, despite

---

12 I do not want to be understood to be suggesting that fairness is relevant only when considering unusual abstract examples. Consider, for example, a case in which a teacher has to decide between using a difficult textbook, which most of the class will learn much from, and an easier one, which will benefit not the majority but those who are lagging behind. Utilitarianism may recommend the difficult book, but the principle of fairness argued for in the text favours the easier.

Mill's insistence in 1.3 and at the end of the *System of Logic*, no reason to think that there must be one single ultimate principle governing practical reason. This is why Mill's argument from conflict (5.26–31) also fails. For in any conflict the claim of the utilitarian principle to be the only means of rational arbitration is not obviously more plausible than that of the other, non-utilitarian principles in play.

It might be asked how, if there are several principles, we are to decide between them when they conflict. The answer can be only that we must use our judgement. But this is not to leave ethics open to arbitrariness or whim. Judgement can be reasonable or unreasonable. And, anyway, it is not as if single-principled theories such as utilitarianism can avoid it. What other than judgement does a utilitarian use to decide which moral theory to accept and then how to live and act in conformity with it?

As we saw in chapter 5, Mill appears to believe that the principle of utility requires little in the way of argument other than an appeal to the claim, attractive enough in itself, that 'equal amounts of happiness are equally desirable' (5.36, n. 2). But in that significant paragraph, Mill demonstrates his unawareness of the importance of the way that utility or welfare is distributed between different people. In other words, Mill fails to give enough weight to the separateness of persons as it enters into not only the rationality of personal concern (as we saw in the last chapter), but the fairness of giving priority to the worse off.

Nevertheless, Mill's project in chapter 5, based as it is on an attempt to understand the phenomenon of morality, is better grounded than many modern attempts at theories of justice which shuffle around beliefs (the origin of which is quite unclear) in whatever ways most appeal to the theorist and their audience. More work on the origin and development of customary morality is urgently required, and it is not unimaginable that Mill will turn out to have been right. It may be that properly understanding the origins of our non-utilitarian moral beliefs will tarnish the principles on which they are based to the point that we allow them to remain with us only for the reasons Mill himself allows, that they 'concern the essentials of human well-being more nearly ... than any other rules for the guidance of life' (5.32).

Chapter 5 concerned the nature of Mill's utilitarianism, and the following two chapters considered two related problems for utilitarianism arising out of its failure to recognize the significance of the separateness of persons. First, utilitarianism cannot account for the reasons each of us have to give some priority to ourselves and those close to us when making decisions about our actions and our lives. That is the sense in which utilitarianism faces a problem with integrity. Secondly, again because of its ignoring separateness, utilitarianism cannot justify giving priority to those who are worse off. Self-interest and fairness both pose difficulties for utilitarianism, and these are the areas on which those who wish to defend utilitarianism should concentrate. As I hinted above, I believe the debate between utilitarianism and its opponents is still quite open.

One important question to ask any utilitarian is what the practical implications of their theory are. Having demonstrated the subtlety and power of Mill's multi-level utilitarianism, I shall now discuss the implications Mill believed that theory had in two important spheres: the liberty of the individual and the relation between the sexes.

Further reading

A comprehensive and insightful discussion of Mill's views on justice is Berger 1984: ch. 4. Essential reading for anyone attempting to interpret Mill on justice are David Lyons's articles: Lyons 1976; 1978; 1982. These are helpfully collected in Lyons 1994. Other useful discussions include Ryan 1970: ch. 12; Harrison 1975. Good general discussions of justice are: Miller 1976; Brown 1986; Hooker 1993.

Utilitarianism and freedom: *On Liberty*

Utilitarianism and liberalism

Utilitarianism is a work both of personal and of social morality; that is, it contains precepts relevant to the question of how each one of us should live our lives, and to the issue of how society's legal and moral institutions should be arranged. Ultimately, of course, the book suggests that both our own lives and the institutions of society should be such that welfare overall is maximized.

Utilitarianism was published in 1861, *On Liberty* in 1859, and they were written almost contemporaneously. The earlier book is more directly concerned with social morality, its subject being 'the nature and limits of the power which can be legitimately exercised by society over the individual' (*L* 1.1).

Mill saw this question as vitally important, and since he provided at least an implicit answer to it in *Utilitarianism*, we must now attempt to understand the relation of the two works.

On the face of it, *On Liberty* is radically inconsistent with *Utilitarianism*. Early in *On Liberty*, Mill tells us that the object of the work is to assert 'one very simple principle' to govern absolutely the legal and moral restrictions society places on the individual. This celebrated principle, often called the *liberty principle*, is: '[T]he sole end for which mankind are warranted, individually or collectively, in interfering with the liberty of action of any of their number, is self-protection' (*L* 1.9).

In other words, as Mill goes on to say, society can exercise power over any individual only to prevent harm to others, never for the good of that individual themselves.

Now consider those laws in various countries which require that anyone travelling in a car wear a seat-belt. On the face of it, this legislation is paternalistic. That is, instead of leaving individuals to make up their own minds about whether to wear seat-belts, legal coercion has been applied in an effort to change the behaviour of individuals for their own good. Of course, there are likely to be non-paternalistic arguments for the legislation, such as that unbelted passengers pose more of a danger to other road-users, that adults with children are not entitled to risk their own lives or those of their children, that the cost to society of treating accident victims justifies the restriction and so on. But certainly one, and perhaps the most influential, of the arguments in favour of such legislation is paternalistic.

The verdict of the liberty principle is that such laws, if they rest on paternalism, are unjustifiable. When one considers the great overall gains in welfare they are likely to produce, however, the principle of utility would seem not only to allow but to recommend or even require them. For this reason, many have taken Mill's views in *Utilitarianism* and *On Liberty* to be irreconcilable. Mill is said to be torn between utilitarianism and liberalism, and some recent interpreters have preferred to see him as 'really' a liberal, who clung on to the vestiges of his utilitarianism out of loyalty to his father, to Bentham and to his own earlier convictions (see e.g. Berlin 1959; Ten 1980).

This view, however, is both intellectually uncharitable and implausible. For not only, as I have said, were the two works roughly contemporaneous, but Mill assures the reader early in *On Liberty* that the principle of utility has not been forgotten:

> It is proper to state that I forego any advantage which could be derived to my argument from the idea of abstract right, as a thing independent of utility. I regard utility as the ultimate appeal on all ethical questions.
>
> (*L* 1.11)

The liberty principle, then, cannot ground any kind of liberalism in Mill's thought which is inconsistent with his act utilitarianism. In *Utilitarianism*, as we saw in chapter 5, Mill recommends on utilitarian grounds the adoption of various 'secondary principles', such as those forbidding murder or theft, which do not in themselves make reference to welfare maximization. *On Liberty* is best seen as an attempt to argue for the adoption of the liberty principle as a secondary principle to govern society's legal and moral treatment of the individual. According to the liberty principle, society should never interfere with individuals paternalistically, in order to protect them from themselves.

We should, then, expect to find utilitarian arguments for the liberty principle. And indeed there are such arguments, as I shall show. But Mill is advocating a place for the liberty principle within 'customary morality', so it is no surprise to find him using arguments which make no direct reference to utilitarianism, but employ concepts which he clearly thought deserved a place in our moral thinking because of their utility. For example, one of his responses to the argument that harsh censorship is justified because truth ought to pass the ordeal of persecution is that it is quite deplorable to reward those who have discovered some important truth with martyrdom (*L* 2.16). But, as Mill points out in *Utilitarianism*, one of the most important secondary principles of justice concerns desert:

> This is, perhaps, the clearest and most emphatic form in which the idea of injustice is conceived by the general mind ... [A] person is understood to deserve good if he does right, evil if he does wrong; and in a more particular sense, to deserve

good from those to whom he does or has done good, and evil
from those to whom he does or has done evil.

(5.7)

It is in this more particular sense that Mill is using the notion
of desert in *On Liberty* 2.16, a sense underpinned by the principle
of utility itself.

So far, I have spoken of the liberty principle as a restriction
on the kinds of justification available for interference with the
conduct of others: paternalistic justification is ruled out. But there
is another side to the liberty principle, which concerns not paternalistic justification but individual sovereignty. As we shall see, Mill
believes that certain parts of a person's life should not be interfered
with *on any ground*, i.e. whether the justification be paternalistic
or not.

The enslavement of the soul

On Liberty is an intensely practical work, far more so than
Utilitarianism. *Utilitarianism* represents Mill's backroom prepara-
tion for engagement in the political debates of his time over what
he saw as 'the vital question of the future' (*L* 1.1).

On Liberty begins with an account of a shift in the relation
between subjects and government, and a correlative change in the
nature of tyranny. In the past, liberty consisted in protection of
subjects from governments in the form of political rights and
constitutional checks. As democratic political systems developed,
Mill claims, many, especially on the Continent (Mill probably has
the French philosopher Jean-Jacques Rousseau (1712–78) in mind),
began to see no good reason for any limit on government, since the
old division between governors and governed had disappeared.

But it soon became clear that democracy has its minorities,
so that the power of 'the people' is in fact exercised by only a
proportion of the population over the rest. The 'tyranny of the
majority' is perceived by most as operating especially dangerously
through the carrying out of its legislative acts by the judiciary. But,

[s]ociety can and does execute its own mandates: and if it issues wrong mandates instead of right, or any mandates at all in things with which it ought not to meddle, it practises a social tyranny more formidable than many kinds of political oppression, since, though not usually upheld by such extreme penalties, it leaves fewer means of escape, penetrating much more deeply into the details of life, and enslaving the soul itself.

(*L* 1.5)

There is little doubt that *On Liberty*, in its details as well as in its themes and general sympathies, owes much to the work of Tocqueville, whose first major work, *Democracy in America*, was enthusiastically reviewed by Mill (Tocqueville 1848; *TD* 18.47–90, 153–204).[1] Tocqueville was the first to describe the tyranny of the majority and its emergence as a peculiarly democratic phenomenon:

The authority of a king is physical and controls the actions of men without subduing their will. But the majority possesses a power that is physical and moral at the same time, which acts upon the will as much as upon the actions and represses not only all contest, but all controversy.

(Tocqueville 1848: 263)

Tocqueville was acutely aware of the importance of socialization, and the boundaries placed on individual autonomy and freedom of thought and action by what he called 'customs'. Customs are what maintain political systems, so any attempt to influence those systems must consist in an attempt to change customs:

The first of the duties that are at this time imposed upon those who direct our affairs is to educate democracy, to reawaken, if possible, its religious beliefs; to purify its morals; to mold

---

1 There are of course important differences between Mill and Tocqueville. First, Tocqueville was much more influenced than Mill by civic republican writers such as Rousseau. Secondly, and relatedly, Tocqueville's moral and political theory is a fairly unsystematic form of pluralism, with fundamental non-utilitarian elements.

its actions; to substitute a knowledge of statecraft for its inexperience, and an awareness of its true interest for its blind instincts, to adapt its government to time and place, and to modify it according to men and to conditions. A new science of politics is needed for a new world.

(Tocqueville 1848: 7)

Mill's central task in *On Liberty* is indeed to 'purify the morals' of his own society, by clarifying the limit of collective opinion over the individual. He notes that the rules governing social conduct in any society tend to appear self-evidently correct to its members, and to rest on the feeling of each person that all should be required to act as that person would like them to act. These ungrounded opinions are nothing other than individual preferences. Now there would be no problem in this were the customary morality which so develops solely the result of the 'tacit influence' of utilitarianism (1.4). Unfortunately, however, there are also other sources: prejudice, superstition, anti-social vices such as envy or arrogance, and – most commonly – self-interest. Mill offers a class-based account of the origin of customary morality. A large portion of the morality of any society will emerge from its dominant class, aided by the tendency to servility of lower classes.

It is in this context, in an 'England' where 'the yoke of opinion is perhaps heavier ... than in most other countries of Europe' (*L* 1.8), that Mill locates *On Liberty*.[2] His aim is to provide a principle to distinguish legitimate from illegitimate legal and moral power exercised over individuals by society. He sees a growing inclination in the world to exert the power of law and opinion over the individual, and 'unless a strong barrier of moral conviction can be raised against the mischief, we must expect, in the present circumstances of the world, to see it increase' (*L* 1.15).

The principle of liberty, then, is Mill's attempt to erect a barrier against the tyranny of the majority. There is no doubt that Mill's book has played a significant rôle both in creating and in sustaining a liberal atmosphere in the UK regarding society's

2   Mill often means 'Britain' as a whole when he speaks of 'England'.

treatment of individuals, and in particular political and moral conflicts. One example is the decriminalization of homosexuality in England. In 1959, the *Wolfenden Report* of the Committee on Homosexual Offences recommended that homosexual acts between consenting adults in private should no longer be subject to criminal sanctions. As Herbert Hart noted in his response to Lord Devlin's attack on the report, the view of the criminal law taken in the report was distinctly Millian. The job of law, according to the report, was not to protect individuals from themselves but from others:

> [The] function [of the criminal law], as we see it, is to preserve public order and decency, to protect the citizen from what is offensive and injurious and to provide sufficient safeguards against exploitation or corruption of others, particularly those who are specially vulnerable because they are young, weak in body or mind or inexperienced
>
> (Wolfenden 1959; quoted in Hart 1963: 14)

Further, Hart's own famous response is explicitly based on Mill (Hart 1963: 5).[3]

Harm to others

The liberty principle, in its first and 'simple' formulation, states that civilized society can exercise power over any individual only to prevent harm to others. Various questions immediately arise, some of which Mill answers later in *On Liberty*.

One is whether the action of the individual justifiably interfered with must *actually* be causing harm to another, or whether interference is permissible in order to ward off *potential* harm. Mill makes it clear that he is construing the liberty principle in the latter, broader form: 'Whenever . . . there is a definite damage, or a definite risk of damage, either to an individual or to the public, the case is

---

3 My own interpretation of Mill below, however, does differ from that of Hart. Hart sees Mill as claiming that morality is not always enforceable; I see him as arguing that morality is by definition enforceable, but only morality as based on the utility principle.

taken out of the province of liberty, and placed in that of morality or law' (*L* 4.10; cf. *L* 5.3, 5, 6).

Another important question, which brings us to the notion of harm itself, concerns the relationship between the various implicit or explicit formulations of the liberty principle throughout the work. Notions other than that of harm are widely used by Mill. Even in *On Liberty* 1.9, he speaks of interference's being justified for the self-protection of society, and refers to the conduct legitimately interfered with as that which is 'calculated to produce evil to some one else' and which 'concerns others'. Elsewhere many other notions are used.[4]

It is important first to note that Mill is not suggesting that causing harm to others, or damaging their interests, is *sufficient* to justify interference. Rather it is merely a *necessary* condition of justification:

> [I]t must by no means be supposed, because damage, or probability of damage, to the interests of others, can alone justify the interference of society, that therefore it always does justify such interference. In many cases, an individual, in pursuing a legitimate object, necessarily and therefore legitimately causes pain or loss to others.
>
> (*L* 5.3)

---

4   The notions used in *On Liberty* include actions which concern the security of others (*L* 1.10) or the interest of others; are hurtful to others; the omission of which causes evil through failure to supply a benefit (*L* 1.11); affect others directly or in the first instance (*L* 1.12); affect the interests of others prejudicially (*L* 4.3); affect the interests of others (*L* 4.6) or need not affect them unless they wish it (*L* 4.3); injure the interests of others (*L* 4.3); are mischievous or injurious to others (*L* 4.6; *L* 5.15) or are an offence against their rights (*L* 4.7); are hurtful to others or lacking in due consideration for the welfare, interests and feelings of others (*L* 4.3; 4.10); constitute a nuisance to others (*L* 3.1); molest others in what concerns them (*L* 3.1); are not purely self-regarding (*L* 4.4); and the evil consequences of which fall on others (*L* 4.7). Mill also speaks of, for example, the part of human life which chiefly interests society (*L* 4.2) and the part of a person's life which concerns others (*L* 4.8); the infringement of the rules necessary for the protection of the individual's fellows (*L* 4.7); the violation of a distinct and assignable obligation to another (*L* 4.10); and immoralities (*L* 4.6).

Mill goes on to give as an example someone's succeeding in a competitive examination. Their performance causes those who fail to lose out, but society 'feels called on to interfere, only when means of success have been employed which it is contrary to the general interest to permit – namely, fraud or treachery, and force' (*L* 5.3).

So harm to others justifies interference *when it is in the general interest to interfere*. Recall that in *Utilitarianism* Mill has already explained how the rules of customary morality, if well grounded, will advance the general interest. These rules, then, already provide us with guidance on when we are entitled to interfere. What Mill wishes to stress in *On Liberty* is that a customary morality grounded on utilitarianism will not permit societal interference with how people live their own lives, unless they are impinging seriously on the interests of others.

So the harmful conduct with which society is entitled to interfere is that conduct which violates the rules of customary morality. Evidence for this understanding of Mill comes in his references, especially in chapter 4 of *On Liberty*, to violations of obligations and to other such moral notions. It is only when I violate a genuine secondary principle of morality that I pose a threat to the welfare of others and can be coerced. Conduct which violates a moral obligation can be punished by law, that which causes perceptible hurt to another individual only by opinion (*L* 4.3). (Mill's distinction here is between action that is wrong in that it violates a right, and action that is wrong not in that it violates a right but in that it violates an 'imperfect' moral duty.) If I am a potential cause of harm to others, a case can be made for interference with my conduct by law or through social opinion. But that case will succeed only if I am violating a moral rule which is itself justified by the utility principle.

But why should customary morality not be assumed to govern those aspects of the lives of individuals which do not seriously impinge on others? Why, that is, should we not interfere with the self-regarding sphere? Because it is not 'for the good of mankind' that people be held accountable in this area of life (*L* 4.6). There is no right to liberty, 'as a thing independent of utility' (*L* 1.12). What gives Mill's liberalism its bite is his view that there are no ordinary moral duties to oneself, at the level of customary morality. So if I am living what appears to you a dissolute life, you are not permitted to attempt to interfere with me using either legal or moral sanctions *unless* I am violating some genuine moral obligation concerning others. I have no duty to myself, and therefore you can have no moral justification for interfering with me.

The relevant moral obligations you can use to justify interference with me are not purely negative (*L* 1.11; see ch. 7). Society can compel the performance of certain actions such as giving evidence in court, taking a part in defence or other joint works, saving another's life or protecting another from abuse, and the justification here, if it is going to make use of the notion of harm, must be that the non-performance of these actions is so harmful to others that the principle of utility justifies their enforcement. It might be thought that Mill is here stretching the notions of causation and harm too far. But he is not; he believes that these customary obligations are securely grounded on the principle of utility, so that failure to fulfil them may well result in harm to others. Nor is Mill open to the charge that his allowing society to compel action will result in the diminishing of the sphere of liberty to vanishing point. For Mill, utilitarianism and the customary morality which it supports are not excessively demanding. So you cannot be coerced by society into constantly collecting for Oxfam on utilitarian grounds. It may be that he is wrong about this, but that would be a different objection.

Offence and slavery

Mill's position, then, is as follows. The actions of individuals and society should conform with the ultimate principle of practical reason, the utility principle. Society has at its disposal two important tools for affecting people's behaviour: the sanctions of law, and blame consequent on the violation of customary moral rules. Mill claims that such interference is justified only to prevent harm to others. Any kind of paternalistic justification for interfering with another person's life is ruled out. Customary moral rules themselves should be directed at preventing harm to others, and breaking such rules is itself what constitutes the level of harm that justifies interference. And since customary morality, if properly developed, will take all possible harms and benefits into account, no interference is justified when a person is not violating one of the customary moral rules justified by utilitarianism. Finally, these customary moral rules will give a much greater latitude to each individual to decide for themselves how they are to live than many of Mill's contemporaries appear to have believed. Not only are paternalistic justifications ruled out, but interference on any ground with the self-regarding sphere is excluded.

Mill's argument allows us to place any action in one of four categories:

1 Actions ruled out by customary morality; e.g. fraud. Harmful to others, and can be interfered with either by law or by opinion.
2 Actions not ruled out by customary morality, but harmful; e.g. succeeding in an examination. Harmful to others, and therefore candidates for interference. But the general happiness is best promoted by non-interference.
3 Actions not ruled out by customary morality, which do affect others, perhaps causing them 'displeasure' (L 3.9), but are not harmful; e.g. drunkenness which does not harm anyone. Within the self-regarding sphere, and so not candidates for interference.
4 Actions not ruled out by customary morality, which do not affect others; e.g. bathing in a private bathroom. Within the self-regarding sphere, and so not candidates for interference.

The self-regarding sphere, then, is not to be confined only to those actions in which no one is interested. Mill's liberalism also concerns those actions in 3, which may cause great offence to others but are nevertheless, we might say, the 'business' only of those who engage in them. My being a drunkard, if I have no obligations to anyone else, is my own concern, and if you say you do not like it I can respond that your displeasure is not enough to constitute a harm. So my action remains within the protected self-regarding sphere. We have rights over our tastes analogous to property rights over things: just as you are not entitled to 'interfere' with my ownership of my wallet (by stealing it), so you are not entitled to interfere with my tastes (by restricting conduct for which I have a taste and you have distaste) (*L* 4.12). Distaste is not injury.

We must ask at this point whether Mill really needs to distinguish between those actions that do cause harm but are not ruled out by customary morality, category (2), and those that cause displeasure but not harm, category (3). The offence some people feel at certain actions, particularly those concerning sex or religion, can be intense, even when those actions are performed in private. How plausible is it to say that it cannot count as injury or harm? Mill has strong utilitarian arguments, to be discussed in the following section, for permitting expression to 'individuality' based on the value of individuality itself to the person expressing it and to others. These arguments would be enough to provide sufficient support for a protected sphere independently of any distinction between harmful and allegedly non-harmful effects on others.

There is anyway something of a grey area in Mill's categorization of particular actions. Sometimes, offence to others *is* enough not only to count as harm but to be ruled out by customary morality and so be preventable by law or opinion. This is the case, for example, with 'offences against decency' (Mill does not say what he has in mind, but such offences presumably include acts such as sexual intercourse in a public place). We can now see that Mill is walking something of a tightrope. On the one hand, he sees the danger of allowing society to inflict its preferences about ways of life on individuals. Thus he appeals to the prejudices of his readers in support of his denial to Muslims of the right to ban pork (*L* 4.14). On the other hand, he believes that certain ways of life or certain actions which society dislikes – such as offences against decency – are indeed just wrong, and should be prohibited. If pressed, Mill would perhaps admit that he believed the British sense of decency to be grounded on the principle of utility in a way that that of Muslims, which Mill after all believed to be based on a seriously mistaken religious assumption, is not. But Muslims might be unpersuaded that pork-eating is clearly in category (3) whereas public sex is clearly in category (1). They might well suggest that pork-eating also falls into category (1).

Because Mill thus leaves open to objectors to any practice the option to claim that their sense of decency is correct, we must ask whether he might not have done better, using the utilitarian arguments in favour of individuality, to collapse category (3) into (2) and rule out *any* interference based on feelings of offence. If certain people really do want to make love in the park, for example, it might well maximize utility in the long run if we restrained ourselves from criticism of them and others like them. But this is perhaps to take Mill's book out of context. His readers would not have tolerated such proto-permissiveness, and any good effects which Mill might have hoped for from his book would have been prevented. Sensitivity to the practicality of *On Liberty* is essential to a charitable interpretation of it. It is a piece of politics as well as of political theory. Nevertheless, Mill might just have omitted mention of offences against decency rather than place them explicitly in category (1).

Offences against decency are not the only case in which the liberty principle might seem to be compromised. Problems arise in category (4) as well as category (3). Adherence to the liberty principle is justified by utilitarianism, and this makes the liberty principle permanently subject to the contingencies of the sources of welfare. To put it bluntly, if social interference will maximize welfare overall, then that legitimizes the interference, even if it might appear to be an encroachment on the self-regarding sphere. A particularly clear example is Mill's refusal to sanction slavery contracts (he almost certainly has marriage contracts in mind; see ch. 9).[5] Our reason for not interfering with the life of an individual, other than to protect others, is that 'his good is on the whole best provided for by allowing him to take his own means of pursuing it' (*L* 5.11). The slave abdicates his liberty and so removes the very justification for allowing him to do what he wishes in this instance. This is a case where society is *not* wrong to interfere, and Mill even imagines an 'ideal public', which might interfere only with the lives of those who are clearly mistaken (*L* 4.12). His principle of liberty is a recognition that the public of his day were so far from ideal

---

5 For a defence of Mill's view of slavery, see Smith 1996.

that they should, in many but not all cases, be forbidden from interference.

Again, Mill has allowed room for a person advocating paternalism in some particular case to argue that it is an exception to the principle, like the case of slavery. And the issue again turns on the empirical consequences of Mill's principle. It could be argued that it might have been more productive of welfare for him to advocate, and for society to accept, a pure principle of liberty which would allow competent, informed and uncoerced adults to sell themselves into slavery, for sexual, financial or other reasons, should they so wish. Mill may be pandering to the abhorrence of slavery many of his readers would have felt, but it may be that his tailoring of his argument to fit these preferences has led to his writing having less rhetorical force in the long term.

Folly and depravation of taste

Mill aimed to erect a barrier against the tyranny of opinion of the majority over the minority. So we might expect him to be against any sort of criticism of self-regarding conduct directed at the improvement of the individual agent in question, other than in exceptional cases such as that of slavery. Indeed, in L 1.7, Mill criticizes those who inquire into what society should like or dislike rather than question 'whether its likings or dislikings should be a law to individuals'.[6] Strangely, however, Mill not only allows but encourages us to respond negatively to certain people in areas where only their own good is at stake:

> There is a degree of folly, and a degree of what may be called (though the phrase is not unobjectionable) lowness or de-
> pravation of taste, which, though it cannot justify doing harm

6   In L 1.9, Mill says we should not 'visit evil' on an individual for his own good. In L 2.19, he implies that the effects of social stigma on someone who expresses banned opinions is an evil. This suggests that the effect of social stigma on someone with a self-regarding fault will likewise be an evil, regardless of whether such stigma is intended to punish that person (which would make it illegitimate) or to help the individual concerned (which Mill allows in L 4.7).

to the person who manifests it, renders him necessarily and properly a subject of distaste, or, in extreme cases, even of contempt.

(*L* 4.5)

One might think that Mill believes that such feelings are natural and desirable, but should be kept to oneself. But he goes on: 'It would be well, indeed . . . if one person could honestly point out to another that he thinks him in fault, without being considered unmannerly or presuming'. Further, we have rights to avoid such people, to warn others against them and to prefer others over them in 'optional good offices'.

How can Mill avoid the conclusion that he is approving of the tyranny of opinion? For though he claims that such reactions and their expression are the 'natural, and, as it were, the spontaneous consequences of the faults themselves', he undoubtedly endorses them. Notice that Mill does not explicitly permit *moral* criticism of self-regarding faults such as the pursuit of lower pleasures. Indeed, he claims that these 'penalties', severe as they are, should not be inflicted 'for the sake of punishment'. We know from our discussion of 5.14 in chapters 5 and 6 that Mill tied morality to punishment: my blaming you for something is analogous to some physical punishment's being inflicted on you for the same action. So the opinions we express should not employ moral coercion. We should not speak of 'duties to oneself', nor claim that pursuit of lower pleasures, when it does not harm others, is wrong.

But two difficulties remain. First, Mill provides us with no clear criterion for distinguishing between moral and non-moral language. If you tell me, albeit perhaps not in an 'unmannerly or presuming' way, that you have contempt for my way of life, are you not expressing a moral attitude, an attitude to which my response might appropriately be guilt? Secondly, even if a criterion can be supplied, it is not clear why a tyranny of opinion could not anyway establish itself using purely non-moral, perhaps aesthetic, language.

The truth of the matter is that Mill would not object to this. Again we can see that he is torn in *On Liberty* between on the one hand his commitment to his own views about welfare and on the other his awareness of the danger in allowing others to use the tyranny of opinion to enforce their own mistaken views of welfare. Lives of animal pleasures, of 'rashness, obstinacy, self-conceit', are just mistaken. And according to Mill's ultimate principle they are indeed wrong, in their failure to maximize welfare. But so afraid is Mill of morality's being misused as a social tool that he advocates its not being employed at all in criticism of purely self-regarding faults.

His acceptance of non-moral self-regarding criticism of some ways of life, however, is another hostage to fortune. He leaves it open to others with conceptions of welfare competing with his to claim that their own reaction against the way of life recommended by Mill is 'natural and spontaneous'. In *On Liberty*, Mill gambles the benefit of allowing society to condemn in non-moral terms ways of life that he saw as clearly mistaken, and indeed morally wrong, against the danger of permitting the erection of a tyranny of opinion which would not be grounded on the principle of utility. Given the continuing vehemence of the debates about the naturalness and unnaturalness ways of life such as homosexuality, and the constant danger of purportedly benevolent oppression of marginalized groups in society, it is arguable that Mill's gamble has not paid off. Perhaps a pure liberal principle, which strictly forbade any comment on or overt response to the self-regarding aspects of the ways of life of others, might have been more productive of welfare.

It may be said that what really matters is that people be allowed to get on with their own personal lives, free in particular from legal restrictions, and this indeed is what most contemporary liberals believe. This does seem right; this is what *really* matters. But my point is that aesthetic coercion can easily lead to moral coercion, and moral coercion can easily lead to legal coercion.

Despite my quibbles in this and the previous section, I must emphasize the power of Mill's utilitarian defence, based on the value of individuality and the danger of social interference, of a self-regarding sphere protected by rights against the interference of others. He is surely correct to claim that widespread recognition of such a sphere will do a great deal of good, in terms of 'utility in the largest sense, grounded on the permanent interests of man as a progressive being' (*L* 1.11). Mill felt that much of the customary morality of his day, properly understood and interpreted, was acceptable, largely because of its origin in the 'tacit influence' of the principle of utility. But he is pessimistic about the worth of *new* interferences with the liberty of individuals (*L* 4.12; cf. *L* 3.6). *On Liberty* is an appeal to the Victorian public to reconsider their existing law and customary morality in the light of the principles of utility and of liberty, and thus to allow individuality to flourish:

> Some rules of conduct, therefore, must be imposed, by law in the first place, and by opinion on many things which are not fit subjects for the operation of law. What these rules should be, is the principal question in human affairs.
>
> (*L* 1.6)

Freedom of expression

Chapter 2 of *On Liberty* – 'Of the liberty of thought and discussion' – is widely held to be the finest, a classic defence of the liberal right to freedom of expression. There is something of a discontinuity between chapter 2 on the one hand, and on the other the outline of the liberty principle in chapter 1 and its application to the question of individuality in chapter 3. The liberty of thought we might expect to fall straightforwardly under the protection of the principle of liberty, since private thoughts, considered in isolation, must, if anything does, fall within the sphere of the self-regarding. But, as Mill recognizes, having an opinion and giving voice to it are quite different:

> The liberty of expressing and publishing opinions may seem to fall under a different principle, since it belongs to that part of the conduct of an individual which concerns other people; but, being almost of as much importance as the liberty of thought itself, and resting in great part on the same reasons, is practically inseparable from it.
>
> (*L* 1.12)

Here Mill admits that the making public of an opinion does fall into the category of actions which concern others, implying that the principle of liberty cannot be invoked directly in its defence. As we have seen, however, the liberty principle is not itself foundational or ultimate, and adherence to it is justified only by the principle of utility. So we might expect to find that the reasons Mill gives for liberty of expression are primarily utilitarian, and similar to those invoked for allowing liberty of thought itself. And indeed this is what we find in chapter 2.[7]

One reason for the absence of the liberty principle from the arguments of chapter 2, perhaps, is that Mill distinguishes opinion from action:

> No one pretends that actions should be as free as opinions. On the contrary, even opinions lose their immunity, when the circumstances in which they are expressed are such as to constitute their expression a positive instigation to some mischievous act. An opinion that corn-dealers are starvers of the poor, or that private property is robbery, ought to be unmolested when simply circulated through the press, but may justly incur punishment when delivered orally to an excited mob assembled before the house of a corn-dealer.
>
> (*L* 3.1)

The implication here is that the liberty principle, though it concerns actions, could in fact be invoked in a revised form in defence of the expression of an opinion in which no harm is done to others. Of course, were Mill to accept the obvious – that expressing an opinion is acting – it could be used in its original form. When your expressing an opinion is likely to cause unjustifiable harm to another person, likely, that is, to violate some part of customary morality grounded on utilitarianism, suppressing you may be legitimate. Here we must remember that very often a censor will claim that the opinion they are censoring is immoral. Mill's chapter can be seen as an attempt to show that many of the

---

7   The structure of Mill's argument in chapter 2 appears to owe much to John Milton's *Areopagitica* of 1644 (see Haworth forthcoming).

expressions of opinion forbidden by censors would not in fact be forbidden by a purified customary morality.

The value of truth

We have seen that Mill does not allow feelings of offence, unless they are responses to indecent or other embarrassing acts, to count as harm sufficient to justify interference. So we might expect to find that racist speakers, for example, cannot be silenced on the ground that they upset others. But at this point we should remember Mill's moralized conception of harm. Offence alone cannot justify suppression, *unless* it is in line with that part of customary morality which is justified by the principle of utility, as is the case with common decency. Now there is a serious question about how we find out what is and what is not permitted by 'customary morality'. Let us assume, however, that customary morality as it is does not prohibit racist speeches. Surely this would be one of the areas in which Mill would claim that customary morality is faulty, given the terrible consequences that flow from racism? And this would provide us with an argument for silencing the racists, just as we forbid people to walk naked or fornicate in the street.

Mill, however, puts such value on truth that he will disagree. At the beginning of chapter 2 we find the following footnote: 'If the arguments of the present chapter are of any validity, there ought to exist the fullest liberty of professing and discussing, as a matter of ethical conviction, any doctrine, however immoral it may be considered' (*L* 2.1, n. 1).

What are Mill's arguments in favour of placing such importance on the freedom of expression and discussion? His defence of any particular expression of an opinion is twofold (*L* 2.1). First, the opinion may be true, in which case suppression deprives those who dissent from it of the opportunity of knowing the truth. Secondly, it may be false, but then what is lost is the 'clearer perception and livelier impression of truth, produced by its collision with error'.

Mill begins by discussing the first line of defence, with his well-known 'infallibility argument' (*L* 2.3–4). He claims that any suppression of opinion is an assumption of infallibility, and that this assumption is unjustified. For, first, many people who have assumed they were infallible, such as those who persecuted Socrates, Christ and the Christian Martyrs, were mistaken, and 'ages are no more infallible than individuals' (*L* 2.4). Mill is decrying the unthinking adherence to customary belief of his fellows. Secondly, you can rationally claim truth for your own view only if you allow it to be tested in the light of the beliefs of others. We have reached the level of rationality in conduct and opinion which now exists only through the yielding of wrong practices and opinions in the past to argument.

A censor of opinion might argue that he is not assuming infallibility so much as protecting beliefs of utilitarian value to society (*L* 2.10). Mill has two arguments against this position. One argument is that the censor is assuming infallibility at a different point, viz. on the question of whether the belief is useful or not. The second, perhaps stronger, argument is that 'no belief which is contrary to truth can be really useful'. Mill describes this view as that of 'the best men', and we can take it that he includes himself among them.

This characteristic piece of nineteenth-century intellectual optimism sits oddly with Mill's own claim, which I shall discuss below, that there is value in the propagation of falsehood. After all, the censors may argue that they are only following Mill's advice, and making sure that sufficient falsehoods remain in circulation for the truth to retain its vitality. But more importantly we can begin to see emerging here the exaggerated emphasis Mill places on truth. Out of social context, his claim about the value of truth sounds plausible. But real societies depend centrally on myths and false-hoods, and often the removal or breaking down of national or local myth can create an emptiness or depression in both individual and society. Consider, for example, the effect of loss of faith on religious believers. Not all religious beliefs could be true, because they are contradictory, and yet the loss of faith in them can be quite destructive.

But what if the opinions generally held in a society are in fact true? What, then, would be wrong with suppressing the expression of false views inconsistent with them? Here lies the second strand of Mill's argument against censorship. This strand depends upon a distinction between knowing the truth and believing a dogma. If I am to be said to know the truth, I must have some knowledge of the grounds for what I believe and be able to defend it against at least some objections (*L* 2.22). There are exceptions, such as mathematics, to which there are no objections to be made. But without free discussion of central issues in morals, politics, religion and so on, the very 'meaning' of what is believed will fade. The belief, that is, will be no longer be 'vivid', 'living' (*L* 2.26). It will be a 'dogma . . ., a mere formal profession, inefficacious for good' (*L* 2.43).

One test of whether one holds a practical belief in this way is to set it against one's actions. In the case of most Christians, for example, Mill argues, belief is dead, and has failed to be realized in the imagination, the feelings or the understanding (*L* 2.28). Hence, their actions do not chime with their beliefs. Rather than give all they have to the poor, they give only as much as anyone else (that is, not much). In this respect, many modern Christians compare badly with those who died for their beliefs in earlier centuries. Mill even goes so far as to argue that where there is consensus on some doctrine, such as that the earth orbits the sun and not *vice versa*, the 'teachers of mankind' should make arrangements for its being questioned, to bring it home to those who believe it (*L* 2.32).

So far we have considered the cases in which received opinion either is false or is true. Mill recognizes that in many situations there will be truth and falsity on both sides. Here he argues that truth is more likely to emerge if free play is given to all opinion. In politics, for example, there should be opinions both on the side of democracy and that of aristocracy, on the side of property and of equality, on the side of co-operation and of competition (*L* 2.36). The 'customary morality' of politics arises from the same sources as morality elsewhere; that is, a combination of a secure grounding in the principle of utility tempered by self-interest, class interest and other distortions. Mill's argument is that the beneficial aspects of various political positions will not emerge without liberty of expression: 'there is always hope when people are forced to listen to both sides' (*L* 2.39).

Close to the conclusion of chapter 2 of *On Liberty*, Mill claims: 'We have now recognised the necessity to the mental well-being of mankind (on which all their other well-being depends) of freedom of opinion, and freedom of the expression of opinion' (*L* 2.40).

Ultimately, then, Mill's arguments for freedom of thought and expression rest on the principle of utility. Knowing the truth, in the full-blooded sense outlined above, is an important constituent of welfare (though of course we have to understand it in terms of Mill's own hedonism). And allowing freedom of expression will enable even 'average' human beings to reach the 'mental stature' of which they are capable (*L* 2.20). Nor is the whole weight of the argument on truth alone. It is good for one to possess a cultivated intellect and capacity to judge (*L* 2.23). Further, liberty of expression will have more practical benefits. In historical periods such as the Reformation, where intellectual authorities are questioned, many improvements 'in the human mind or in institutions' will result (*L* 2.20). We might also expect or hope that the enervation which Mill decries in Christianity would be expunged from customary morality, in such a way that individuals are more highly motivated to morality and can accept greater moral burdens than at present.

How powerful is Mill's case? It is certainly overstated. Consider his historical claim: in fact, benefits in many areas of life have resulted from the Victorian age which he so castigates for its intellectual conformity. But his arguments are generally sufficient to outweigh those who oppose freedom of expression. Understanding and the exercise of the intellect are plausible constituents of welfare, and are certainly harder to obtain in a repressive society. And there are likely to be many indirect practical and intellectual advantages in permitting freedom of expression.

Nevertheless, Mill's faith in human rationality is excessive. He underrates the human capacity to believe and act on the patently absurd. Consider the propaganda campaign run by Joseph Goebbels in Germany before the Second World War. Whatever the implications for liberalism, the principle of utility would have sanctioned the silencing of his campaign. Nor is it at all plausible to argue that those who believed Jews and other minority groups to be morally equal to other human beings would have been led by the silencing of the Nazis into holding their belief as dead dogma. Nor again does the distinction between long-term and short-term consequences, which may be what Mill has in mind when he speaks of 'the permanent interests of man as a progressive being' (*L* 1.11), help Mill. The long-term interests of humanity will be better served by encouraging the end of racism rather than allowing it to have its day. That particular list is better closed (*L* 2.8).

It might perhaps be possible to draw analogies between Nazi propaganda and the utterances of the person in front of the corn-dealer's house. But this just opens up the same set of issues that we found in our discussion of the principle of liberty: what constitutes harm sufficient to justify interference? In the end, we shall often in practice fall back on the proper application of the principle of utility.

Individuality

We have seen how many of Mill's central arguments in *On Liberty* take us inexorably back to the principle of utility of *Utilitarianism*. In the case of freedom of expression, Mill suggests that the cultivation of our intellectual faculties, and their employment in full-blooded understanding of the truth, is an essential component of welfare. Further, such freedom will lead to social progress and so has instrumental value.

When Mill returns to the question, as he sees it, of action as opposed to opinion, in chapter 3 of *On Liberty*, we find arguments that individuality also is instrumental to social progress, advancing the welfare of all, arguments intended to convince even those unimpressed by the claims of individuality as a component of welfare itself (see Friedman 1966). We see also that his arguments for liberty rest on his sophisticated conception of welfare, with individuality as a self-standing constituent:

It is desirable, in short, that in things which do not primarily concern others, individuality should assert itself. Where, not the person's own character, but the traditions or customs of other people are the rule of conduct, there is wanting one of the principal ingredients of human happiness.

(*L* 3.1)

What is individuality? This quotation shows that at least part of it will involve one running one's life for oneself, and not merely on the basis of social custom. We might call this *autonomy*, though that term is not found in Mill (see ch. 3). It is clear that Mill is thinking of autonomy not as a mere human capacity, the possession of which adds to one's welfare, but as the exercise of that capacity in self-government (*nomos* is the Greek word for 'government', while the prefix *auto*- means 'self').

Good government is rational, and Mill allows us to draw an analogy between his claims about the value of intellectual development in chapter 2 and what he says about autonomy in chapter 3. Autonomy, though it involves spontaneity (*L* 3.2), is not just that. For autonomy to count as a constituent of individuality and so of welfare, it must be exercised in the development of one's own potentialities. Just as one constituent of welfare is the reflective arrival at belief – ideally, true belief – so the exercise of autonomy consists in the cultivation and use of the capacities of the practical intellect:

The human faculties of perception, judgment, discriminative feeling, mental activity, and even moral preference, are exercised only in making a choice ... The faculties are called into no exercise by doing a thing merely because others do it, no more than by believing a thing only because others believe it.

(*L* 3.3; cf. *L* 3.4)

Nor is Mill optimistically assuming that individuals will never make mistakes, despite his claims elsewhere in the book about each individual's knowing what is best for him or her (e.g. *L* 4.4). He allows that it is indeed in some cases possible to interfere to prevent a person's exercise of his practical capacities leading to his being harmed. But, Mill asks, 'what will be his comparative worth as a human being? It really is of importance, not only what men do, but also what manner of men they are that do it' (*L* 3.4).

Consider also Mill's view of the higher pleasures in the second chapter of *Utilitarianism*. In *On Liberty*, he encourages society to allow individuals to make their own decisions about how to run their lives, and we are beginning to see how this encouragement is grounded in the view that welfare will be so promoted. But in *Utilitarianism* 2.7, Mill admits that many people who are capable of the higher pleasures fall into ways of life involving the lower. But, Mill claims:

> I do not believe that those who undergo this very common change, voluntarily choose the lower description of pleasures in preference to the higher . . . Capacity for the nobler feelings is in most natures a very tender plant, easily killed, not only by hostile influences, but by mere want of sustenance; and in the majority of young persons it speedily dies away if the occupations to which their position in life has devoted them, and the society into which it has thrown them, are not favourable to keeping that higher capacity in exercise.

In other words, society, present society, is to blame. In an improved society, Mill implies, individuals would choose higher over lower pleasures.

On the whole, Mill's claim that one's own plan for life is best because it is one's own is plausible enough (*L* 3.14). This is not just because, *on the whole*, individuals do in fact know their own tastes and interests best, but because autonomy itself is valuable. You may remember that it was one of the goods in my 'ideal' in chapter 3 above.

So far, then, we have disentangled several components of individuality: the running of one's life for oneself rationally – which, incidentally, allows one to have a *character* (*L* 3.5) – and in the way which most develops one's own particular potentialities and is most in line with one's own peculiar tastes. But this is not the whole story. For so far Mill might be committed to allowing individuality to someone who rationally and deliberately chooses the quiet life of custom. Again, however, just as Mill encourages liveliness and vigour in the intellectual sphere in chapter 2 of *On Liberty*, so in chapter 3 we learn that an important further component of individuality is an *energetic* character, with strong desires and impulses (*L* 3.5). Part of individuality is '"Pagan self-assertion"' (*L 3.8*), almost the only outlet for which Mill saw in the Britain of his day to be business (*L* 3.16).

Mill is again here showing his influences. We are reminded of Aristotle's stress on the importance of *activity* in happiness, and Tocqueville's praise of the 'energetic passions . . . and wild virtues' found in the aristocracies from which modern democracies descend (Aristotle *c* 330 BC: 1098b31–1099a7; Tocqueville 1848: 9). Mill explicitly quotes the claim of Baron Wilhelm von Humboldt (1767–1835) that there are two necessary conditions for individuality to flourish in a society: freedom and diversity (*L* 3.2). By freedom, here, he means what Isaiah Berlin calls 'negative freedom', that is, in this context, freedom from the legal or moral coercion of others (Berlin 1958). Diversity of ways of life – 'experiments in living' (*L* 3.1) – will bring us closer to practical truth, that is, to the truth about their worth, just as diversity of opinion will allow us to advance intellectually nearer truth (*L* 3.11). Indeed this plurality is what has characterized and what lies behind the past success of Europe (*L* 3.18). But so depressed is Mill by the apparent conformity surrounding him that he encourages eccentricity for its own sake, as the only way to break the tyranny of custom (*L* 3.13). Moreover, those who exercise their individuality in living originally and differently will 'keep the life' in ways of life which already exist, just as opinions at variance with the norm keep received opinions alive (*L* 3.11).

Mill even believes that the 'average' citizens of democracies must take their lead from those one or two men of genius who exercise their individuality to rise above mediocrity (*L* 3.13). But he does not advocate dictatorship. That would be self-defeating, in that it would not allow the citizens to rise to the level of individuality of which they are capable, and would anyway corrupt the dictators themselves. The rules of justice constrain any person in the exercise of their individuality, and this is not, Mill claims, a sheer loss even to the person constrained. For the constraint of justice will itself encourage the development of the moral feelings (*L* 3.9).

Mill's book, then, is as much 'on diversity' as on liberty. Neither, if we understand freedom in the negative sense, is valuable in itself. Rather, their value lies in their making possible the attainment of human lives in which individuality is prominent in all its guises. Without individuality, there is no life of higher pleasures. In that sense, at least, individuality is the highest of all pleasures.

In this chapter, we have seen how Mill applied his utilitarian principle to the question of the limits of social interference with the lives of individuals. The principles he recommends in *On Liberty*, even though they make no explicit reference to the utility principle, derive their plausibility from that principle. The liberty principle states that such interference is justified only to prevent harm to others, and this principle not only rules out paternalistic justifications for interference, but provides the underpinning for a protected self-regarding sphere. The liberty principle rests upon individuality, which has welfare value in itself when instantiated in people's lives, as well as being of great instrumental value as humanity progresses. The same sorts of justification underlie Mill's defence of freedom of speech: the value of understanding, and the importance of vivid belief, both of which can be productive of welfare for society as a whole. Mill states that the liberty principle is 'absolute' (*L* 1.9), but I noted that his own arguments – concerning offence, slavery and the depravation of taste – show that he himself allows his utilitarianism to temper its application. I suggested that it is at least arguable that utilitarianism might support a self-regarding sphere even more strictly bounded by rights than Mill's own. But whatever the merits of that suggestion, I hope that this chapter has at least provided some insight into the subtlety and power of Mill's version of utilitarianism and its application to pressing practical problems. In the final chapter of the book, we shall examine another issue which Mill thought extremely important, and on which he again shone his utilitarian spotlight.

Further reading

On Liberty is well worth studying carefully in its entirety. A large secondary literature has grown up around it over the last few decades. The standard 'liberal' interpretation of Mill is Berlin 1959. A book-length version is Ten 1980. A 'utilitarian' interpretation, along the lines of my own, can be found in Sartorius 1975. A book-length version is Gray 1983, which also includes a good discussion of individuality. See also Strasser 1984. Standard interpretative articles include Rees 1960; Friedman 1966; Brown 1972; Wollheim 1973; Riley 1991b; Wolff 1997. Feinberg 1971 and Dworkin 1972 are classic discussions of paternalism. An excellent pair of papers on freedom of expression is McCloskey 1970 and Monro 1970; see also McCloskey 1963. The importance of self-development in Mill is discussed in Donner 1991. An interesting essay discussing the relation of *On Liberty* to pluralistic scientific methodology is Feyerabend 1970. The most important recent work in liberal political philosophy concerns itself with many of the questions that Mill discusses: Raz 1986.

Chapter 9

Utilitarianism and equality: *The Subjection of Women*

Unmasking the morality of marital slavery

We have seen how the cornerstone of Mill's practical view is the principle of utility. According to this principle, the right act is that which maximizes overall welfare. Some of our acts involve our taking part in the practices of everyday, or 'customary', morality. Because my child is less likely to attack others if I encourage her to feel proud at her self-control and kindness, and shame and guilt at her cruelty, it makes utilitarian sense to bring her up to feel these emotions at the proper times, and thus to guide her conduct in a utilitarian direction.

As we have already seen, Mill accepts that some parts of customary morality may well be grounded on the promotion of human welfare (*SW* 1.5; cf. *SW* 1.4). These include certain 'secondary principles', such as principles of justice, which have been initiated and continued reflectively, and tested against alternatives. Other parts of customary morality, however, such as what he saw as the common readiness to permit interference with individuals for their own good, he finds abhorrent, and wishes to see replaced. In other words, the mere fact that a certain moral principle is widely accepted does not justify it. Custom itself has no authority.

Another area in which Mill thinks the customary morality of his day is in need of radical reform concerns the relations between the sexes. Here Mill recognized that he had a great battle on his hands, and it was one he fought throughout his life, from the time he was arrested at the age of 17 for handing out leaflets on contraception until the final period of his life, in which he attempted in Parliament to extend suffrage to women. The battle, as he sees it, is against custom, and the intense and irrational feelings which protect it (*SW* 1.2). One of Mill's primary tasks in *The Subjection of Women* is to reveal the reality of oppression behind the genteel appearance of Victorian chivalry:

> It was inevitable that this one case of a social relation grounded on force, would survive through generations of institutions grounded on equal justice, an almost solitary exception to the general character of their laws and customs; but which, so long as it does not proclaim its own origin, and as discussion has not brought out its true character, is not felt to jar with modern civilization, any more than domestic slavery among the Greeks jarred with their notion of themselves as a free people.
>
> (*SW* 1.6)

What, then, was the origin of the relative positions of men and women? According to Mill, fully to understand this requires one to grasp the history of morality itself, so that one can see how those relations are still governed by a morality which has in other areas of life become obsolete.

Mill suggests that in the very earliest human societies each woman, because of her physical weakness and sexual attractiveness, would be enslaved to a man. Out of this primitive Hobbesian state of nature developed legal systems which merely legitimized these ownership relations:

Slavery, from being a mere affair of force between the master and the slave, became regularized and a matter of compact among the masters, who, binding themselves to one another for common protection, guaranteed by their collective strength the private possessions of each, including his slaves.

(*SW* 1.5)

Primitive slavery, then, is the source of the inequality of women. And in the legitimation of this primitive relation is to be found the origin of social or legal obligation: those who disobeyed the 'law of force' were thought guilty of the most serious crime, and duly punished with great cruelty (*SW* 1. 7). Here we must not forget Mill's brief but important account of morality's origin in the desire to punish in *Utilitarianism* 5.14 (see ch. 5 and ch. 7).

Gradually, a certain sense of obligation developed in some superiors towards some inferiors (though not slaves), as the result of the development of consciences which motivated the keeping, from a sense of duty, of promises originally made for convenience. This evolution out of the pure law of force was the beginning of what we might recognize as a morality:

[T]he banishment of that primitive law even from so narrow a field, commenced the regeneration of human nature, by giving birth to sentiments of which experience soon demonstrated the immense value even for material interests, and which thenceforward only required to be enlarged, not created.

(*SW* 1.7)

Then the view arose among the Stoics, and was taken up in Christianity, that there are obligations to slaves (*SW* 1.7; cf. *SW* 2.12). Though not widely adopted, this was the clearest example of a new stage in morality – the morality of chivalry, in which the strong would be praised for refraining from oppressing the weak (*SW* 2.12).

Chivalry and justice

Women, in fact, had from very early times played a rôle in creating the conditions for the morality of chivalry (*SW* 4.8). Because of women's vulnerability, they encouraged men not to be violent, and because of female weakness, to settle disputes by non-violent means. Women did not, however, wish their men to be cowards, because, after all, they themselves needed protection. So courage was always encouraged in sons by their mothers, and in young men by their female lovers. A possessor of military virtue would also be admired by other men, and such admiration would provide another opportunity of entry into the affections of women. The morality of chivalry, then, consists in an apparently odd mix of militarism and gentleness, especially towards women, who used their sexual power to their best advantage.

The morality of chivalry, however, is a thing of the past (*SW* 4.9). The individualism of the warrior has been replaced by co-operation in business and industry: 'The main foundations of the moral life of modern times must be justice and prudence; the respect of each for the rights of every other, and the ability of each to take care of himself' (*SW* 4.9).

Chivalry was not entirely successful. It depended on praise rather than blame and punishment, and for that reason left untouched the behaviour of the majority, unimpressed by the rewards of honour. With the morality of justice, society has the collective means to enforce decency on the part of the strong without relying on their higher feelings, and indeed it has done so – except as regards the relation of women and men. The behaviour of most men towards most women is governed not by the morality of justice, nor even the morality of chivalry, but the morality of submission – the law of force.

The morality of justice is grounded on the equality of human beings. One's birth does not determine rigidly the course one's life must take; rather one is free to employ the talents one has in whatever career one wishes (*SW* 1.13; *SW* 4.5). And this freedom, as we saw in the previous chapter, protects autonomy, one of the most important sources of welfare. It is recognized both as an injustice to the individuals concerned, and as damaging to the interests of society as a whole, to place needless obstacles in the way of individual advancement: 'Nobody thinks it necessary to make a law that only a strong-armed man shall be a blacksmith.'

There is clearly some hyperbole in Mill's claims about the morality of justice, and indeed he does become more sanguine when reflecting upon the constraints placed on its development in society by the present relations of the sexes. But it is no doubt true that Mill is writing at at a time in which sexual inequality is not widely recognized as a serious injustice. What is Mill's explanation?

One main cause is the continuing physical weakness of women (*SW* 1.6). Men have nothing to fear from women, and so have seen no good reason to concede ground to them. Mill notes that less than forty years before the publication of *The Subjection of Women*, British citizens could own other human beings, and that absolute monarchy or military despotism as systems of government had only recently begun to decline in Europe. 'Such is the power of an established system' (*SW* 1.8). Since every man has the advantage of despotism over those closest to him, is it any wonder that he has not resigned his power?

More support for the customary morality of sexism, Mill believes, is provided by the sentiments and feelings (*SW* 1.2). Given that men have inculcated in women duties of submission and self-abnegation (*SW* 1.11), it is no surprise that many women do not desire any reform.

But Mill realizes that many women have not been taken in (*SW* 1.10). Many women complain of sexism in their writings, and are petitioning vociferously for the vote and for education. In addition, even more women, though they do not complain of men as a whole, resent the tyranny of their own husband. Yet more would complain if the hold of husbands over wives were not so tight.

Mill believes that wives are in a position of slavery (*SW* 2.1). His hope is that once this is recognized, radical changes will follow. What those changes will be, and how they are to come about, we must now begin to consider.

Marriage, equal opportunity and the liberation of women

Mill is appalled by the position of women in his society. He is particularly concerned by the nature of marriage, which he sees women as being coerced into by the lack of any serious alternative (*SW* 1.25). The history of marriage as he describes it is part of the history of morality. It has its origin, as did ordinary slavery, in the law of force, and women are owned either by their husbands or by their fathers (*SW* 2.1). A woman has no legal rights against her husband, who has literal sovereignty over her; under 'the old laws of England', murder of a husband had been considered high treason, the penalty being death by burning. Even now, Mill notes, a woman's avowal of obedience at the altar is upheld by the law, her property passing to her husband (but not *vice versa*). A woman has no time of her own; she is constantly at her husband's beck and call. Nor does she have any rights over her body; there is no crime of rape within marriage in the law of England. The husband has legal rights over the children, and most women have no real opportunity of escaping the tyranny of their husbands.

Sexism, of course, is not confined to the private sphere. Here Mill finds it unnecessary to go into detail (*SW* 3.1), since it is an undeniable fact that women are prohibited from applying for places at university, and from the 'greater number of lucrative occupations, and from almost all high social functions'. In particular, of course, women can neither vote nor stand for parliament (*SW* 3.2).

What is to be done? Mill says that the object of *The Subjection of Women* is to advocate 'a principle of perfect equality, admitting no power or privilege on the one side, nor disability on the other' (*SW* 1.1). Marriage should be on equal conditions (*SW* 1.25). As a voluntary association, it should be governed jointly, with a division of powers between wife and husband analogous to that between partners in a business (*SW* 2.7). Women should of course be given the vote, and be allowed admittance to the same positions in government, business and so on as men.

Mill's views, especially those on marriage, were considered dangerously radical even by most of those otherwise sympathetic to him. James Fitzjames Stephen, one of Mill's ablest critics, thought his position on female equality to be verging on the indecent (Stephen 1874: 134–5). It is no surprise, therefore, that Mill delayed the publication of the book, and strove to avoid particularly delicate issues such as divorce (*SW* 2.1).[1]

---

1 A tricky subject for him anyway, given his relationship with Mrs Taylor: see ch. 1.

Nevertheless, a common criticism of Mill by modern writers is that he does not go far enough. Mill can be seen at best as a proponent of the rights of women, not their liberation (see e.g. Goldstein 1980). He advocates mere equality of opportunity for women, not seeing that the social conditioning of women, of which he was so aware, would prevent the majority's taking up any opportunities made available to them.

This criticism might be thought a little unfair to Mill. We know that he considers both law and customary morality to be important social tools for the maximizing of welfare, so it is to be expected that he will concentrate on reform within these institutions as a means to progress. He is quite aware of the indoctrination in women by society of exaggerated views about the moral and sexual importance of female meekness and submissiveness (*SW* 1.11). He believes, however, that equality in law and customary morality will result in important changes in the nature of the family and the relationships within it, and indeed in the character of society at large:

> The family, justly constituted, would be the real school of the virtues of freedom ... What is needed is, that it should be a school of sympathy in equality, of living together in love, without power on one side or obedience on the other. This it ought to be between the parents. It would then be an exercise of those virtues which each requires to fit them for all other association, and a model to the children of the feelings and conduct which their temporary training by means of obedience is designed to render habitual.
>
> (*SW* 2.12)

Removing sexual discrimination would also allow women 'a life of rational freedom' (*SW* 4.19). Here Mill speaks of the 'liberation' of women, and he is clearly to be understood as speaking of women's being not only uncoerced by men, but positively free to make for themselves important decisions about the shape of their lives.

So Mill is concerned with the liberation of women, and with enabling them to exercise equal rights, not merely to possess them.

And there is much in what he says. Were most in society, whether female or male, to begin to see women as the legal and moral equals of men in both private and public spheres, and not to view sex as relevant where it clearly is not, then the position of women would be greatly advanced. Nevertheless, as I shall show in the next section, the modern objection to Mill I have been discussing is not completely off target.

Mill's empiricism and the power of ideology

Mill recognizes the authority of custom. His error, perhaps, is not to see how entrenched are the views of women in modern society. In an early essay, Mill had claimed that there was no natural inequality between the sexes, except perhaps in physical strength (*O* 21.42). In *The Subjection of Women*, Mill is more circumspect. The debates about the nature of women raged during his day as they do in ours, and he was concerned to sidestep them. As a strict empiricist, ready only to accept the evidence of experience, Mill says that we can know nothing of the nature of women, other than, presumably because we are aware of the forces of distortion at work, that their present state is not the natural one (*SW* 1.18). History teaches us of the great openness of human beings to external influence (*SW* 1.19). Domination has always appeared natural, and indeed the unnatural is little more to most people than what is unusual (*SW* 1.9). Views of what is natural vary wildly (*SW* 1.9; *SW* 3.14). Women themselves have been permitted to say little of their own experience, and frankness is anyway hardly a common quality in unequal relationships (*SW* 1.21). But, Mill says, from the moral point of view this is all by the by: 'For, according to all the principles involved in modern society, the question rests with women themselves – to be decided by their own experience, and by the use of their own faculties' (*SW* 1.23).

Unfortunately, however, in speaking of women as they are at present, Mill is less careful. While attempting to explain why women should be permitted to enter business and public life, Mill offers a set of generalizations about women's capacities which are unsupported in just the way he elsewhere criticizes (*SW* 3.8–13).

Women are said to be more practical than men, and to possess 'intuition' and a sensitivity to particular facts instead of the male capacity to reason abstractly. They tend to be more nervous, their minds more mobile than men's, but less able to concentrate.

Admittedly Mill takes pains to stress that he is not making claims about the universal nature of women, but only women as they are. Nevertheless, his 'mere empirical generalizations, framed, without philosophy or analysis' (*SW* 3.14) not only make Mill the first to enter the quagmire of the sameness/difference debate which concerns many contemporary feminists, but suggest that it was perhaps fortunate that time did not permit him to carry out the programme of 'ethology' he describes at the end of the *System of Logic*. Whether Mill's claims be true or false, they are both irrelevant to the practicalities of his argument and based on no more evidence than claims about the nature of women as, say, instinctively maternal or sexually insatiable.

Even worse, Mill allows himself to express opinions about which choices women should make once liberated, and they are somewhat conservative:

> In an otherwise just state of things, it is not . . . a desirable custom, that the wife should contribute by her labour to the income of the family . . . Like a man when he chooses a profession, so, when a woman marries, it may in general be understood that she makes choice of the management of a household, and the bringing up of a family, as the first call upon her exertions.
>
> (*SW* 2.16)

One might think Mill says these things merely to ingratiate himself with his sexist audience, and so perhaps win them over to a more liberal position (compare his comments on Muslims and on common decency in *On Liberty*). But this is probably not the case. Mill believed that mothers were closer to children than their fathers ('Letter to Hooker' (1869) 17.1640), and does not raise the possibility that men could be involved in the raising of children (*SW* 3.1).

Mill's mistake is not just to generalize about women without good evidence when he has explicitly warned against so doing. He makes two further errors analagous to some I outlined in *On Liberty*. Recall that in the discussion of our attitude to self-regarding faults in *On Liberty*, Mill failed to see that social despotism might be based on the criticism of others which he permitted. Here, he fails to note that, if it is widely believed that women should raise children and not work, this will create an atmosphere in which it is difficult for women to make a free choice. Other options may just not occur to them, and there may be social pressure to conform. Further, in the passage of *On Liberty* on self-regarding faults, Mill seems temporarily unaware not only of the authority of custom, but also of the authority of his own text. The same is true in *The Subjection of Women*. By advocating a domestic rôle for women, Mill was playing into the hands of those sexists who wished to prevent women from competing on equal terms with men by any means available.

The tension in Mill's writing on women demonstrates the power of the very ideology he attempted to reveal. On the one hand, he sees very clearly the intricate methods of subjection employed by men against women over the ages. On the other, he fails to recognize that he himself has been taken in by the myth that the rôle of the vast majority of women is to raise children, along with other myths, such as that the age of a husband, or the fact that he earns money, entitles him to a greater say in marriage (*SW* 2.9).

These blemishes, however, should not blind us to the force and eloquence of Mill's case for the equality of women. He does anyway allow that 'the utmost latitude ought to exist for the adaptation of general rules to individual suitabilities' (*SW* 2.16). And we find in his spelling out of the morality of justice a position which not only provides a resource for modifying his own position on child-rearing but is still important in debates about sexual equality:

> [I]t is felt to be an overstepping of the proper bounds of authority to fix beforehand, on some general presumption, that certain persons are not fit to do certain things. It is now thoroughly known and admitted that if some such

presumptions exist, no such presumption is infallible. Even if it be well grounded in a majority of cases, which it is very likely not to be, there will be a minority of exceptional cases in which it does not hold: and in those it is both an injustice to the individuals, and a detriment to society, to place barriers in the way of their using their faculties for their own benefit and for that of others. In the cases, on the other hand, in which the unfitness is real, the ordinary motives of human conduct will on the whole suffice to prevent the incompetent person from making, or from persisting in, the attempt.

(*SW* 1.13; cf. *SW* 3.1)

In 1869, Elizabeth Cady Stanton, a pioneer of women's liberation in America, wrote to Mill concerning his book:

I lay the book down with a peace and joy I never felt before, for it is the first response from any man to show he is capable of seeing and feeling all the nice shades and degrees of women's wrongs and the central point of her weakness and degradation.

(Lutz 1940: 171–2; cited in Rossi 1970: 62)

In the final section of this chapter, let me show how Mill employed the theory he had developed in *Utilitarianism* and *On Liberty* to argue for women's equality.

The benefits of reform

Mill advocates that, rather than allow the question of women's position in society to be decided by prevailing custom, one should think of it

as a question of justice and expediency: the decision on this, as on any of the other social arrangements of mankind, depending on what an enlightened estimate of tendencies and consequences may show to be the most advantageous to humanity in general, without distinction of sex.

(*SW* 1.17)

The morality of justice, then, is the customary morality which Mill believes suits modernity. In the circumstances in which we find ourselves, equality is to govern our relations with one another, because in this way human welfare will be best promoted.

In his discussion of justice in *Utilitarianism*, Mill suggests that there is more disagreement about equality than about any other component of justice (5.10). It is clear, however, what he means by equality between the sexes: a substantive equality of rights, allied with an attitude of equality of respect by each citizen towards every other, male or female. Equality for Mill is closely tied to desert: 'We should treat all equally well (when no higher duty forbids) who have deserved equally well of us' (5.36). And he is acutely aware, as we shall see below, of the distress caused to women who saw that the arrangements in their society prevented their exercising their talents as they wished.

What, then, would be the consequences of equality? The most important, of course, would be for women. First, they would be relieved from the terrible suffering inflicted by many husbands upon their wives (*SW* 2.1; *SW* 4.2). Mill, a husband himself, is of course aware that not all husbands are tyrants; but he is equally, and painfully, aware of the level of violence against women in the home and the lack of protection offered them by society and the law. Nor is it any surprise that women love their husbands whether they batter them or not: similar attachments were forged between slave and master in Greece and Rome.

Secondly, women might find a positive benefit in a marriage based on equality (*SW* 4.15–18). There might be far greater similarity in interests, tastes, wishes and inclinations, and a consequent decrease in painful disagreement. Mill compares the ideal marriage to friendship, in which association and sympathy enable each partner to enrich himself or herself through insight into the other's view of the world. There is little doubt that Mill is speaking here from the experience of his relationship with Harriet Taylor, and, given his view of sexual intercourse as an 'animal function' (*SW* 2.1), it is to be expected that he emphasize the non-sexual aspect of the marriage relationship.

Thirdly, and no less importantly, Mill's reforms would allow women a life of rational freedom in place of one of subjection to the will of men (*SW* 4.19–20). Here we see that Mill's case depends not only on *Utilitarianism*, and the conceptions of justice and human welfare there developed, but on the understanding of liberty and individuality worked out in *On Liberty*. Mill argues that, after food and clothing, freedom is the most important want of any human being. Mill asks his reader not to concentrate on how much freedom matters to others, but on how much it matters to the reader themselves – and then to base their conclusions about others on their own case:

> Whatever has been said or written, from the time of Herodotus to the present, of the ennobling influence of free government – the nerve and spring which it gives to all the faculties, the larger and higher objects which it presents to the intellect and feelings, the more unselfish public spirit, and calmer and broader views of duty, that it engenders, and the generally loftier platform on which it elevates the individual as a moral, spiritual, and social being – is every particle as true of women as of men. Are these things no important part of individual happiness?
>
> (*SW* 4.20)

The experience of freely running one's own life, then, is a central component of human welfare. Mill stresses two further elements which women will be able to incorporate in their lives through exercising this freedom: achievement, and the enjoyment of contemplating it (*SW* 4.21–2). As we have seen, Mill believes women should remain in the home, so his proposals as he conceives them concern mainly women who have brought up a family. He suggests that the only active outlet available to such women at present is charity, in which the effect is merely to remove the capacity for autonomy from those who are helped (*SW* 4.11). Not only could women achieve in the spheres in which men currently achieve, but they could enjoy their achievement, something again 'vitally important to the happiness of human beings', and be spared the undeserved disappointment and dissatisfaction of a wasted life.

Mill realizes that he cannot rest his case on the advantages of equality to women alone. Some benefits, he argues, will accrue to men. Like women, they will be able to enjoy a marriage of friendship with an equal. And there will be less obvious improvements to their position. For example, a man who wishes to live his life according to his own conscience and in accordance with the truth as he sees it will be able to do so, even if his opinions are at odds with those of the masses (*SW* 4.13–14; cf. *S* 2.5). At present, he would probably not attempt it, because of the social sacrifice he would be imposing on his family: 'Whoever has a wife and children has given hostages to Mrs Grundy.'[2] Mill was quite aware of the effects of social ostracism after the way he and Mrs Taylor were treated by society at large (see ch. 1).

But the main advantages for men will come from those to society as a whole. Society will benefit from the constructive, as opposed to the mischievous, influence of women (*SW* 4.8–12, 20). At present, women denied liberty seek whatever power they can, without regard for its wider social implications. Sheer power depraves, whether it be held by a woman or a man. With equality, not only will women's interests move beyond the sphere of Mrs Grundy, but they will extend to combine the virtues of gentleness with a distinterested concern for society at large.

Discrimination is inefficient, resulting in the failure to realize or use the potential of those discriminated against (*SW* 1.13–14, 24; *SW* 3.1; *SW* 4.6–7). The equal education of women and their entry into professions previously prohibited to them would make available huge mental resources, as well as spur men to great competition.

Equal education would also affect the characters of both men and women: women would become more assertive, men more self-sacrificial (*SW* 2.10). And, as we saw above, there would be other effects on the morality of society, emerging from the family as a 'school of sympathy in equality' (*SW* 2.12). Present institutions result in men's becoming 'depraved' (*SW* 2.13; cf. *SW* 2.4). Mill is quite adamant about this: 'All the selfish propensities, the

---

2 Mrs Grundy, in Thomas Morton's *Speed the Plough* (1798), represents a narrow-minded sense of propriety.

self-worship, the unjust self-preference, which exist among mankind, have their source and root in, and derive their principal nourishment from, the present constitution of the relation between men and women' (*SW* 4.4).

It might be thought that Mill is exaggerating. Certainly he is again sticking his neck out further than his empiricism might allow. But it is not implausible to suggest that were sexism to be rooted out, for the right reasons, from the family at all levels, many of those brought up within the institution would live up to the morality of justice elsewhere: 'Though the truth may not be felt or generally acknowledged for generations to come, the only school of genuine moral sentiment is society between equals' (*SW* 2.12).

The vision of a society in which all are granted the rights and respect they deserve is at the heart of the liberalism and egalitarianism which Mill's act utilitarianism supported. That vision is as important now as it ever was, and modern utilitarians have stressed that the boundaries of such a society should extend to include not only women, but human beings in all countries, and indeed non-human animals. Because of the depressing fact that Mill's ideal remains in many respects as distant as it did in his time, his moral and political writings, all of which must be read in the light of *Utilitarianism*, will rightly remain at the centre of moral and political debate for many years to come.

Further reading

In addition to *The Subjection of Women*, it is worth reading Mill's 'On marriage' essay; this is printed along with an essay by Harriet Taylor, in Mill and Mill 1970. General discussions of *The Subjection of Women* include: Millett 1970: 89–108 (compares Mill and Ruskin); Annas 1977; Okin 1979: pt 4; Berger 1984: 195–204; Hekman 1992; Donner 1993. On marriage, see Mendus 1989; Shanley 1991; Urbinati 1991. On sameness and difference, see Di Stefano 1989.

Bibliography

This bibliography contains items mentioned in the text as well as other items I have found useful.

Adams, R.M. 1976: 'Motive utilitarianism', *Journal of Philosophy* 73.

Altham, J.E.J. and R. Harrison (eds) 1995: *World, Mind, and Ethics: Essays on the Ethical Philosophy of Bernard Williams*, Cambridge.

Annas, J. 1977: 'Mill and the subjection of women', *Philosophy* 52.

Anscombe, G.E.M. 1957: *Intention*, Oxford.

Archard, D. 1990: 'Freedom not to be free', *Philosophical Quarterly* 40.

Aristotle *c* 330 BC: *Nicomachean Ethics*, standard Greek edn: ed. J. Bywater, Oxford, 1894; mod. edn trans. T. Irwin, Indianapolis, 1985.

Arneson, R. 1980: 'Mill versus paternalism', *Ethics* 90.

Arneson, R. 1989: 'Paternalism, utility and fairness', *Revue Internationale de Philosophie* 43.

Atkinson, R.F. 1957: 'J.S. Mill's "proof" of the principle of utility', *Philosophy* 32.

Ayer, A.J. 1965: *Philosophical Essays*, London.

Bain, A. 1882: *John Stuart Mill*, London; repr. Bristol, 1993.

Baker, J.M. 1971: 'Utilitarianism and secondary principles', *Philosophical Quarterly* 21.

Baker, J. 1980: 'Mill's captivating "proof" and the foundations of ethics', *Social Theory and Practice* 6.

Barry, B. 1995: *Justice as Impartiality*, Oxford.

Bentham, J. 1789: *An Introduction to the Principles of Morals and Legislation*, London; mod. edn ed. H.L.A. Hart and F. Rosen, Oxford, 1995.

Berger, F. 1984: *Happiness, Justice, and Freedom*, Berkeley, California.

Berger, F. 1985: 'Reply to Professor Skorupski', *Philosophical Books* 26.

Berlin, I. 1958: 'Two concepts of liberty', Oxford.

Berlin, I. 1959: 'John Stuart Mill and the ends of life', repr. in J. Gray and G.W.Smith (eds) *On Liberty in Focus*, London, 1991.

Bogen, J. and D.M. Farrell 1978: 'Freedom and happiness in Mill's defence of liberty', *Philosophical Quarterly* 28.

Bond, E.J. 1983: *Reason and Value*, Cambridge.

Bradley, F.H. 1927: *Ethical Studies*, Oxford, 2nd edn.

Brandt, R.B. 1979: *A Theory of the Good and the Right*, Oxford.

Brink, D.O. 1992: 'Mill's deliberative utilitarianism', *Philosophy and Public Affairs* 21.

Britton, K. 1953: *John Stuart Mill*, Harmondsworth.

Broad, C.D. 1930: *Five Types of Ethical Theory*, London.

Brown, A. 1986: *Modern Political Philosophy: Theories of the Just Society*, Harmondsworth.

Brown, D.G. 1972: 'Mill on liberty and morality', *Philosophical Review* 81.

Brown, D.G. 1973: 'What is Mill's principle of utility?', *Canadian Journal of Philosophy* 3.

Brown, D.G. 1974: 'Mill's act utilitarianism', *Philosophical Quarterly* 24.

Brown, D.G. 1978: 'Mill on harm to others' interests', *Political Studies* 26.

Butler, J. 1726: *Fifteen Sermons*, mod. edn in *Collected Works*, ed. J. Bernard, London, 1900, vol. 1.

Carr, S. 1975: 'The integrity of a utilitarian', *Ethics* 86.

Cohen, S. 1990: 'Proof and sanction in Mill's utilitarianism', *History of Philosophy Quarterly* 7.

Conly, S. 1983: 'Utilitarianism and integrity', *Monist* 66.

Cooper, N. 1969: 'Mill's "proof" of the principle of utility', *Mind* 78.

Cooper, W.E., K. Neilsen and S.C. Patten (eds) 1979: *New Essays on John Stuart Mill, Canadian Journal of Philosophy*, suppl. vol. 5.

Copp, D. 1979: 'The iterated-utilitarianism of J.S. Mill', in W.E. Cooper, K. Nielsen and S.C. Patten (eds), *New Essays on John Stuart Mill, Canadian Journal of Philosophy*, suppl. vol. 5.

Cottingham, J. 1983: 'Ethics and impartiality', *Philosophical Studies* 43.

Cottingham, J. 1996: 'Impartiality and the virtues', in R. Crisp (ed.), *How Should One Live? Essays on the Virtues*, Oxford.

Crisp, R. 1992: 'Utilitarianism and the life of virtue', *Philosophical Quarterly* 42.

Crisp, R. 1994: 'Aristotle's inclusivism', *Oxford Studies in Ancient Philosophy* 12.

Crisp, R. 1996a: 'Mill on virtue as a part of happiness', *British Journal for the History of Philosophy* 4.

Crisp, R. 1996b: 'The dualism of practical reason', *Proceedings of the Aristotelian Society* 96.

Cupples, B. 1972: 'A defence of the received interpretation of J.S. Mill', *Australasian Journal of Philosophy* 50.

Dahl, N.O. 1973: 'Is Mill's hedonism inconsistent?', *American Philosophical Quarterly*, Monograph 7.

Davis, N. 1980: 'Utilitarianism and responsibility', *Ratio* 22.

Diggs, B.J. 1964: 'Rules and utilitarianism', *American Philosophical Quarterly* 1.

Dinwiddy, J. 1989: *Bentham*, Oxford.

Di Stefano 1989: 'Re-reading J.S. Mill: interpolations from the (m)other world', in M. Barr and R. Feldstein (eds), *Discontented Discourses*, Urbana, Illinois.

Donner, W. 1991: *The Liberal Self*, Ithaca.

Donner, W. 1993: 'John Stuart Mill's liberal feminism', *Philosophical Studies* 69.

Downie, R.S. 1966: 'Mill on pleasure and self-development', *Philosophical Quarterly* 16.

Dryer, D.P. 1969: 'Essay on Mill's *Utilitarianism*', introduction to J.S. Mill, *Collected Works*, 33 vols, ed. J. Robson, Toronto, vol. 10.

Dryer, D.P. 1979: 'Justice, liberty, and the principle of utility in Mill', in W.E. Cooper, K. Nielsen and S.C. Patten (eds), *New Essays on John Stuart Mill, Canadian Journal of Philosophy*, suppl. vol. 5.

Dworkin, G. 1972: 'Paternalism', *Monist* 56.

Dworkin, R. 1984: 'Rights as trumps', in J. Waldron (ed.), *Theories of Rights*, Oxford.

Ebenstein, L. 1985: 'Mill's theory of utility', *Philosophy* 60.

Edwards, R.B. 1979: *Pleasures and Pains*, Ithaca.

Feagin, S. 1983: 'Mill and Edwards on the higher pleasures', *Philosophy* 58.

Feinberg, J. 1971: 'Legal paternalism', *Canadian Journal of Philosophy* 1.

Feyerabend, P. 1970: 'Against method', *Minnesota Studies in the Philosophy of Science* 4.

Finnis, J. 1980: *Natural Law and Natural Rights*, Oxford.

Fox, C. 1882: *Memories of Old Friends*, ed. H.N. Pym, London.

Friedman, R. 1966: 'A new exploration of Mill's essay *On Liberty*', *Political Studies* 14.

Gibbard, A. 1965: 'Rule-utilitarianism: just an illusory alternative?', *Australasian Journal of Philosophy* 43.

Gildin, H. 1964: 'Mill's *On Liberty*', in J. Cropsey (ed.), *Ancients and Moderns*, New York.

Glover, J. 1984: *What Sort of People Should There Be?*, Harmondsworth.

Glover, J. (ed.) 1990: *Utilitarianism and its Critics*, New York.

Godwin, W. 1798: *Enquiry Concerning Political Justice*, 3rd edn, London; mod. edn ed. I. Kramnick, Harmondsworth, 1985.

Goldstein, L. 1980: 'Mill, Marx and women's liberation', *Journal of the History of Philosophy* 18.

Goodin, R. 1991: 'Utility and the good', in P. Singer (ed.), *A Companion to Ethics*, Oxford.

Gray, J. 1983: *Mill On Liberty: A Defence*, London, 1983.

Gray, J. and G.W. Smith (eds) 1991: *On Liberty in Focus*, London.

Green, T.H. 1883: *Prolegomena to Ethics*, Oxford.

Griffin, J. 1986: *Well-Being*, Oxford.

Griffin, N. 1972: 'A note on Mr Cooper's reconstruction of Mill's "proof"', *Mind* 81.

Grote, J. 1870: *An Examination of the Utilitarian Philosophy*, Cambridge.

Hall, E.R. 1949: 'The "proof" of utility in Bentham and Mill', *Ethics* 60.

Hare, R.M. 1952: *The Language of Morals*, Oxford.

Hare, R.M. 1981: *Moral Thinking: Its Methods, Levels, and Point*, Oxford.

Harris, G. 1989: 'Integrity and agent-centred restrictions', *Nous* 23.

Harris, J. 1974: 'Williams on negative responsibility and integrity', *Philosophical Quarterly* 24.

Harrison, J. 1975: 'The right, the just and the expedient in Mill's *Utilitarianism*', in T. Penelhum and R.A. Shiner (eds), *New Essays*

in the History of Philosophy, Canadian Journal of Philosophy,
suppl. vol. 1.

Harrison, J. 1979: 'Rule utilitarianism and cumulative-effect utilitarianism', in N.E. Cooper K. Nielsen and S.C. Patten (eds), *New Essays on John Stuart Mill, Canadian Journal of Philosophy,* suppl. vol. 5.

Harrison, R. 1983: *Bentham,* London.

Harrod, R. 1936: 'Utilitarianism revised', *Mind* 45.

Hart, H.L.A. 1963: *Law, Liberty, and Morality,* Oxford.

Harvie, C. 1976: *The Lights of Liberalism: University Liberals and the Challenge of Democracy 1860–86,* London.

Haworth, A. forthcoming: *Freedom of Speech,* London.

Hearns, S.J. 1992: 'Was Mill a moral scientist?', *Philosophy* 67.

Hekman, S. 1992: 'John Stuart Mill's *The Subjection of Women*: the foundations of liberal feminism', *History of European Ideas* 15.

Herman, B. 1983: 'Integrity and impartiality', *Monist* 66.

Hoag, R.W. 1986: 'Happiness and freedom: recent work on John Stuart Mill', *Philosophy and Public Affairs* 15.

Hoag, R.W. 1987: 'Mill's conception of happiness as an inclusive end', *Journal of the History of Philosophy* 25.

Hoag, R.W. 1992: 'J.S. Mill's language of pleasures', *Utilitas* 4.

Hobbes, T. 1651: *Leviathan,* London; mod. edn ed. C.B. Macpherson, Harmondsworth, 1968.

Hollis, M. 1995: 'The shape of a life', in J.E.J. Altham and R. Harrison (eds), *World, Mind, and Ethics: Essays on the Ethical Philosophy of Bernard Williams,* Cambridge.

Honderich, T. 1974: 'The worth of John Stuart Mill on liberty', *Political Studies* 22.

Hooker, B. 1993: 'Political philosophy', in L. McHenry & F. Adams (eds), *Reflections on Philosophy,* New York.

Hooker, B. 1995: 'Rule-consequentialism, incoherence, fairness', *Proceedings of the Aristotelian Society* 95.

Hume, D. 1739–40: *A Treatise of Human Nature,* London; mod. edn ed. L. Selby-Bigge, rev. P.H. Nidditch, 2nd edn, Oxford, 1978.

Hume, D. 1751: *An Enquiry Concerning the Principles of Morals,* London; mod. edn ed. L. Selby-Bigge, rev. P.H. Nidditch, 3rd edn, Oxford, 1975.

Hurka, T. 1993: *Perfectionism,* Oxford.

Hutcheson, F. 1755: *A System of Moral Philosophy,* London; mod. edn in *Collected Works,* Hildesheim, 1969, vols 5–6.

Irwin, T.H. 1997: 'Mill and the classical world', in J. Skorupski (ed.), *Cambridge Companion to Mill*, Cambridge.

Jones, H. 1978: 'Mill's argument for the principle of utility', *Philosophy and Phenomenological Research* 38.

Kagan, S. 1992: 'The limits of well-being', in F. Miller, E.F. Paul and J. Paul (eds), *The Good Life and the Human Good*, Cambridge.

Kant, I. 1785: *Groundwork of the Metaphysics of Morals*, mod. edn. trans. L.W. Beck, 2nd edn, Upper Saddle River, NJ, 1995.

Kleinig, J. 1970: 'The fourth chapter of Mill's *Utilitarianism*', *Australian Journal of Philosophy* 48.

Kretzmann, N. 1958: 'Desire as proof of desirability', *Philosophical Quarterly* 8.

Kupperman, J. 1978: 'Do we desire only pleasure?', *Philosophical Studies* 34.

Locke, J. 1690: *An Essay Concerning Human Understanding*, London; mod. edn ed. P.H. Nidditch, Oxford, 1975.

Long, R. 1992: 'Mill's higher pleasures and the choice of character', *Utilitas* 4.

Lutz, A. 1940: *Created Equal: A Biography of Elizabeth Cady Stanton*, New York.

Lyons, D. 1965: *The Forms and Limits of Utilitarianism*, Oxford.

Lyons, D. 1976: 'Mill's theory of morality', *Nous* 10.

Lyons, D. 1977: 'Human rights and the general welfare', *Philosophy and Public Affairs* 6.

Lyons, D. 1978: 'Mill's theory of justice', in A. Goldman and J. Kim (eds), *Values and Morals*, Dordrecht.

Lyons, D. 1979: 'Liberty and harm to others', in W.E. Cooper K. Nielsen and S.C. Patten (eds), *New Essays on John Stuart Mill, Canadian Journal of Philosophy*, suppl. vol. 5.

Lyons, D. 1982: 'Benevolence and justice in Mill', in H.B. Miller and W.H. Williams (eds), *The Limits of Utilitarianism*, Minneapolis.

Lyons, D. 1994: *Rights, Welfare, and Mill's Moral Theory*, Oxford.

Mabbott, J.D. 1956: 'Interpretations of Mill's *Utilitarianism*', *Philosophical Quarterly* 6.

McCloskey, H.J. 1957: 'An examination of restricted utilitarianism', *Philosophical Review* 66.

McCloskey, H.J. 1963: 'Mill's liberalism', *Philosophical Quarterly* 13.

McCloskey, H.J. 1970: 'Liberty of expression: its grounds and limits (I)', *Inquiry* 13.

McCloskey, H.J. 1971: *John Stuart Mill: A Critical Study*, London.

Mackie, J.L. 1977: *Ethics*, Harmondsworth.

Mandelbaum, M. 1968: 'Two moot issues in Mill's *Utilitarianism*', *Journal of the History of Philosophy* 6.

Marshall, J. 1973: 'The proof of utility and equity in Mill's *Utilitarianism*', *Canadian Journal of Philosophy* 3.

Martin, R. 1972: 'A defence of Mill's qualitative hedonism', *Philosophy* 47.

Martineau, J. 1885: *Types of Ethical Theory*, Oxford.

Mayerfeld, J. 1997: *The Morality of Suffering*, Oxford.

Mendus, S. 1989: 'The marriage of true minds: the ideal of marriage in the philosophy of John Stuart Mill', in S. Mendus and J. Rendall (eds), *Sexuality and Subordination*, London.

Mill, J.S. 1961–91: *Collected Works*, 33 vols, ed. J. Robson, Toronto.

Mill, J.S. 1997: *Utilitarianism*, ed. R. Crisp, Oxford.

Mill, J.S. and H.T. Mill 1970: *Essays on Sex Equality*, ed. A.S. Rossi, Chicago.

Miller, D. 1976: *Social Justice*, Oxford.

Miller, H.B. and W.H. Williams (eds) 1982: *The Limits of Utilitarianism*, Minneapolis.

Millett, K. 1970: *Sexual Politics*, London.

Mitchell, D. 1970: 'Mill's theory of value', *Theoria* 36.

Monro, D.H. 1970: 'Liberty of expression: its grounds and limits (II)', *Inquiry* 13.

Moore, A. 1991: *A Theory of Well-Being*, D.Phil. thesis, Oxford.

Moore, G.E. 1903: *Principia Ethica*, Cambridge.

Moser, S. 1963: 'A comment on Mill's argument for utilitarianism', *Inquiry* 6.

Nagel, T. 1986: *The View from Nowhere*, New York.

Nakhnikian, G. 1951: 'Value and obligation in Mill', *Ethics* 62.

Nelson, M. 1991: 'Utilitarian eschatology', *American Philosophical Quarterly* 28.

Nielsen, K. 1973: 'Monro on Mill's "third howler"', *Australian Journal of Philosophy* 51.

Nozick, R. 1974: *Anarchy, State, and Utopia*, Oxford.

Okin, S.M. 1979: *Women in Western Political Thought*, Princeton.

Oldenquist, A. 1982: 'Loyalties', *Journal of Philosophy* 79.

Packe, M. 1954: *The Life of John Stuart Mill*, London.

Parfit, D. 1984: *Reasons and Persons*, Oxford.

Persson, I. 1992: *The Retreat of Reason – A Dilemma in the Philosophy of Life*, unpublished typescript, Lund.

Plato *c*. 390 BC: *Gorgias*, standard Greek edn ed. J. Bywater, Oxford, 1902; mod. edn trans. T. Irwin, Oxford, 1979.

Plato *c*. 380 BC: *Republic*, standard Greek edn ed. J. Bywater, Oxford, 1902; mod. edn trans. G.M.A. Grube, rev. C.D. Reeve, Indianapolis, 1992.

Plato *c*. 360 BC: *Philebus*, standard Greek edn ed. J. Burnet, Oxford, 1901; mod. edn trans. J. Gosling, Oxford, 1975.

Prichard, H.A. 1912: 'Does moral philosophy rest on a mistake?', *Mind* 21.

Prior, A.N. 1949: *Logic and the Basis of Ethics*, Oxford.

Putnam, H. 1981: *Reason, Truth, and History*, Cambridge.

Quinton, A. 1973: *Utilitarian Ethics*, London.

Railton, P. 1984: 'Alienation, consequentialism, and the demands of morality', *Philosophy and Public Affairs* 13.

Raphael, D.D. 1955: 'Fallacies in and about Mill's *Utilitarianism*', *Philosophy* 30.

Raphael, D.D. 1994: 'J.S. Mill's proof of the principle of utility', *Utilitas* 6.

Rashdall, H. 1907: *The Theory of Good and Evil*, Oxford.

Rawls, J. 1955: 'Two concepts of rules', *Philosophical Review* 64.

Rawls, J. 1971: *A Theory of Justice*, Cambridge, Mass.

Raz, J. 1986: *The Morality of Freedom*, Oxford.

Rees, J.C. 1960: 'A re-reading of Mill on liberty', *Political Studies* 8.

Rees, J.C. 1985: *John Stuart Mill's* On Liberty, Oxford.

Riley, J. 1988: *Liberal Utilitarianism*, Cambridge.

Riley, J. 1991a: 'One very simple principle', *Utilitas* 3.

Riley, J. 1991b: 'Individuality, custom, and progress', *Utilitas* 3.

Riley, J. 1993: 'On quantities and qualities of pleasure', *Utilitas* 5.

Robinson, D.N. 1982: *Toward a Science of Human Nature: Essays on the Psychologies of Mill, Hegel, Wundt, and James*, New York.

Robinson, D.N. 1995: *An Intellectual History of Psychology*, 3rd edn, Madison, Wisconsin.

Rossi, A.S. 1970: 'Sentiment and intellect: the story of John Stuart Mill and Harriet Taylor', introduction to J.S. Mill and H.T. Mill, *Essays on Sex Equality*, ed. A.S. Rossi, Chicago.

Ryan, A. 1965: 'J.S. Mill's art of living', *The Listener* 74; repr. in J. Gray and G.W. Smith (eds), *On Liberty in Focus*, London, 1991.

Ryan, A. 1966: 'Mill and the naturalistic fallacy', *Mind* 75.

Ryan, A. 1970: *The Philosophy of John Stuart Mill*, London.

Ryan, A. 1974: *J.S. Mill*, London.

Ryan, A. (ed.) 1993: *Justice*, Oxford.

Sartorius, R. 1975: *Individual Conduct and Social Norms*, Encino, California.

Scanlon, T. 1993: 'Value, desire, and quality of life', in M. Nussbaum and A. Sen (eds), *The Quality of Life*, Oxford.

Scheffler, S. 1982: *The Rejection of Consequentialism*, Oxford.

Schneewind, J.B. 1977: *Sidgwick's Ethics and Victorian Moral Philosophy*, Oxford.

Schwartz, T. 1982: 'Human welfare: what it is not', in H.B. Miller and W.H. Williams (eds), *The Limits of Utilitarianism*, Minneapolis.

Sen, A. 1980–1: 'Plural utility', *Proceedings of the Aristotelian Society* 81.

Sen, A. and B. Williams (eds) 1982: *Utilitarianism and Beyond*, Cambridge.

Seth, J. 1908: 'The alleged fallacies in Mill's "Utilitarianism"', *Philosophical Review* 17.

Shanley, M.L. 1991: 'Marital slavery and friendship: John Stuart Mill's *The Subjection of Women*', in M.L. Shanley and C. Pateman (eds), *Feminist Interpretation and Political Theory*, Cambridge.

Sidgwick, H. 1907: *The Methods of Ethics*, 7th edn, London.

Simmons, A.J. 1982: 'Utilitarianism and unconscious utilitarianism', in H.B. Miller and W.H. Williams (eds) *The Limits of Utilitarianism*, Minneapolis.

Singer, M.G. 1955: 'Generalization in ethics', *Mind* 64.

Singer, P. 1972: 'Is act-utilitarianism self-defeating?', *Philosophical Review* 81.

Skorupski, J. 1985: 'The parts of happiness', *Philosophical Books* 26.

Skorupski, J. 1989: *John Stuart Mill*, London.

Skorupski, J. (ed.) 1997: *Cambridge Companion to Mill*, Cambridge.

Smart, J.J.C. 1956: 'Extreme and restricted utilitarianism', *Philosophical Quarterly* 6; rev. in P. Foot (ed.), *Theories of Ethics*, Oxford, 1967.

Smart, J.J.C. 1973: 'An outline of a system of utilitarian ethics', in J.J.C. Smart and B. Williams, *Utilitarianism For and Against*, Cambridge.

Smith, A. 1759: *A Theory of the Moral Sentiments*, London; mod. edn ed. D.D. Raphael and A.L. Macfie, 2nd edn, Oxford, 1979.

Smith, G.W. 1991: 'Social liberty and free agency: some ambiguities in Mill's conception of freedom', in J. Gray and G.W. Smith (eds), *On Liberty in Focus*, London.

Smith, S.A. 1996: 'Future freedom and freedom of contract', *Modern Law Review* 59.

Spence, G.W. 1968: 'The psychology behind Mill's "proof"', *Philosophy* 43.

Sprigge, T.L.S. 1988: *The Rational Foundations of Ethics*, London.

Stephen, J.F. 1874: *Liberty, Equality, Fraternity*, 2nd edn; mod. edn ed. S.D. Warner, Indianapolis, 1993.

Stocker, M. 1969: 'Mill on desire and desirability', *Journal of the History of Philosophy* 7.

Stocker, M. 1976: 'The schizophrenia of modern ethical theory', *Journal of Philosophy* 73.

Stove, D. 1993: 'The subjection of John Stuart Mill', *Philosophy* 68.

Strasser, M. 1984: 'Mill and the utility of liberty', *Philosophical Quarterly* 34.

Sumner, L.W. 1974: 'More light on the later Mill', *Philosophical Review* 83.

Sumner, L.W. 1979: 'The good and the right', in W.E. Cooper, K. Nielsen and S.C. Patten (eds), *New Essays on John Stuart Mill, Canadian Journal of Philosophy*, suppl. vol. 5.

Sumner, L.W. 1981: *Abortion and Moral Theory*, Princeton.

Sumner, L.W. 1992: 'Welfare, happiness, and pleasure', *Utilitas* 4.

Ten, C.L. 1980: *Mill On Liberty*, Oxford.

Thomas, W. 1985: *Mill*, Oxford.

Tocqueville, A. de 1848: *Democracy in America*, 12th edn; mod. edn trans. P. Bradley, ed. A. Ryan, London, 1994.

Urbinati, N. 1991: 'John Stuart Mill on androgeny and ideal marriage', *Political Theory* 19.

Urmson, J.O. 1953: 'The interpretation of the moral philosophy of J.S. Mill', *Philosophical Quarterly* 3.

Vallentyne, P. 1993: 'Utilitarianism and infinite utility', *Australasian Journal of Philosophy* 52.

Varouxakis, G. 1995: *John Stuart Mill on French Thought, Politics, and National Character*, Ph.D. thesis, London.

Warnock, M. 1960: *Ethics Since 1900*, Oxford.

Watkins, J. 1966: 'John Stuart Mill and the liberty of the individual', in D. Thomson (ed.), *Political Ideas*, Harmondsworth.

Wellman, C. 1959: 'A reinterpretation of Mill's proof', *Ethics* 69.

West, H.R. 1972: 'Reconstructing Mill's "proof" of the principle of utility', *Mind* 81.

West, H.R. 1975: 'Mill's naturalism', *Journal of Value Inquiry* 9.

West, H.R. 1976: 'Mill's qualitative hedonism', *Philosophy* 51.

West, H.R. 1982: 'Mill's "proof" of the principle of utility', in H.B.

Miller and W.H. Williams (eds), *The Limits of Utilitarianism*, Minneapolis.

Williams, B. 1973a: 'Egoism and altruism', in *Problems of the Self*, Cambridge.

Williams, B. 1973b: 'A critique of utilitarianism', in J.J.C. Smart and B. Williams, *Utilitarianism For and Against*, Cambridge.

Williams, B. 1976: 'Persons, character, and morality', in A.O. Rorty (ed.), *The Identities of Persons*, Berkeley; repr. in B. Williams, *Moral Luck*, Cambridge, 1981. Page numbers refer to the latter.

Williams, B. 1976: 'Moral luck', *Proceedings of the Aristotelian Soceity*, suppl. vol. 50; repr. in B. Williams, *Moral Luck*, Cambridge, 1981.

Williams, B. 1981: *Moral Luck*, Cambridge.

Williams, B. 1985: *Ethics and the Limits of Philosophy*, London.

Williams, B. 1995: 'Replies', in J.E.J. Altham and R. Harrison (eds), *World, Mind, and Ethics: Essays on the Ethical Philosophy of Bernard Williams*, Cambridge.

Williams, G. 1976: 'Mill's principle of liberty', *Political Studies* 24.

Williams, G. 1996: 'The Greek origins of J.S. Mill's happiness', *Utilitas* 8.

Wilson, F. 1982: 'Mill's proof that happiness is the criterion of morality', *Journal of Business Ethics* 1.

Wilson, F. 1983: 'Mill's "proof" of utility and the composition of causes', *Journal of Business Ethics* 2.

Wolfenden 1959: *The Wolfenden Report*, London.

Wolff, J. 1997: 'Mill, indecency, and the liberty principle', *Utilitas* 9.

Wollheim, R. 1973: 'John Stuart Mill and the limits of state action', *Social Research* 40.

Index